LONG-RANGE PRECISION RIFLE

The Complete Guide to Hitting Targets at Distance

Anthony Cirincione II

Paladin Press
Boulder, Colorado

Long-Range Precision Rifle: The Complete Guide to Hitting Targets at Distance
by Anthony Cirincione II

Copyright © 2013 by Anthony Cirincione II

ISBN 13: 978-1-61004-869-9
Printed in the United States of America

Published by Paladin Press, a division of
Paladin Enterprises, Inc.,
P.O. Box 1307
Boulder, Colorado 80306 USA
+1.303.443.7250

Direct inquiries and/or orders to the above address.

Visit our website at www.paladin-press.com.

✦
CONTENTS

Chapter 1:

Rifle and Ammunition Selection 1

What is a Precision Rifle? 1

Purposes for Precision Rifles 3

Caliber and Cartridge Selection 3

Choosing a Rate of Twist 12

Accuracy Guarantee 14

Putting It All Together 15

Action Screws 15

Attaching the Scope Base 16

Attaching the Bottom Ring Halves 16

Setting Your Cheek Height 17

Setting the Eye Relief of Your Riflescope and Attaching the Top Ring Halves 17

Verify Your Barrel is Floated in the Stock 18

Let's Shoot 18

Chapter 2:

Scope Mechanics: Minutes of Angle and Mils 21

All Scopes Are Not Created Equal 22

True and Consistent Riflescope Adjustments 22

Using Minutes of Angle in Riflescopes 24

Using a Riflescope with Target Knobs 25

Two Ways to Zero Using Target Knobs, and One Method to Avoid 26

Using a BDC Elevation Knob 27

Using a Mil-Dot Reticle for Ranging Targets, Holding during Shots, and Obtaining a Zero . .29

Practical Exercise 31

Capabilities of Different Riflescopes and Selecting the One for You 38

Scope Tube Diameter 40

First Focal Plane vs. Second Focal Plane 41

Chapter 3:

**Gathering Data, Manipulating Ballistic
Software, and Creating a Ballistic Card** 45

Getting on Paper at Range 46

Making the Ballistic Card 50

Shooting Two Different Types of Loads Out of the Same Gun 52

Keeping and Using a Sniper Data Book 59

Chapter 4:

High-Angle Shooting 67

Adjusting for High Angle Based on Flat-Ground Distance 68

Flat-Ground Distance Tailored to Your Ballistic Profile 69

Chapter 5:
Compensating for Changing Environmental Conditions 71
    Compensating for Windage 72
    Fabricating a Custom Wind Chart 74
    Compensating for Temperature 80
    Compensating for Altitude 85
    Compensating for Barometric Pressure 88
    A Quick Word about Humidity 90
    Practical Exercise 90

Chapter 6:
Shooting Over or Under Obstructions 95
    Practical Exercise 99

Chapter 7:
Hand Loading for Precision Rifles 101
    Performance Analysis: Factory Match-Grade Ammunition vs. Quality Hand Loads 101
    Building Precision Cartridges 104
    Determining Your Accuracy Load 105
    A Quick Word on Velocity 106
    Case Prep: Resizing, Depriming, and Cleaning 107
    Lot Your Brass by Weight! 110
    Weighing a Powder Charge 112
    Seating the Bullet 113
    Crimping the Bullet 117
    Hand Loading for the .338 Lapua Magnum 118
    More Hand-Loading Techniques 120
    Trajectory Difference Between Fired and Unfired Brass 124
    Determining Your Most Accurate Cartridge Overall Length 127

Chapter 8:
Barrel Care: Extending Barrel Life, Accuracy,
and Understanding Cold-Bore Shift 133
    Avoiding Pitting the Bore 133
    Clean-/Cold-Bore Adjustments 134
    Bore-Cleaning Process 136
    Avoiding Throat Erosion 139

Chapter 9:
The Fundamentals of Marksmanship and the
Importance of a Steady Firing Position 141
    The Fundamentals of Marksmanship 141
    Applying the Fundamentals 145
    Natural Firing Position 146

A Final Word to the Reader 147

DEDICATION

This book is dedicated to my father for introducing me to firearms and taking the time to teach me the fundamentals of marksmanship, strict firearms safety, and responsibility at a very early age.

I also thank those specific fellow soldiers who have provided me with further training, especially First Sergeant Jason Rogers for sending me to Sniper School, and my leadership from HHC 1-327 INF Scouts.

Most of all, I dedicate this book to my daughter, Ava. I can't wait until you're old enough to shoot with Daddy!

AUDIENCE AND
MISSION STATEMENT

This book is intended for those who already know how to shoot, and who wish to take their game to the next level by pushing their weapon systems to their maximum effective ranges.

I believe this book to be an easy-to-read, easy-to-understand instructional text with everything the reader needs in order to achieve a high level of success while shooting at medium and long range. My hope is that after you achieve this success, you'll have greater confidence in your rifle and fall in love with the high level of precision, just as I have.

This is the book I wish I'd had when I first learned to shoot long range.

CHAPTER ONE

RIFLE AND
AMMUNITION SELECTION

WHAT IS A PRECISION RIFLE?

For our purposes here, we'll define a "precision rifle" as a rifle that consistently prints groups 1.047 inches or smaller at 100 yards, or 1.152 inches or smaller at 100 meters . . . in other words, 1 minute of angle (MOA) accuracy or better. The expected accuracy for any U.S. military sniper rifle is 1 MOA.[1] A rifle accurate to 1 MOA holds approximately 1-inch groups at 100 yards, 2-inch groups at 200 yards, 3-inch groups at 300 yards, and so on. Long-range shooters often take the necessary steps to tune their rifles to shoot more accurately than 1 MOA.

Accepting less than the 1-MOA standard for precision shooting is out of the question for this reason: Let's say the rifle holds a group of 1.5 inches at 100 yards instead of 1.047 inches. A rifle yielding 1.5 inches at 100 yards is a 1.43-MOA rifle. A 1.43-MOA rifle is capable of producing groups that measure 7.48 inches at 500 yards, 10.48 inches at 700 yards, and 14.97 inches at 1,000 yards in theory, providing that the bullet is stabilized during flight at those distances. (We'll address how to ensure a bullet is stabilized later in this

Figure 1-1. M24 SWS—7.62x51mm.

1

chapter in the section called "Choosing a Rate of Twist.") Folks who require a precision rifle need better group measurements than those. People who hunt at long range should be able to hold a 4-inch group (maximum size) in order to take ethical shots on medium-sized and big-game animals. Equally important to acceptable group size, a shooter also must be able to place that group center-center on his target.

Long-range precision marksmanship is more than just shooting nice looking, sub-minute groups at long range . . . it's also about shot placement. If a hunter's quarry is 15 inches—such as a coyote—and the shooter knows he can produce 4-inch groups out to 550 yards, that doesn't mean he can achieve a guaranteed hit out to 550 yards on a coyote! This book is not only geared toward getting you to print tiny groups but also toward getting you to place those groups center-center on your target despite the range to the target.

Many varmints, such as groundhogs, are small in size and therefore require a sub-MOA rifle in order to guarantee a hit at long range. Competition shooters not only require a sub-MOA rifle, but also require even more accuracy if they plan on being competitive. Most of these shooters hand load—build their own ammunition so as to fine tune the powder type, powder charge in grains, bullet type, and bullet weight to achieve hopefully .25-MOA results or better.

As of today, the type of rifle most trusted for accuracy and consistency is a bolt-action rifle with a heavy, floated barrel, and a bedded action. It should be built by a reputable rifle manufacturer. In addition, many shooters have a gunsmith fit a custom barrel of their choice to a receiver of their choice. By doing this, the shooter can get exactly what *he* wants. As an example, a shooter could choose a heavy contour, 28-inch Krieger barrel with a 1:10 twist rate, fitted to a Lawton short action for .308 Winchester ammunition. The choices for receivers and barrels are vast; some are high quality, some are less than that. (I'll note here that I use *he* to refer to a shooter for simplicity's sake. Shooting is a gender-neutral sport—many women are simply amazing at this game. So please don't take offense when I refer to a hypothetical shooter as *he*.)

As stated, for accuracy, a bolt-action rifle built by a reputable manufacturer with a heavy, floated barrel and a bedded action is the way to go. A floated barrel ensures that the only thing the barrel touches is the receiver, even during the act of firing. The rifle stock does not touch the barrel, so there is no opportunity for the rifle stock to put pressure on the barrel as the metal of the barrel heats up and expands. If the stock were to touch the barrel, as the barrel heated and expanded more and more with each shot, the stock would place a different amount of pressure in one or more areas of the barrel. To achieve a consistent level of sub-MOA accuracy, everything needs to be the same with each shot.

Having a bedded action means that epoxy, aluminum, or pillars have been fitted to the rifle stock where the receiver lies. This is done so that there is zero movement of the receiver during the rifle shot. An action can be "bedded" at home with an epoxy kit or by a gunsmith.

A barrel that is thicker than a sporter barrel is considered a heavy barrel, and there are many options for thickness, length, and rate of twist. There are several benefits to a heavy barrel. A heavy barrel is less subject to heating as the rifle is repeatedly fired but, more importantly, it is stiffer. I've had a .308 Win with a sporter barrel, and currently have a .308 Win with a heavy contour barrel. After sending eight shots down the sporter barrel, heat would noticeably affect bullet placement in relation to the rest of the group at 100 yards. However, I've shot 40 rounds in one sitting with my heavy-barreled rifle, and have yet to notice my group placement being affected by heat.

It's also nice that my heavy-barreled .308 Win, which weighs 14.5 pounds, is comfortable to fire. The recoil feels more like that of a .243 Winchester, and I can shoot the rifle as much as I need to in the course of a day at the range. The recoil from the lightweight Ruger M77, chambered in .308 Win, began to get noticeable after about five shots. Physical pain to the shooter during the act of firing can result in flinching or anticipating recoil during the shot. This produces movement in the gun, and group size and placement suffers as a result.

Although the Army's new M2010 is chambered in .300 Winchester Magnum, the gun weighs more than 17 pounds, has a muzzle brake, and an Advanced Armament Corps Titan sound suppressor.

This gun is very comfortable to shoot all day long and has less recoil than my 14-pound .308 Winchester. Whatever caliber you choose, your gun can be set up in such a way that will not cause pain upon firing.

The added weight of a heavy barrel is also useful for added consistency. When you get a chance, assume a steady firing position and look through the scope. Dry fire a shot—allow the firing pin to fall forward with no round in the chamber. The more the rifle weighs, the less the reticle of your riflescope will twitch due to the movement in the action of your rifle. When the trigger is squeezed, a lighter weight rifle will experience more movement, if only a little. I'll cite another drawback of thin rifle barrels. Upon firing a rifle shot, on a microscopic level the barrel performs a wavelike motion. Thin, long barrels wave more due to lack of stiffness. Thick, short barrels wave the least. If fitting a custom barrel to your action, the longer your barrel, the thicker it needs to be. A 1-inch thick, 28-inch long barrel may do well for a .223 Remington, but poorly for a .300 Winchester Magnum. Thicker barrels heat more slowly than thin barrels while firing, but the stiffness of thicker barrels is the primary reason why thicker barrels tend to be more accurate.

The rifle pictured in Figure 1-2 is the one that Brian Bowling uses. As of this writing (September 2012), he is the F-Class Open state champ for Mississippi. The barrel is thicker than necessary to provide enough stiffness for a 6.5mm bullet. But this added thickness provides more weight, which in turn provides him with very little recoil and very stress-free shooting throughout the 60 to 100 rounds required for competing in the F-Class Open. This rifle has served Brian well.

PURPOSES FOR PRECISION RIFLES

Precision rifles are used for different applications. Civilian uses include varmint hunting, hunting game animals, plinking, competitive shooting, and target shooting. Precision rifles are not required for most of the previous fields mentioned, but I would argue that all shooting sports using long guns become more rewarding and enjoyable when the shooter gains a useful understanding of the external ballistics of his rifle. Target shooters can enjoy putting tightly grouped shots on targets at odd distances. Varmint hunters and plinkers can gain confidence by hitting their targets with greater consistency, whether using a "flat-shooting" rifle or not. And hunters have the opportunity to engage game animals at greater distances, while still keeping their shots ethical.

A hunter who can shoot minute-of-angle groups consistently understands the ballistic profile of his rifle, *and* possesses the know-how to adjust his optics for each different situation (range, wind, etc.), is able to ethically engage more game, bagging some animals that he would normally have to pass up primarily due to distance to the target. Those who've experienced hunting in Wyoming, New Mexico, or some other place where you can "see forever," are likely to understand. It's just not as much fun letting game pass by without taking a shot because you don't know how to shoot as far as your rifle is capable.

CALIBER AND CARTRIDGE SELECTION

Avoid buying or placing an order for a precision rifle too soon after deciding that a precision rifle is for you. Don't succumb to thinking, "I want a rifle

Figure 1-2. Caliber .260 Remington, 1.5-inch diameter Krieger barrel.

Figure 1-3. Local Precision Marksmanship Competition at the Montgomery County Shooting Complex, Clarksville, Tennessee.

capable of accurate, long-range shooting. Lots of people shoot the .308 Winchester. The US Army uses the 7.62x51mm NATO (.308 Win) in its M110 SASS and it served well in the dearly departed M24 SWS, so *I'm* gonna get a rifle in .308 Winchester. So many people trust the .308 Win that it must be the best caliber for successful long-range shooting!"

Yes, the .308 Winchester does a fine job, and I love it, but it's not for everyone. The .308 Winchester is a popular competition caliber and can do the job on taking large game while hunting but, for example, the 6.5mm Creedmoor can be an excellent caliber choice for 1,000-yard shooting, bucks wind better than the .308 Winchester, and has a flatter trajectory—which is nice if you're a little off on your range estimation. The caliber bullet you choose for your rifle, and the cartridge you choose your rifle to be chambered in, should be based on what the primary use of your rifle will be. Varmint hunters generally don't need 1,000-yard capability, and big-game hunters often require bullets with calibers .30 inches in diameter or bigger (sometimes due to state law). Shooters who are new to centerfire high-power shooting tend to be most successful using rifles firing a lighter-kicking cartridge, which allows them to relax without flinching or anticipating harsh recoil. If flinching is a prob-

lem, it's better to sacrifice the power of firing a larger cartridge in order to maintain accuracy. What primary function will your rifle serve?

As a general rule, the smaller-diameter, faster-moving bullet will shoot flatter; and the bigger, slower-moving bullets will require more upward MOA or mil compensation than smaller-diameter bullets as distance to the target increases. Variables are thrown into that rule though. Cartridge manufacturers put massive amounts of powder behind some larger caliber bullets to increase their range and/or make them shoot flatter. A .308 Winchester bullet is of smaller diameter than the .338 Lapua Magnum bullet, but the .338 Lapua Magnum is flatter shooting given the same zero distance, due to the massive amount of powder behind the projectile—99.5 grains of Hodgdon Retumbo for a 250-grain .338 Lapua Magnum bullet versus 44.8 grains of Alliant Reloder 15 for a 180-grain .308 Winchester bullet.

Manufacturers also make small caliber bullets with different-sized casings to allow for different-sized powder charges. With so many caliber and cartridge choices, shooting is made so much more successful and rewarding by choosing the right cartridge for the job.

Answer these two questions and bullet choice is narrowed down quickly: between what *distances* will your targets be, and what *will* your targets be? Also, you may consider any secondary purpose the rifle is going to serve. Let's say you plan to shoot varmints anywhere from 75 yards to 600 yards from a single, stationary, sturdy firing position. For a secondary purpose, the rifle will be used for plinking at unspecified distances, both for fun and to get ready for shooting those varmints.

For this scenario, varmints are smaller animals, usually anywhere from 5 to 30 pounds in body weight. Therefore, a bullet of any caliber placed correctly on the animal would likely result in a kill, as long as the bullet has enough mass and velocity to penetrate the animal after impact. Bullets having diameter as small as .17 inch are OK for smaller varmints such as groundhogs, but the caliber is limited on range. Bullets having diameters at or above .223 inch can do the job for heavier varmints, such as coyotes. In past years, bullet diameter was key when it came to putting down game of a given size.

4

With technological advancement, many companies have made smaller-diameter bullets more lethal. In this regard, I would be doing you a disservice if I didn't mention the Barnes TSX bullet. I use a 62-grain Barnes TSX in my 5.56x45mm AR-15 for one of my hand load recipes. It is a hollow-point boattail, built for rapid expansion, and features 100 percent copper construction—no lead core. Because it's 100 percent copper, the weight and length of each bullet is closer to the average bullet—i.e., the specifications are "tighter." The importance of this will be identified in Chapter 7: Hand Loading for Precision Rifles. Further, if you don't think a 6.5mm Creedmoor bullet can put down large game effectively, make a hand load for it using the Barnes TSX and find yourself happily surprised.

Because such a range of cartridges can be selected for varmint hunting, cost may be the deciding factor. Let's compare a few cartridges commonly used for shooting varmints.

After comparing those three common varmint-hunting cartridges by using a ballistic calculator—Remington Shoot!, for this example—we can see that the .223 Rem and the .243 Win are similarly affected by wind, and that the wind takes the .22-250 Rem for more of a ride. The lighter bullet and lower ballistic coefficient of the .22-250 result in more wind drift, despite its higher velocity, in comparison to the other two cartridges. Any of the three cartridges could be used for shooting small, 600-yard targets, as all three cartridges are supersonic beyond 600 yards—and therefore considered consistent at that distance—although 600-yard shots would be noticeably more difficult with the .22-250 Rem. Given the same rifle-zero-distance, the .243 Win appears to be the cartridge requiring the least amount of optical adjustment to be put on target.

I chose the above zero distance of 300 yards for a quick comparison of the three loads. Using the ballistic software application, we can determine the optimal zero distance for each load in order to figure out how to make the rifle shoot its flattest. What I mean by this is that there is one zero distance for every cartridge whereby the bullet will not strike higher or lower than 1 inch from the point of aim, up to a specified distance. I call this my "hunting zero." This is what my rifle remains zeroed at to pull quick, precise shots within a specified range without an elevation adjustment being necessary prior to the shot. Let me demonstrate this with a visual aid.

Figure 1-4 is a graph showing the trajectory of

PERFORMANCE COMPARISON OF THREE COMMON VARMINT LOADS

.22-250 REMINGTON 55-grain Sierra GameKing HPBT 3,650 fps .185 Ballistic Coefficient	.223 REMINGTON 77-grain Sierra MatchKing HPBT 2,720 fps .362 Ballistic Coefficient	.243 WINCHESTER 85-grain Sierra GameKing HPBT 3,300 fps .282 Ballistic Coefficient
YARDS		
100 -3.1 MOA	-4.87 MOA	-3.23 MOA
200 -2.04 MOA	-2.86 MOA	-2.01 MOA
300 Weapon Zero	Weapon Zero	Weapon Zero
400 2.89 MOA	3.45 MOA	2.58 MOA
500 6.92 MOA	7.62 MOA	5.74 MOA
600 12.58 MOA	12.4 MOA	9.65 MOA

8 MPH FULL VALUE WIND @ 600 YARDS

59.92 inches	34.96 inches	36.78 inches

MAXIMUM EFFECTIVE RANGE

620 yards	880 yards	850 yards

our .243 Winchester cartridge from the example, given a 191-yard zero on a rifle with a 1.97-inch bore height (elevation of scope above centerline of the barrel).

Between 20 yards and 220 yards, our bullet will impact all targets within 1 inch of our point of aim. It is very helpful to know how to determine your "hunting zero." We figured that out by using Remington Shoot! Ballistic Software. Figure 1-5 shows the main page of this software program and that is

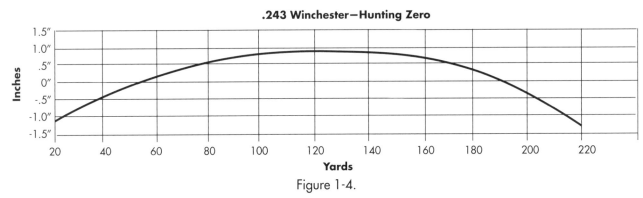

Figure 1-4.

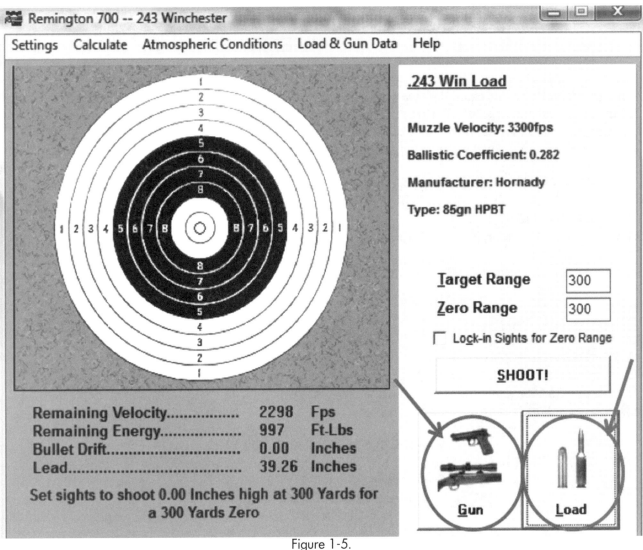

Figure 1-5.

where we start. First we click on "Gun" and "Load" to insert our bore height, bullet diameter, muzzle velocity, ballistic coefficient, and bullet weight among other marginal data.

In Figure 1-6 you can see that our .243 Win is currently zeroed for 300 yards. Go to "Calculate" and "Ballistic Report."

Look at Figure 1-7 to see the path, or trajectory, of our bullet. You can see the corresponding range just to the left of the "Path" column. To help you read this, you can see that at 200 yards our bullet will hit 4.10 inches above our point of aim. This 300-yard zero is definitely not our "hunting zero." We want no more than a 1-inch deviation above or below our point of aim.

By changing our weapon zero on the "Main

Page" to 191 yards, we achieve the results shown in Figure 1-8. You can see that between 25 and 200 yards, our bullet does not deviate from the point of impact more than one inch in either direction. If you click "Range Increment," you can change the range increment from 25-yard increments to 10-yard increments. You'll then be able to identify that our hunting zero is between 20 and 220 yards. We've simply determined the ideal zero distance for the flattest shooting, given our cartridge and bore height. This can also be done with traditionally non-flat shooting cartridges—so try not to let "flat-shooting" be a factor in deciding which caliber your new rifle will be chambered in.

It may be very useful when hunting bigger varmints, such as coyotes or foxes, to determine a

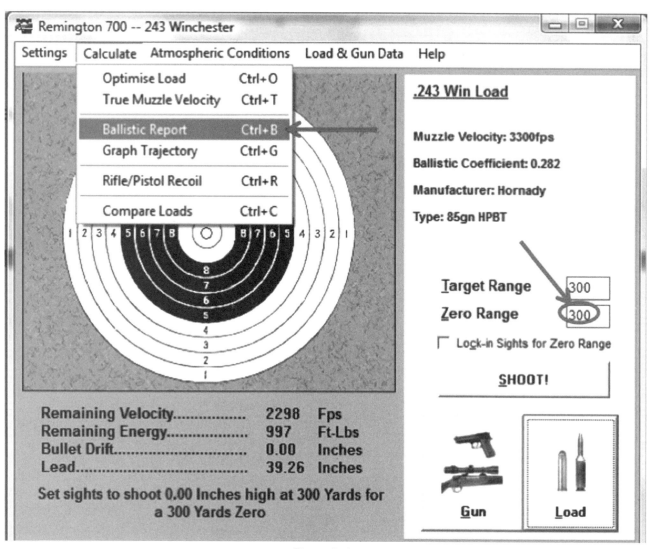

Figure 1-6.

.243 Win Load

Range Increment   Report Options   Save Report...

Ballistic Report

Range	Path	Velocity	Energy	Drop	Drift	TOF	Zero Adj
(Yards)	(Inches)	(FPS)	(FT-LBS)	(Inches)	(MOA)	(Sec)	(MOA)
0	-1.97	3300	2055	0.00	0.00	0.000	0.00
100	3.09	2940	1631	-1.72	0.00	0.096	-2.95
200	4.10	2607	1283	-7.50	0.00	0.205	-1.96
300	0.00	2298	997	-18.38	0.00	0.327	0.00
400	-10.74	2010	763	-35.90	0.00	0.467	2.57
500	-30.13	1746	575	-62.08	0.00	0.627	5.76
600	-60.99	1508	429	-99.72	0.00	0.812	9.71
700	-107.54	1307	322	-153.05	0.00	1.026	14.68
800	-174.47	1150	249	-226.77	0.00	1.272	20.83
900	-267.61	1042	205	-326.69	0.00	1.546	28.40
1000	-390.40	967	177	-456.27	0.00	1.846	37.28

100 Yards increment out to 1000 Yards

Print Preview   ✗ Exit

Figure 1-7.

2-inch or even a 3-inch hunting zero. This would extend their range beyond 220 yards without adjusting the scope prior to the shot, if time is of the essence. Use the ballistic software and determine what the 2-inch hunting zero would be for our .243 Win above. You'll find that the 2-inch hunting zero is 233 yards, and extends the range to 270 yards with a minimal sacrifice in bullet placement. To go from one hunting zero to the other, you can simply change your rifle zero using your elevation turret to go from the 191-yard zero to the 233-yard zero ... whichever you'd like to use.

Most of this book is not about preparing for quick shots while hunting—exactly the opposite, actually. I wanted to mention the above information though, because I do stalk game with my rifle dialed in for what I call a hunting zero. I'll identify in great depth how to change the zero of your rifle for each shot based on the distance to the target in Chapter 3, when we'll fabricate a custom ballistic card for your rifle.

Any of those three varmint loads would be fun to shoot and would get the job done, but now the discussion moves to those sportsmen requiring 1,000-yard capable rigs. These rifles are necessary to do any good in rifle competition, such as F-Class Target Rifle or F-Class Open Class. A rifle capable of long-range sub-MOA consistency is also a useful tool to have when hunting in wide-open spaces— say on a pronghorn hunt in New Mexico. During

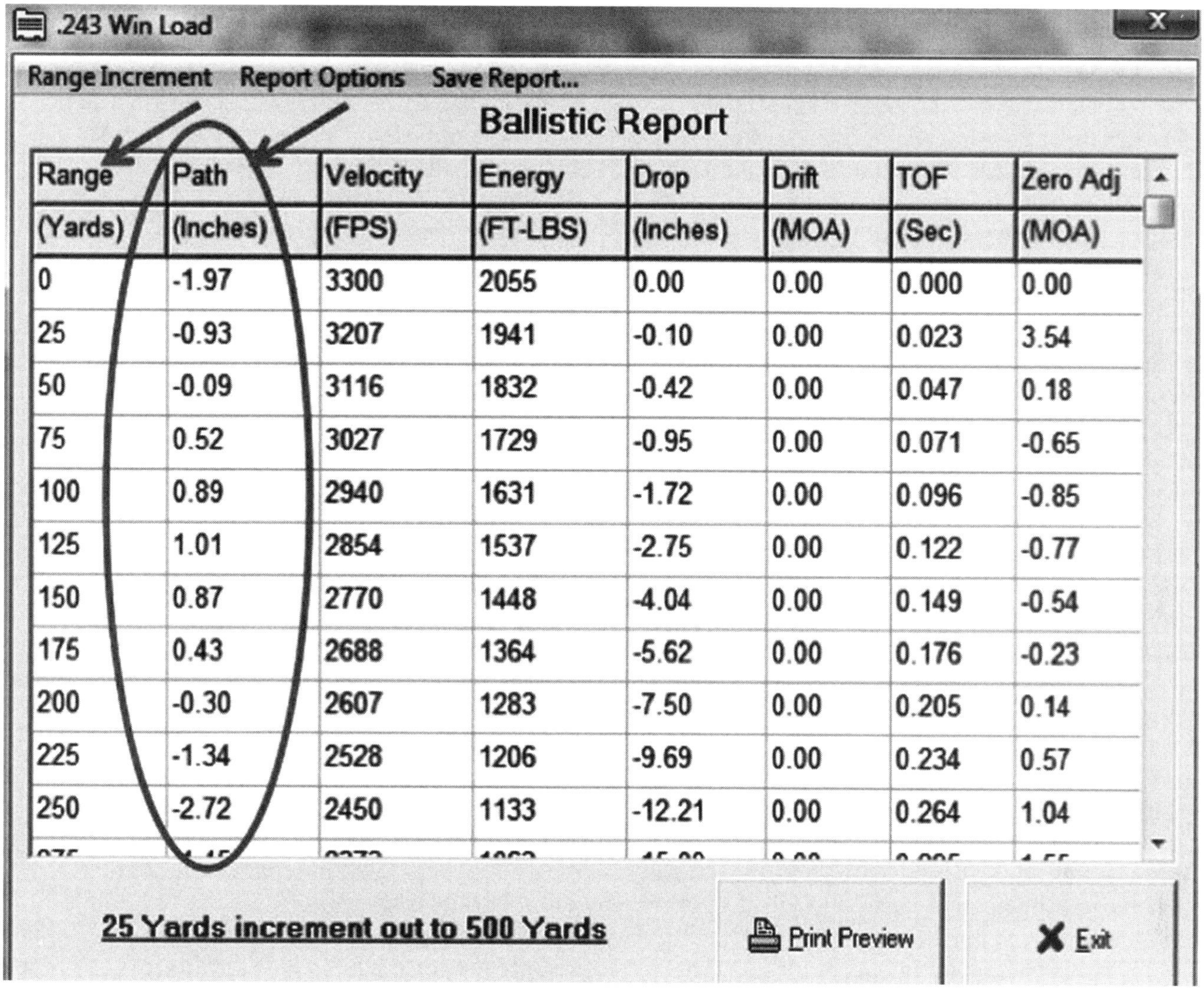

.243 Win Load

Range Increment   Report Options   Save Report...

Ballistic Report

Range	Path	Velocity	Energy	Drop	Drift	TOF	Zero Adj
(Yards)	(Inches)	(FPS)	(FT-LBS)	(Inches)	(MOA)	(Sec)	(MOA)
0	-1.97	3300	2055	0.00	0.00	0.000	0.00
25	-0.93	3207	1941	-0.10	0.00	0.023	3.54
50	-0.09	3116	1832	-0.42	0.00	0.047	0.18
75	0.52	3027	1729	-0.95	0.00	0.071	-0.65
100	0.89	2940	1631	-1.72	0.00	0.096	-0.85
125	1.01	2854	1537	-2.75	0.00	0.122	-0.77
150	0.87	2770	1448	-4.04	0.00	0.149	-0.54
175	0.43	2688	1364	-5.62	0.00	0.176	-0.23
200	-0.30	2607	1283	-7.50	0.00	0.205	0.14
225	-1.34	2528	1206	-9.69	0.00	0.234	0.57
250	-2.72	2450	1133	-12.21	0.00	0.264	1.04

25 Yards increment out to 500 Yards

Print Preview   Exit

Figure 1-8.

those hunts, my dad used to joke that the reason there were no ancient Indian paintings of pronghorn in caves or on rock faces was because it was too damn hard to "put the sneak on 'em." Given the terrain and concealment available in most places we hunted, it's no lie to say that they could see you coming a mile away. If the animals spotted us from far enough away, I think they just didn't care about the threat of our presence. This can be taken advantage of with a long-range rifle and a shooter behind it who uses it correctly.

I'll mention here that having a rifle capable of printing sub-MOA groups at 1,000 yards does not mean that it is ethical to attempt to kill game at 1,000 yards! Shot placement is key. My .308 Win-chester Tikka T3 with 1:11 rate of twist barrel prints sub-MOA groups out to 950 yards consistently. I know that I can only ethically attempt shots at game animals out to 700 yards, though. No matter the day, I know that at every distance from 50 to 700 yards, I can place a single shot in a 4-inch circle. Any farther than that, my groups may still be sub-MOA, but the shot placement isn't always perfect on that first shot. The moral is to know your limitations, abilities, and at what distance you can drop your animal, guaranteed 100 percent of the time.

In addition to competitors and hunters, others who may need a 1,000-yard rifle include recreational target shooters. Military/law enforcement shooters who just want to have fun or stay sharp off the job often desire them as well. It also may be a useful suggestion for military/law enforcement shooters who are issued precision rifles to purchase a rifle of the same barrel length, rate of twist, and caliber as that of their issue. By doing this the shooter can work up an extremely accurate hand load for his duty weapon (unit policy dependent)— rifle accuracy depending most upon ammunition quality in precision firearms.

Finding a hand load that outperforms the cartridges provided by the military or your department and using them in your issued rifle may not always be legal without specific permission, but after having worked up an optimal hand load recipe and having put some rounds on paper with your personal rig, it couldn't hurt your status with your first-line supervisor to suggest or request using your personal cartridges after showing him the difference in accuracy between your loads and the department/unit's issued loads. Be sure to note that your better shot groups were achieved with the same type of rifle as your rig at work. Permission to develop a hand load for your gun at work may be denied, but it will absolutely show that your interest in your job extends beyond that of the workplace—and that whether or not your unit is training regularly, *your* skill with your rifle is always going to be proficient, because your job at work is also your hobby at home.

There are two requirements a rifle must meet in order to be considered a "1,000-yard rifle." The projectile must be traveling 1,116 feet per second (supersonic)—or faster, preferably—as it passes the 1,000-yard point, and the rifle must be accurate enough to be on target with each shot at 1,000 yards. Naturally it is preferred that the shots be tightly grouped, not just on target.

The reason a bullet must be supersonic at whatever distance a shooter decides to shoot at, is that once a bullet of any caliber begins traveling less than 1,116 fps, the bullet is considered "inconsistent," and accuracy tends to suffer greatly. At common ground elevations, less than 1,116 fps is subsonic. In order to print the best groups on paper, you'll need to keep the projectile supersonic to at least Mach 1, based on the ground elevation you're firing from. Look back at the chart labeled "Perfor-

mance Comparison of Three Common Varmint Loads." At the bottom of the comparison, "Maximum Effective Range" simply shows the maximum distance at which each load remains above 1,100 fps, based on our ballistic software's yield in the "Calculate" and "Ballistic Report" tabs. This is the part of the software we were using to view the path of our bullet, given our specified zero distance when we were finding our hunting zero for the .243 Winchester earlier this chapter. On that same screen is a "Velocity" column for each range as the bullet passes by. Be advised that many ballistic software products do not account for the fact that as the bullet loses velocity during flight, the ballistic coefficient of the bullet is reduced. I've found Remington Shoot! Ballistic Software to yield nearly perfect elevation correction predictions out to 700 yards; beyond that, I find the rounds of my .308 Winchester striking low by up to 2 MOA. Despite this, the software is excellent for comparing different cartridges and getting on paper at ranges beyond that which I've fired.

Of the rifle cartridges that remain supersonic at 1,000 yards, which one should you choose? One way to decide on a 1,000-yard capable caliber, if the gun's primary purpose is hunting, is to determine the maximum weight you're willing to carry. If you're not willing to carry a gun that weighs more than 22 pounds, don't purchase a caliber that is painful to shoot if weighing less than 22 pounds. I enjoy precision shooting, but if it stings every time I pull the trigger, the fun goes away pretty quickly. A heavy gun is definitely worth its weight, especially if you're moving straight to a static position to sit or lie in wait for your game to show itself. Despite the .338 Lapua Magnum cartridge having over twice the amount of rifle powder weight as a .308 Winchester, the rifle in Figure 1-9 has less felt recoil than does my .308 Winchester. While the .338 is has a heavier barrel, its muzzle brake is the significant factor in its reduced recoil.

Another way to decide would be to research the costs of ammunition, based on the calibers you are considering. Or you could decide on a 1,000-yard capable caliber by determining which cartridge and bullet for whatever caliber features the least amount of drift due to the presence of a crosswind, the most difficult environmental factor to compensate for correctly after making the adjustment for

Figure 1-9. Savage .338 Lapua Magnum.

range to the target. By using the bullet that is comparatively less susceptible to horizontal movement during flight due to wind, the shooter has more room for error. So if a shooter were off in his wind estimation by one or two miles per hour, the bullet least susceptible to horizontal movement due to the presence of wind would strike closer to the point of aim. For target shooting, it could be the difference between a high score and a low score. For hunting, it could be the difference between taking a quick-killing, ethical shot or taking an unethical shot and causing the animal's slow death. (Beside the obvious desire to avoid causing unnecessary pain to the animal, a slower death means more difficult tracking. A slow death also results in less desirable meat

flavor due to the release of adrenaline into the muscle tissue while the animal is waiting to die. Well-placed shots are important.)

Below are a few examples of how an 8-mph crosswind affects three common long-range cartridges, all of which remain supersonic at 1,000 yards at all land elevations.

The .300 Winchester Magnum yields the least amount of wind drift at every distance, compared to the .308 Winchester and the .260 Remington loads. The cartridge with the least amount of wind drift, given the same wind condition, is not necessarily the best cartridge for everyone. The specific accuracy of the rifle itself—an even bigger factor if the shooter tunes his loads to his spe-

1,000-YARD RIFLE—WIND DRIFT COMPARISON

8 MPH FULL VALUE WIND
(from the 3 o'clock or 9 o'clock)

.308 Winchester 175-grain Sierra MatchKing 2,600 fps .496 ballistic coefficient	.300 Winchester Magnum 190-grain Sierra MatchKing 2,900 fps .535 ballistic coefficient	.260 Remington 120-grain Nosler Ballistic Tip 2,950 fps .417 ballistic coefficient

YARDS

800 48.13 inches drift	37.13 inches drift	50.22 inches drift
900 63.35 inches drift	48.70 inches drift	66.71 inches drift
1,000 80.92 inches drift	62.18 inches drift	86.00 inches drift

The above ammunition is based on Federal Premium ammunition.[2]

11

Figure 1-10. Glassing target area from abandoned fighting position in Afghanistan.

cific rifle, as shown in Chapter 7—plus the skill of the person shooting the rifle, plus the quality of ammunition used will result in the highest score on paper. The cartridge yielding the least amount of wind drift *does* allow for more human error while shooting, though.

Let's see what effect a judgment error of 2 miles per hour of wind-speed has, while shooting at 1,000 yards. In our scenario there are three rifles at the range: a .308 Win, a .300 WinMag, and a .260 Rem. All three rifles are using the cartridges from the example below. In the chart below are the conditions at the range today.

There is something to be gained by choosing a rifle based on which caliber is least susceptible to wind drift, but it is only one of many factors that may be used to choose a 1,000-yard capable rifle.

CHOOSING A RATE OF TWIST

After you find a cartridge that fits your needs, you probably need a rifle to put it in to make it useful. Before deciding on a rifle, decide whether you want/need a custom barrel, or if the barrel you require is easy to find on the rifle you plan to purchase. Different bullets have different ideal conditions for their best long-range performance. One of those conditions is the rate of twist of the rifle barrel. *It is important that you match the length of the bullet you intend to use with a rifle barrel of the proper twist rate.* By ignoring this important factor, your rifle may be able to hold sub-MOA accuracy at shorter distances from 50 to 200 yards—depending on the caliber—but the bullet will not be stabilized for shooting farther out, especially at 400 yards plus.

A good example of this is a scenario I experienced while setting up a rifle for an F-Class Target Rifle (T/R) competition. In F-Class Target Rifle, the caliber options are .223 Remington and .308 Winchester—all other calibers go into the Open Class. I knew I wanted to select .308 Winchester as my cal-

R	(Range)	1,000 yards
A	(Angle)	0 degrees
W	(Wind)	3 mph (but the shooters think it's 5 mph)
P	(Pressure)	28.53 inches Hg
A	(Altitude)	0 ft
T	(Temperature)	59 degrees F
		. . . and the humidity measures 78 percent

Given: a 2 mph miscalculation of wind-speed downrange by all three shooters

	.308 Winchester	.300 Winchester Magnum	.260 Remington
Yards			
1,000	off by 20.23 inches	off by 15.55 inches	off by 21.5 inches

Figure 1-11. This Tikka T3 caliber .308 Winchester has a heavy varmint barrel with a 1:11 rate of twist.

iber of choice. I figured the heavier, higher-ballistic coefficient bullet would buck the wind better than any .223 Remington bullet. After some research, I found that there was no hope for a 168-grain .308 caliber bullet to achieve sub-MOA results out to 1,000 yards. I therefore chose a 1:11 rate of twist Tikka T3 Varmint for the job. The hand load I built for this gun yields sub-MOA performance for me out to 950 yards. So close, but I fell short of my goal! I use this rifle and ammunition combination for 600-yard F-Class T/R, but it is out of the question for shooting at the 1,000-yard mark. The gun and ammo is sub-MOA, the bullet is stabilized at long range and is therefore sub-MOA at long range, but it just doesn't have the legs for consistent sub-MOA performance at 1,000 yards. The first 600-yard F-Class event I shot at, I noticed the .308 Winchester guys all were mostly shooting 190-grain bullets out of 1:10 twist barrels. This setup would've been the effective choice for using a caliber .308 Winchester rifle at all distances up to 1,000 yards.

Now we'll explore how to determine the ideal rate of twist for a specific bullet in a given diameter. First, a couple of terms need to be defined in order to ensure understanding. The *bearing surface* of a bullet is the part of the bullet that is in direct contact with the bore of the rifle, more specifically, in contact with the lands of the bore. The bearing sur-face lands on the lands—makes sense. The longer the bearing surface of a bullet is, the faster the bar-rel's rate of twist needs to be in order to stabilize the bullet. Unfortunately, most bullet manufactur-ers don't report the lengths of the bullets they pro-duce, though you can call the manufacturer's toll-free number and ask a service technician what weight bullets in a specified caliber have what length. The technicians at Sierra Bullets, for exam-ple, have always been helpful to me.

Manufacturers *do* report bullet weight, though, and bullet weight and bullet length share a positive correlation—the heavier the bullet, the longer the bullet tends to be, and the longer the bullet, the longer the bearing surface.

The other term to understand is *rate of twist* (ROT). The rate of twist of a barrel is defined as how many inches of travel down the bore it takes a bullet to make one full rotation. For example, a pop-ular twist rate for the .308 Winchester is 1 twist in 10 inches. This can be stated many different ways —1/10, 1-10, 1 in 10, or 1 twist in 10 inches—but we will be using 1:10. The bigger the number repre-sented in inches, the slower the twist rate of the barrel is. A 1:10 rate of twist is a faster twist rate than 1:12, because a barrel with a 1:10 twist rate will cause a bullet to spin more times given the same length of travel down the bore.

13

Accuracy seriously suffers if the bullet is unstable during flight. The bullet will begin to wobble if unstable—the wobble growing exponentially worse as the projectile continues downrange. This wobble will be present if the bearing surface of the bullet is too short *or* too long for the rate of twist of your rifle barrel.

The Greenhill Formula was formerly considered the best way to obtain the perfect twist rate for whatever bullet you wanted to use at whatever speed. Updated methods for obtaining the ideal twist rate for rifles are based on the original Greenhill Formula. The difference between the original Greenhill Formula and the best current method of obtaining ideal twist rate is that the constant (150 or 180 in the Greenhill Formula) fluctuates in accordance with the rifle's muzzle velocity—the higher the muzzle velocity, the larger the constant gets.

Using the Greenhill Formula, let's figure out the ideal rate of twist for the 175-grain Sierra Match-King bullet that is used in the Federal Gold Medal Match .308 Winchester cartridges. After having contacted Sierra Bullets, we know that the 175-grain Sierra MatchKing bullet averages 1.242 inches long. When fired out of a factory-loaded Federal Gold Medal Match cartridge, the bullet reportedly has a muzzle velocity of 2,600 fps. What twist rate would be best to stabilize this bullet?

$$\frac{(.308)(.308)}{1.242} \times 150 = 11.46 \text{ inches}$$

Well, they don't traditionally make a 1:11.46 ROT barrel for off-the-shelf rifles chambered in .308 Winchester. You could get a barrel with custom rifling. There *are* ready-to-purchase rifles that come with barrels that will stabilize this bullet though. A 1:12 rate of twist would be too slow to stabilize this bullet. A 1:11 twist rate would work, but a 1:11.25 rate-of-twist barrel would work even better, such as is standard for the U.S. Army's M24 SWS. The ammunition provided for the Army's M24 SWS happens to be the 175-grain M118LR (long range) cartridge, yielding +/- 2,650 fps.

There are common twist rates for each rifle caliber. If the bullet you intend to use is a common weight for that caliber of rifle, chances are you won't need to fit a custom barrel to a receiver—you can just get a full rig, already set up, and use the proper length/weight bullet for that given caliber and muzzle velocity. I should note here that I've found the Greenhill Formula to be an extremely effective tool to match the rate of twist of a bore to the length of a .30 caliber bullet. I've found the Greenhill Formula to be much less effective with bullets not having a .30-inch diameter, such as my .223 Remington caliber rifle, which has a 16-inch barrel. Using the Greenhill Formula, I was pointed in the direction of a 77-grain projectile. I found that my 1:9 rate of twist stabilized 55-grain projectiles more successfully than any other bullet weight. Be advised.

ACCURACY GUARANTEE

There are a handful of rifle manufacturers that guarantee the accuracy of the rifles they produce. Among them are Sako, Tikka, and Weatherby for noncustom built bolt-action rifles, and Rock River Arms and Armalite for AR-style semiautomatic rifles. Depending on the model, these rifles guarantee sub-MOA accuracy—absolutely essential for shooting long range. There are also pricier makes and models, some custom built, some not, that guaran-

GREENHILL FORMULA

$$\frac{(\text{Diameter of the Bullet}) (\text{Diameter of the Bullet})}{(\text{Length of the Bullet})} \times 150 = \text{Ideal Twist Rate in Inches}$$

For muzzle velocities over 2,800 fps, the number "150" should be replaced by the constant "180."

tee 1/2-MOA or even 1/4-MOA accuracy when firing factory match-grade ammunition. Ed Brown builds custom rifles with such guarantees. Doing research is important before deciding on which rifle is for you. Find out what the manufacturer has to say about the rifle you're interested in, read some consumer reviews on the rifle, and determine pros and cons. A little bit of research will most likely get you into a rig you'll want to keep for the rest of your life, pending new barrels should you shoot this much. If you fire that rifle to the point that you shoot the barrel out, you may then consider re-barreling the receiver and trying out a faster twist rate to shoot a heavier/longer bullet in that caliber.

You're likely to find that shooting a heavier, higher ballistic coefficient bullet will increase the max effective range of your rifle within the same caliber. Again, you must select a rate of twist that will stabilize this heavier bullet. Having said that, if your current rate of twist isn't stabilizing those heavier bullets that you desire to use, don't trash your current barrel quite yet! Through hand loading, if you can safely increase the muzzle velocity by 100 or 200 feet per second, you may be pleasantly surprised to see that the same heavier bullet that once failed to be stable in your rifle is now stable in flight due to the increase in muzzle velocity.

As for me, the day that my Tikka barrel gets shot out is nearing. As Krieger does not accept Tikka as a receiver type to fit their barrels, I've made the decision to put the money from the current rig toward a Surgeon 591 R Action—for .308 Winchester, yet again—and fit a heavy contour 1.25-inch-diameter Krieger 28-inch barrel with a 1:10 twist rate for the heavier 190-grain Sierra MatchKing. This will make the rifle much more effective at 1,000 yards, although yield similar accuracy results from 950 yards and closer. Also, the heavier bullet, having a higher ballistic coefficient, will buck the wind better.

PUTTING IT ALL TOGETHER

By now you should have a good idea of the caliber that will best fit the primary and secondary purposes of your desired style of shooting. At the very minimum, you have the tools to use to determine your caliber and bullet weight, rate of twist, barrel type as per weight and length, and whether a bolt action or semiautomatic action will be best for you.

You can fit your 1.5-pound Timney trigger to your top-of-the-line Surgeon or Stiller action with a trued receiver and bolt face, headspace a heavy contour 1.25-inch straight Krieger or Bartlein cut-rifled barrel to the action, and have a chamber cut with a custom reamer by your favorite gunsmith. This will allow you to fit your carefully neck-turned cases just .005-inch from your chamber neck. You can drop this barreled action into an Accuracy International Chassis System to solve the action bedding and pillar bedding issue. On top of this product you can put your favorite NightForce 5.5-22x56mm riflescope with MOAR reticle wearing 30mm Badger Ordnance rings that you already share between two other rifles. I consider all these products to be top of the line. If you don't put this system together correctly, the performance at the range is sure to disappoint you.

Materials needed to set up your rifle are a scope base, scope rings, riflescope, cheek piece, torque wrenches graduated in inch-pounds, necessary attachments for the torque wrenches that fit in your action screws and the screws of your top ring halves, a small level that can fit on the top of your scope's elevation knob, blue Loctite, and red Loctite. The torque wrenches can be purchased from Belknap Tools. Read the rest of this book before placing any orders for the above equipment.

ACTION SCREWS

The action screws of a bolt-action rifle are found on the bottom of the action. These screws hold the action to the stock. These action screws must be torqued to 65 inch-pounds so that during recoil they do not come loose. If these screws loosen during the act of firing, accuracy goes out the window. If your bottom metal (the metal around the trigger) is actually plastic or polymer, you may not be able to torque this prescribed amount. Replacing the plastic with metal would be the best course of action. You could instead elect to buy a high enough quality rifle that the manufacturer doesn't use plastic on this important part. If the action screws begin to strip prior to reaching the 65 inch-pound mark, this too is a bad sign. I'd recommend replacing your action screws with heads for use with Allen wrenches instead of flat-head screwdrivers.

ATTACHING THE SCOPE BASE

The scope base is that 1913 or Picatinny rail that goes on top of the receiver. The bottom halves of the scope rings attach to this rail. Some scope bases are integral to the receiver, such as on Surgeon Action products. Therefore, the base can never come loose, as it is machined from the same piece of metal as the rest of the receiver. The scope base of most bolt-action receivers is (or was at one time) separate. Most scope bases are held to the top of the action with screws that fit into the top of the rail, and secure the scope base to the top of the receiver. Clean up the top of the action and bottom of the scope base with acetone to remove any old oil or debris. Apply a very light coat of Hoppes 9 to the bottom of the scope base—just enough to see visible wetness. Torque the scope base to the action using the provided screws using a torque wrench set to 15, 20, or 25 inch-pounds. After all screws are torqued to this specification, remove one screw at a time. Add a small amount of red Loctite to the screw threads and torque the screw back into place. Use red Loctite (permanent) if you know you're never going to put a different scope base on this rifle. Use blue Loctite (breakable using hand tools) if you may one day put a different scope base on the gun.

A person who may one day be in the market for a night sight to put in front of his day scope may want a MARS rail one day. This person should use blue Loctite for the scope base that he may one day replace.

After all screws are in place with Loctite on the threads, re-torque each one to ensure that there is no more movement. If you get any movement on one screw, re-torque them all.

You may be asking yourself, "What's wrong with just using the dovetail that's already there? Why pay another $100 for a rail?"

If you stick with this sport long enough, eventually you'll acquire one great riflescope for your primary precision rifle. After being successful with this gun, you'll probably build another one. If every rifle you have has a rail, you can share that one amazing riflescope on all rifles. The change in zero is 100-percent consistent. My NightForce riflescope sits with the front scope ring two rails away from the front of the scope base. When I remove the rifle-scope using my 65 inch-pound torque wrench and put the scope on my AR-10 (and torque to 65 inch-pounds), I place the front scope ring in the farthest-forward available rail on my AR-10 to produce the correct eye relief. By adjusting the optic 4.25 MOA up and .75 MOA right, my optic is now zeroed at 100 yards for the AR-10. After throwing on this adjustment, I slip the turrets back to zero and proceed. Why would I buy a bunch of midgrade optics—one for each rifle? I just use the one great optic on all my rifles. I can only shoot one gun at a time, so they don't all need to be wearing scopes at the same time. The zero change is so perfectly consistent, that if I zero the scope on one gun and put the scope on a different gun—having applied the required zero change—I don't even have to confirm zero on the new rifle. It's that perfect.

I once took my AR-10 to the nearby 600-yard rifle range. I had two 20-inch-tall targets downrange. After doing all the work I needed to do with my AR-10, I pulled my bolt-action rifle out of the bag, took the optic off the AR-10, and torqued it to my bolt-action rifle. I re-zeroed the scope for 100 yards, applied the zero-slip for the different gun, slipped the rings, put on my 600-yard adjustment, and proceeded to shoot my second target at 600 yards, this time using my bolt-action rifle. I got a few crazy looks from my friends. After we drove downrange and my company saw that I was center-center on both targets—both vertically and horizontally—the crazy looks turned into questions.

This will save you some time. If your scope rings are high enough that your scope can fit on an AR-15 or AR-10 without the bell of the scope touching the gun, then the scope height is tall enough to be shared on every rifle that has a 1913 or Picatinny scope base.

ATTACHING THE BOTTOM RING HALVES

If the scope rings move during the recoil of the rifle shot, the point of impact on the target will change. I'll show you how to do your part to keep this movement between the scope rings and the scope base from occurring; however, selecting high quality scope rings is a prerequisite. I trust Night-Force, Badger Ordnance, and LaRue Tactical products for both scope bases and scope rings. I'm sure there are other high-grade products out there that I haven't tested. Do more research if you want to find the cheapest product that can withstand the recoil of your gun, but the above-mentioned brands are the only names you're getting from me. I find what works, and I stick with it. Why look for more equipment that works if I'm satisfied with what I have?

Ultimately, you want your scope rings as far from the adjustment turrets as possible without touching where the bell of the scope starts on either side. There are only two critical things that must happen here: within whatever rail slot the bottom ring half is sitting, it needs to be pushed forward toward the muzzle as far as possible; and the bottom ring half needs to be torqued to 65 inch-pounds if it features a 1/2-inch nut. If the bottom ring half is attached with a flat-head screw driver, buy a different product.

Put a loose bottom ring half on your rail. You can slide it forward and back within whichever slot it's sitting in. By pushing it forward toward the muzzle end of the gun, the bottom ring half cannot move during recoil. It will want to move forward during a rifle shot, but it cannot if it is already as far forward as it can go within its slot.

SETTING YOUR CHEEK HEIGHT

I'm not afraid to admit when I reach a failure point, especially if others can benefit from the experience. Despite all the marksmanship training I've received in the military and from civilian trainers, not one instructor has touched on this subject in this manner. The instruction I've received on the proper setting for cheek height is that it needs to be high enough that you don't need to use your neck muscles to lift your head high enough to acquire a sight picture, and your cheek rest cannot disable your bolt (for bolt-action rifles) while in the fully open position and your cheek rest cannot disable the charging handle (for AR-style rifles) when pulled all the way to the rear position. Both of these are important.

While training I set my cheek height to a comfortable position for shooting in the prone firing position—i.e., lying down. When I was on a combat deployment, the cheek rest was exactly the same as during training. During a firefight, we identified one of the points of origin of enemy fire as coming from within a cave to our north 955 meters away. I quickly threw the proper elevation on my optic, kneeled behind the ledge of the rooftop I was on, and established my steady firing position. Mashing my head down against the cheek rest, I couldn't get down low enough to get a proper sight picture. Lowering the cheek rest took all of five seconds. But really, this was terrible timing. By setting your cheek height from a bench, you'll be able to shoot from the prone, but you'll have to raise your head ever so slightly while in the prone position. By setting your cheek height to be perfect from the prone, your cheek piece will be too high for firing from a bench.

Set your cheek height from a bench, even if you never plan to shoot from a bench.

SETTING THE EYE RELIEF OF YOUR RIFLESCOPE AND ATTACHING THE TOP RING HALVES

Eye relief is the distance from your eye to the ocular lens—the back of the scope. Without your scope on the gun, bring it close to your eye, almost touching. Slowly pull it away while still looking through the scope. You should have a full field of view until the ocular lens is about 3 to 3.5 inches from your eye, depending on the model. The farther you take it away from your eye, the thicker the black ring around your cross-hair gets. If you pull the scope far enough away from your eye, the sight picture is completely blacked out. Bring the scope back to your eye very slowly. The black ring around your sight picture will start getting thinner and thinner. As soon as the black ring is about to disappear, that is your perfect eye relief.

When you get down behind your rifle in the prone (lying down) position, you want to be completely comfortable behind the gun. Don't stretch your neck forward or pull it back. Have a friend place the scope on the bottom ring halves. Don't move your head! Have your friend move the scope forward or back until you achieve that same thin black ring described above. Get off the gun and look at the position of the scope. With the scope in this ideal position, can you move the bottom ring halves farther from the turrets without touching the bell on either side? If so, do so.

Mark the scope tube with a pencil on the outside of the rings and remove the scope. Clean up the inside of the scope rings with acetone to remove any oil or debris. Place a thin layer of Hoppes 9 on the inside of the scope rings, just enough to see visible wetness. This will serve as a rust preventative. No, your scope will not slide during a rifle shot due to this application of solvent. Place a level on the scope base and level the gun by twisting it right and left as needed. Remove the level. Put the scope back on the bottom ring halves, where you marked it earlier, without moving the gun. Place your level on top of the elevation knob and turn the scope to the left or right until the level looks the same as when it was on the scope base. Place the top scope ring halves on top of the bottom ring halves. Tighten the screws by hand softly until you feel resistance. Tighten each screw to 15, 20, or 25 inch-pounds. Each set of scope rings will specify which torque setting to use. If not, simply call the company that built them to get this answer. After all screws are tightened to this specification and none of them move when you pass over all of them once more, you scope is good to go for now. Do not apply any form of Loctite to the screws at this time.

VERIFY THAT YOUR BARREL IS FLOATED IN THE STOCK

Take two business cards or two index cards and slide them between the barrel and the stock all the way back to where the barrel meets the receiver. Did you make it all the way there without resistance? If not, you need to remove material from the inside of your stock. As the barrel heats up during a course of fire, the metal will expand no matter how thick your barrel is. If any part of the barrel is touching the stock, as the barrel heats, the stock will put pressure on the barrel at different amounts and at different points for each subsequent rifle

shot. This will destroy your accuracy. Fire a string of 20 shots. With the barrel hot, can you still fit one business card or index card all the way under your barrel all the way back to the receiver? If so, the relationship between your barrel and stock is OK.

I am a big Remington 700 fan. However, most of Remington's factory, lower-grade stocks do not float the barrel. If you buy a Rem700 off the rack at a gun shop, there's a good chance it doesn't have a floated barrel. Many shooters will take that new Rem700 home and put it in a better stock right away. There are many high-grade rifle stock options, including McMillan. Yet other shooters will take their Rem700 home and proceed to sandpaper the inside of their stock until the barrel is floated. There are then those unfortunate few who just don't know and shoot the gun without a floated barrel only to print 2-inch groups at 100 yards using match-grade ammunition. Get a good stock or invest in sandpaper and time. Chassis systems are an excellent choice, and not all of them are exceedingly heavy.

Some bolt-action rifles do not require the barrel to be floated. Many rifles require a pressure point impacting the bottom of the barrel near the end of the rifle stock. Avoid these rifle models for the applications discussed in this text.

LET'S SHOOT

Be sure to bring your torque wrenches to the range with you. Whether you're breaking in a barrel, zeroing and going straight into gathering ballistic data, or jumping right into hand load development, torque your action screws and bottom ring halves to 65 inch-pounds and torque the screws on your top ring halves to 15, 20, or 25 inch-pounds—whichever specification you selected at home. After the first five shots, re-torque everything! Your action screws and bottom ring halves were likely just fine. But it is very common to get movement on those tiny screws on your top ring halves after they've experienced a bit of violent recoil.

While the barrel is still hot is a great time to verify whether the barrel is still floated. Slide that business card under there. Having spent your ammunition that you planned to shoot that day, re-torque your top ring halves. There should be zero movement this time. If you'd like to remove each screw one at a time and apply blue Loctite, you may. If there is no chance this rifle scope will ever go on any other rifle, it is wise to apply the blue Loctite. Remove one screw at a time, apply the Loctite to the threads, and re-torque the screw. Move on to the next screw in a crisscross fashion, just as if you're changing a tire on a truck. From now on, you won't have to re-torque these before shooting. You'll still have to torque the action screws and bottom ring halves to 65 inch-pounds before each shooting event to eliminate the possible variable of their coming loose. I like to mark the heads of my action screws and the piece of bottom metal in contact with the action screws with a sharpie. Before shooting, I look at the bottom of the action screws. If the sharpie markings have not separated, the action screws didn't come loose. There is no need to torque.

If you choose not to use the blue Loctite on the top ring half screws, be sure to torque them before each shooting event

ENDNOTES

1. http://en.wikipedia.org/wiki/Precision_rifle#Classification
2. http://www.federalpremium.com

CHAPTER TWO

SCOPE MECHANICS: MINUTES OF ANGLE AND MILS

Figure 2-1. Hasty scan of a target area with vector laser rangefinder, Afghanistan.

You're trying out a new rifle range. You brought your sub-MOA-capable .308 Winchester bolt-action rifle with you today, along with some match-grade factory loads—175-grain HPBT, Federal Gold Medal Match. The range safety officer tells you that the 10 targets downrange in front of you are staggered in increments of 100 yards, going from the 100-yard target to the 1,000-yard target. You verify the distance to each target with your laser rangefinder.

The range safety officer made a mistake, however. The range is actually staggered in 100-*meter* increments, not 100-*yard* increments. Honest mistake, of course, but this would have seriously affected the data you're about to gather. You adjust your riflescope *up* for a 660-yard shot (600 meters)—14.25 MOA *up*. A 5-mph wind is blowing to the left, from the 3 o'clock. You lay your crosshairs over the target. You know that when you have achieved a steady position and proper sight picture, you will either hold the crosshair center-center over the target, or .8 mils to the right to compensate for wind. If the wind has calmed by the time you're ready to fire, you'll aim with no hold; if the wind is back to 5 mph when you're ready to fire, you'll hold .8 mils to the right of the desired point of impact.

You've achieved a steady position and proper sight picture. You pause your breathing and slowly squeeze the trigger. Your rifle recoils into your shoulder. Dust splashes around the target indicating a hit at just about the time your rifle comes out of its recoil. You put four more shots into the same target, taking your time, slow and controlled, waiting for that wind to calm down completely to 0 mph or kick up to what you believe to be 5 mph, because those are the holds you're prepared to use—no hold or .8 mils to the right. Dust splashes from the base of the target about one second after each time you squeeze the trigger.

Understanding how to effectively use MOA and mils is essential for effectively shooting at long range, and is extremely rewarding. By knowing *exactly* where to set your riflescope's adjustment knobs or where to place your target on a mil-dot reticle, you reap the reward of feeling confident in your ability to be on target at any distance within the maximum effective range of your rifle.

ALL SCOPES ARE NOT CREATED EQUAL

Using a precision rifle is useless if the riflescope mounted is not recoil-proof for the given caliber being fired, or the elevation and windage adjustments are not both "true" and "consistent." Unfortunately, sportsmen generally get what they pay for when it comes to optics. Maybe guys try to save money on the riflescope because of how hard it would be to explain to the wife why the scope costs as much as the rifle—I don't know.

As far as price range is concerned, the least costly riflescope I've found and used—which was capable of handling the recoil of centerfire rifle calibers, magnums included, and that possessed true and consistent elevation and windage adjustments—came out to $300. That optic was a Super Sniper riflescope that I purchased from SWFA. Top-of-the-line glass can run more than $2,000. Premier Reticles, U.S. Optics, Schmidt and Bender, and NightForce are among the top-of-the-line riflescope manufacturers.

Be wary of purchasing a Swarovski, Kales, or any other European, Australian, or other foreign-built riflescope; many of them do not use minutes of angle for their adjustments, because minutes of angle are based on inches. The United States is gradually making the transition to .1-mil-per-click riflescopes so that the turret adjustments communicate with the mil-dot reticles but, for precision, 1/4 MOA is a smaller adjustment than .1 mil. There is good in both methods. You will learn how to use mils in this text, as they are very useful for shot placement.

Some riflescopes use MPI, or mean point of impact, and should be avoided if you wish to achieve your best shot-placement results. These turrets use friction plates, which you slip to zero, instead of traditional target knobs. The turret is calibrated to one cartridge fired out of one rifle, not your ammo or your rifle. They are generally a bit off. Friction plates are neither good nor bad, but imperfect shot placement is bad. Just be aware.

Be sure to do sufficient research prior to buying a scope in order to ensure that it is recoil-proof for the caliber you are shooting. Also make certain that the scope has true and consistent windage and elevation adjustments. A riflescope that isn't recoil-proof will not stay zeroed as shots are fired and, in addition, may be destroyed due to recoil. A riflescope that doesn't have true and consistent adjustments isn't useful for what we need either. We need to be able to change the zero from, say, the preset zero of 300 yards to a zero of 470 yards in order to place a shot on a deer or other target at that distance. After the shot we need to be able to put the riflescope back to its desired zero distance of 300 yards. The same requirement applies to compensating for wind. We need to be able to put the windage turret back to its original zero position and know that the crosshairs are in fact in the same place as before the adjustment was made.

As with the rifle you decide to use, you should read some consumer reviews on the piece of glass you plan to buy to better ensure that it will work for you. Some names in riflescopes are trusted, some are not, and some manufacturers make some of their models well and other models poorly. NightForce, Premier Reticles, and U.S. Optics are among the trusted names that deserve consideration. One that deserves special mention is the Leupold Custom Shop, where you can select what type of knobs you want on your scope (BDC or target knobs), and what type of reticle shape you desire—to include a reticle based on the ballistic profile of your rifle and ammunition combination.

TRUE AND CONSISTENT RIFLESCOPE ADJUSTMENTS

The Box Test

After obtaining the riflescope that you'll be using on your precision rifle, it is important to test that the minute of angle increments are in fact "minutes of angle." This means that every minute equals 1.047 inches at 100 yards, or 1.152 inches at 100 meters. Mount the scope to the rifle in accordance with the directions, select a box of match-grade ammunition, such as Federal Gold Medal Match, and take a trip to the range.

After zeroing your optic to yourself and the ammunition you're using, prepare a target at 100 yards.

This is how we will go about conducting the "box test."

Step 1. (Figure 2-2) We need to put a two-shot group in the target, from a zeroed riflescope.

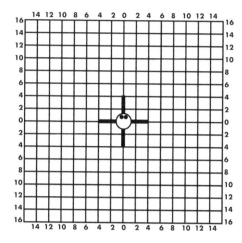

Figure 2-2.

Step 2. (Figure 2-3) Adjust the riflescope *up* 10 minutes of angle. On a 1-MOA-per-click riflescope, you will need 10 clicks; on a 1/4-MOA-per-click riflescope, it will be 40 clicks, and on a 1/8-MOA-per-click riflescope it will be 80 clicks. After making the 10-MOA adjustment in the up direction, fire another two shots—making sure to use the same point of aim as before. The placement of these two shots should be 10.47 inches above the first two shots, if firing at a 100-yard target, and should appear to be 3.0 mils above the first shot group (10 MOA = 2.96 mils).

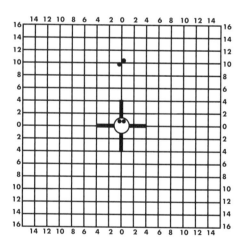

Figure 2-3.

Step 3. (Figure 2-4) Now, adjust the riflescope *left* 10 MOA. Fire another two shots using the same point of aim as the first two shots.

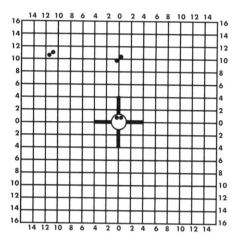

Figure 2-4.

Step 4. (Figure 2-5) Adjust the riflescope *down* 10 MOA, and fire another two shots while maintaining the same point of aim as the first two shots placed on the target.

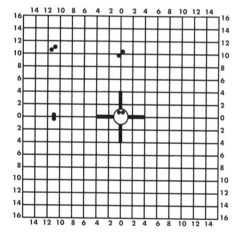

Figure 2-5.

23

Step 5. (Figure 2-6) Finally, adjust the riflescope *right* 10 MOA, and fire the final two shots. The last two shots you fire should be right on top of the first two shots you fired at the target.

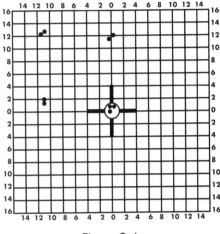

Figure 2-6.

If your last two shots landed on top of your first two shots—and the scope is thus back to its original zero point—your riflescope has "consistent" adjustments. You'll need to recover the target and take a measuring tape to the target to determine if your adjustments are "true." If your target was 100 yards away and the distance between each shot group *was not* 10.47 inches, record how many inches each shot group was from the last, and record that information in your data book. This will allow you to determine how many inches at 100 yards 1 MOA is for your riflescope. For example, one of my riflescopes features elevation adjustments in increments of 1.017 inches per MOA at 100 yards—not a huge difference, but important to know.

If you fired at a target exactly 100 yards away, then the distance from the first group to the second group, second group to the third, third group to the fourth, and fourth group to the fifth should all measure 10.47 inches apart. Ten MOA at 100 yards = 10.47 inches. If the shot groups measure 10.47 inches from one another, your riflescope has "true" adjustments—meaning that the number of clicks your scope requires to move the point of impact 1 MOA is correct.

Be aware that 1 minute of angle is a different amount of inches at every distance! The 10.47 inches that was required at 100 yards is not the

amount of inches required at, say, 110 yards. At 110 yards, 10 MOA is 11.52 inches. You should bring a rangefinder to ensure the exact distance to the target for this drill. Don't just take the range safety officer's word for it that the target is exactly 100 yards away. For all we know, the guy who put the target out there walked out, counting every time his left foot hit the ground, stopped at 60, and stuck the target in the ground.

USING MINUTES OF ANGLE IN RIFLESCOPES

A minute of angle, or MOA, is approximately 1/60 of a degree. See the math below:

A circle = 360 degrees, or 6,400 mils. To convert mils to MOA, multiply by 3.375.

(6,400 mils) (3.375)= 21,600.0 MOA

So, there are 21,600 MOA in a circle.

$$\frac{\textbf{21,600 MOA}}{\textbf{360 degrees}} = \textbf{60 MOA per degree}$$

A minute of angle is a fraction of a degree. Regardless what fraction of a degree it is, the important point is that it is a *consistent* fraction of a degree. Most American-made riflescopes use micro-adjustments calibrated in minutes of angle for the windage and elevation turrets.

Imagine pointing your rifle downrange. If you take a look through the riflescope, you see some style of crosshair with a chunk of terrain behind it. But while a riflescope sees in a straight line, we know that bullets do not travel in straight lines. Say we have a target we'd like to shoot using a rifle chambered in .243 Winchester. The target is sitting at 525 yards. Our rifle is zeroed at 300 yards. We know the bullet we're using will reportedly hit 36.61 inches low at 525 yards, given our 300-yard zero. If we determine how many MOA to adjust the optic up, we can re-zero our rifle for the 525-yard shot, take the shot, then set the rifle back to its original 300-yard zero. Here is how to convert inches to MOA based on any given distance.

$$\frac{\text{Inches}}{\text{Distance}/100} = \text{Answer} \qquad \frac{\text{Answer}}{1.047} = \text{MOA}$$

or

Inches/Distance in Hundreds/1.047 = MOA

In order to adjust our riflescope for this 525-yard shot, we need to compensate for 36.61 inches at 525 yards.

36.61 inches/5.25 yards/1.047 = 6.66 MOA.

Therefore, we round 6.66 to 6.75 MOA and adjust in the up direction.

Adjusting the scope up 6.75 MOA for a rifle shot at 525 yards moves the impact of the bullet 37.1 inches, which places the shot on target. After you are finished shooting, remember to reset your riflescope to its original zero. This is especially easy to remember if using a riflescope with target knobs or a BDC knob where the elevation turret is. After shooting with a target-knob style riflescope, simply set the elevation knob back to "0." A similar concept applies to resetting the BDC knob. We'll go more into specifics about using target knobs and BDC knobs later.

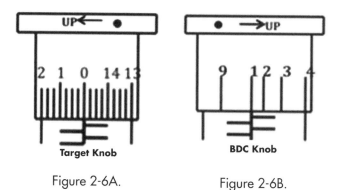

Figure 2-6A.   Figure 2-6B.

Note: the reason we include the constant "1.047" in the formula is because 1 MOA does not equal 1 inch at 100 yards. One MOA equals 1.047 inches at 100 yards. If working in meters, the constant is 1.152 inches instead of 1.047 inches. One inch at 100 meters equals 1.152 inches.

Here are the required formulas for going from MOA to inches, whether working in meters or yards:

YARDS
(MOA)(distance/100)(1.047) = inches

METERS
(MOA)(distance/100)(1.152) = inches

For example, to find how many inches 6 MOA is at 200 meters, we set up the formula like this:

(6 MOA)(2.00 meters)(1.152) = 13.82 inches

It is important to throw the constant into the formula, especially when working in meters. That 1.152 inches per hundred meters per minute of angle adds up as distance increases.

USING A RIFLESCOPE WITH TARGET KNOBS

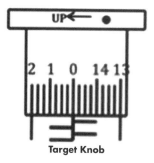

Figure 2-7.

Represented in Figure 2-7 is a target knob for a 1/4-MOA-per-click riflescope. Four clicks of this knob are required to move the impact of the bullet 1 MOA on the target. As you can see in the figure, each minute of angle is clearly marked on the knob by a number representing how many MOA you've moved by spinning the knob. Understand that each number *does not* represent the distance to the target! Each number represents one minute of angle. Refer to the example in the last section, when we simulated a 525-yard shot with a .243 Win. In order to be on target, we needed to adjust the riflescope up 6.75 MOA. On a riflescope with target knobs, that adjustment would look like Figure 2-8 on the elevation knob.

25

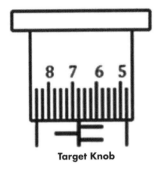

Target Knob

Figure 2-8.

25 yards	Must hit .05 inches above point of aim
50 yards	Must hit 1.38 inches above point of aim
100 yards	Must hit 3.38 inches above point of aim

One option to obtain a 300-yard zero is to measure and mark the desired impact point above the bull's-eye on the target (Figure 2-9).

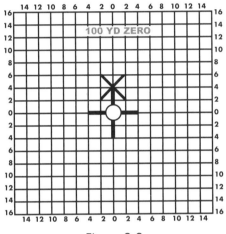

Figure 2-9.

Figure 2-8 is what a 6.75-MOA adjustment in the up direction looks like on a target knob. It is important to note that spinning the knob rotates a screw within the scope, and that screw tilts a piece of glass to change the relationship with the crosshair and the image in the riflescope. Going in the up direction on a riflescope tends to yield a "true" scope adjustment, but when going back down to your zero point, it is wise to pass the "0" by three or four clicks, then go back up to the "0" mark. The last few clicks on the scope should be in the up direction to ensure that the screw and the glass within the riflescope are sitting the same way as before the scope's zero was changed for the shot. This also applies to the windage turret if you compensated for wind speed during the shot. Always make the last few clicks of any adjustment in the same direction. On my riflescope, spinning the elevation knob counterclockwise is the *up* direction, and spinning the windage knob counterclockwise is the *right* direction. Every correction I make with my target knobs ends in a counterclockwise rotation of either knob.

TWO WAYS TO ZERO USING TARGET KNOBS, AND ONE METHOD TO AVOID

We'll use a common .243 Winchester load for this example. By utilizing a personal ballistic software application, we find that in order to obtain a 300-yard zero for our .243 Win, the impact of the bullet must be as follows at 25 yards, 50 yards, and 100 yards:

I drew the "X" on this 100-yard target 3.38 inches above the point of aim. Now I just have to aim at the bull's-eye and zero my rounds to hit the black "X" I drew on the target. After getting my bullets on that "X," my rifle is zeroed for 300 yards. *This is the method I'd like you to avoid.* Do not trust ballistic software in this manner.

A better way to zero the same rifle—the riflescope having target knobs—is to zero the rifle to hit the bull's-eye at 100 yards, such as in Figure 2-10, then to "slip the rings" to obtain that 300-yard zero.

The rifle is now zeroed at 100 yards, but we need it to be zeroed for 300 yards. Simply refer to the ballistic card you created for your cartridge fired from your rifle to see what minute-of-angle setting is required for a 100-yard shot when your rifle is zeroed for 300 yards. The riflescope on our .243 Win needs to be adjusted 3.25 MOA down in order to be zeroed for a shot at 100 yards. Therefore, having zeroed at 100 yards, simply "slip the ring" to the 3.25 MOA *down* position. To "slip the ring" means to remove the elevation knob from the riflescope by loosening the screw/screws on

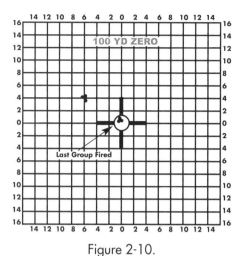

Figure 2-10.

the knob itself, and reattaching the knob to the riflescope at the desired MOA setting. See Figures 2-11A through 2-11E for a visual aid of this concept.

The most effective method of zeroing is to zero your rifle at the desired distance, then slip the ring to read 0.00 MOA. I recommend having a zero distance of 100 or 200 yards, but that's not a function of performance or how high or low the bullet hits with the same point of aim at multiple distances. It's much simpler than that—it is a huge timesaver to be able to see the bullet holes in your target.

With my 16x42mm riflescope, I can clearly see .30-caliber bullet holes in paper at 200 yards. This is my zero distance for my .308 Winchester rifle. With my 10x42mm riflescope, I can clearly see .223 caliber holes in paper at 100 yards. This is the zero distance for my AR-15. The timesaver is the fact that you don't have to travel downrange to see where you're hitting. If the target has inch rings or an inch grid, you can simply convert the number of inches you have to move to hit center-center to MOA. I find that using a mil-dot reticle or MOA works just as well if not better. I just convert mils to MOA, which we'll begin to cover at length later in this chapter.

USING A BDC ELEVATION KNOB

A riflescope with a bullet-drop compensating (BDC) knob uses minutes of angle for its increments of adjustment, as does a riflescope with target knobs. The BDC knob, though, is an elevation knob that is calibrated to compensate for the drop of a bullet of a given caliber and muzzle velocity, at distances in increments of 100 yards or meters.

The riflescope wearing the BDC knob in Figure 2-12 is currently zeroed for 100 yards. If the shooter rotates the knob to the number "3," the rifle will then be zeroed for a 300-yard rifle shot. If he rotates it to the "4," the

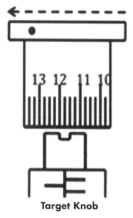

Figure 2-11A.
I just zeroed the rifle at 100 yards.

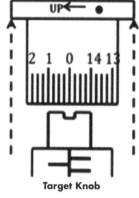

Figure 2-11B.
Pop the elevation knob off the riflescope.

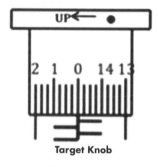

Figure 2-11C.
Rotate the elevation knob to the *down* 3.25-MOA position.

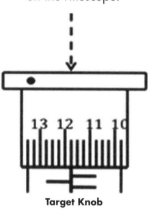

Figure 2-11D.
Lower the elevation knob back onto the riflescope, maintaining that down 3.25-MOA position.

Figure 2-11E.
Adjust the elevation knob in the *up* direction 3.25 MOA, back to the "0" position. The rifle is now zeroed for 300 yards.

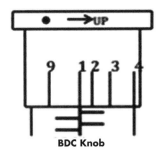

Figure 2-12.
The bullet-drop compensation knob.

rifle is then zeroed for a 400-yard rifle shot, and so on. Some riflescopes, such as the Leupold M3A, which was issued for use with the M24 SWS (Sniper Weapon System) that was used by the U.S. Army, are fitted with BDC knobs that are graduated in 1-MOA-per-click increments. The Leupold Mark 4 features either 1-MOA-per-click elevation adjustments or 1/2-MOA-per-click adjustments, model dependent. The BDC knobs that come with the Leupold M3A and the Leupold Mark 4 are calibrated for the M118LR, 7.62x51mm NATO cartridge that was fired from the M24, and is still used in the M110 SASS.

By using a riflescope with a BDC elevation knob, shots may be taken more quickly after ranging a target. This is because—in theory—the shooter doesn't need to view a reference card to see how many MOA up or down he needs to adjust in order to be on target at whatever distance. As an example, a shooter using *target knobs* with his .243 Win rifle needs to look at a reference card in order to see that, "Oh, for this 500-yard shot, I need to adjust up 5.75 MOA." After viewing the reference card and dialing in the elevation correction, the shooter can then reassume his cheek-weld to take the shot. A shooter using a BDC knob can simply range the target and spin his BDC knob to the "5" (representing 500 yards) . . . in theory.

The advantage of using a BDC elevation knob is that shots may be taken more quickly, which can be a serious plus on a tactical rifle, for example. Also, the rings can be slipped in the same manner as target knobs. One drawback of using a BDC elevation knob is that a BDC knob is only correct for one set of environmental conditions (altitude, temperature, humidity, and air pressure). Also, each number on a BDC elevation knob represents 100 yards or meters. For tactical applications or hunting scenarios, it is likely that most

shots will not be at exactly 100-yard or -meter increments. Shots come at odd distances. If a desired target appears at 430 yards, the shooter may be able to closely estimate where between the "4" and the "5" the 430-yard mark lies on the BDC knob, but it would only be estimation. The amount of error produced by using this method is OK given a man-sized object, especially if time is an issue, but for a varmint shooter trying to hit a groundhog at the same distance, sacrificing a little time for accuracy by using a riflescope with target knobs would likely be more necessary. Also, I have yet to use a BDC knob on an M24, M110 SASS, or M2010 that is perfect.

There is a way to overcome having to estimate when using a BDC elevation knob. Shooters who use BDC knobs will often carry a reference card, as shooters who use riflescopes with target knobs should carry. Figure 2-13 is an example of a BDC Knob Reference Card made for the .308 Winchester load listed below. In this chart, the BDC knob perfectly matches the trajectory of the cartridge used in the rifle. Again, I have yet to experience a BDC knob of the "perfect" type.

.308 Winchester BDC Knob Reference

175-grain, HPBT Sierra MatchKing
2,600 fps .496 BC

Yards	Adjust	Yards	Adjust
25	**1** + 2 clicks	425	**4** + 1 click
50	**1**	450	**4** + 2 clicks
75	**1**	475	**4** + 3 clicks
100	**1**	**500**	**5**
125	**1**	525	**5** + 1 click
150	**1** + 1 click	550	**5** + 2 clicks
175	**1** + 1 click	575	**5** + 3 clicks
200	**2**	**600**	**6**
225	**2** +1 click	625	**6** + 1 click
250	**2** +1 click	650	**6** + 2 clicks
275	**2** +2 clicks	675	**6** + 4 clicks
300	**3**	**700**	**7**
325	**3** + 1 click	725	**7** + 1 click
350	**3** + 2 clicks	750	**7** + 3 clicks
375	**3** + 3 clicks	775	**7** + 4 clicks
400	**4**	**800**	**8**

Figure 2-13

USING A MIL-DOT RETICLE FOR RANGING TARGETS, HOLDING DURING SHOTS, AND OBTAINING A ZERO

Having a mil-dot reticle, and understanding how to use it, is useful for a few reasons. By understanding how to use a mil-dot reticle, a shooter will use less ammunition to acquire a zero. A mil-dot reticle can be utilized to obtain a semi-accurate range to a target when a laser rangefinder is unavailable—or if the shooter simply doesn't want to pay the money for a rangefinder. Most importantly, a mil-dot reticle may be used to acquire an accurate "hold" on a target, for example if there is not enough time to click away on the elevation knob before the shot. The shooter may also compensate for wind if he is using a riflescope with a mil-dot reticle.

Mil-Dot Reticle Dimensions

Mil-dots are different sizes depending on the riflescope. Be sure to check your specific riflescope reticle dimensions. For example, a Leupold mil-dot measures .2 mils tall, whereas a Super Sniper riflescope mil-dot measures .25 mils tall. The dimensions of a Leupold mil-dot reticle are shown in Figure 2-14.

Converting MOA to Mils and Mils Back to MOA

There are 3.375 MOA in one mil. That means the distance from the crosshair to the center of the mil-dot just above it equals 1 mil, or about 3 1/2 MOA. Here are the conversion formulas:

$$\text{MOA}/3.375 = \text{mils} \qquad (\text{mils})(3.375) = \text{MOA}$$

or

$$(\text{MOA})(.296) = \text{mils} \qquad \text{mils}/.296 = \text{MOA}$$

Using a Mil-Dot Reticle for Ranging

Our man-sized silhouette in the next example measures 36 inches tall. We can use either of the sight pictures in Figure 2-15 to measure the height of the object in mils. We can use either the crosshair as the base for the object, or the thick part of reticle that lies 5 mils below the crosshair as the base for the object.

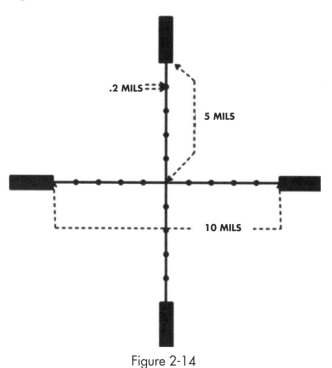

.2 MILS

5 MILS

10 MILS

Figure 2-14

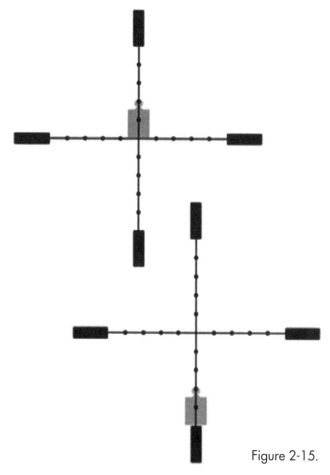

Figure 2-15.

Whether using the first sight picture in Figure 2-15 or the second, the man-sized silhouette measures 2 mils tall. Provided below are the formulas required to range the object in either yards or meters

$$\frac{(\text{height in inches})(27.94)}{\text{mils}} = \text{yards}$$

$$\frac{(\text{height in inches})(25.4)}{\text{mils}} = \text{meters}$$

In this example, the formula to range the object in yards is built like this:

$$\frac{(36)(27.94)}{2} = 502.92 \text{ yards}$$

The formula to range the object in meters is built like this:

$$\frac{(36)(25.4)}{2} = 457.2 \text{ meters}$$

Holding for a Shot Using Mil-Dots

Let's continue to use the example wherein the target is a 36-inch-tall, man-sized silhouette, which measures 2 mils tall in our optic. We've already dis-

covered that the target is sitting at 457 meters. Let's say that the rifle we're using requires a 7-MOA adjustment in the up direction to be zeroed at 450 meters. In order to use the mil-dot reticle to hold for the shot, the sight picture should look like Figure 2-16.

Zeroing a Rifle Using a Mil-Dot Reticle

A shooter who has and knows how to use a mil-dot reticle while zeroing at *any* distance will spend less time while zeroing and will save money on ammunition. Without a mil-dot reticle, the shooter would need to put a three-shot group in paper at a known distance, measure how far in inches the three-shot group is away from the bull's-eye, convert inches to MOA, adjust the riflescope as needed, then fire again in order to put the next three-shot group in the bull's-eye. A shooter using a mil-dot reticle while zeroing does not need to know how many inches high, low, left, or right his shots are hitting in relation to the bull's-eye. Next, we will view an example of how easy it is to zero when using a riflescope with a mil-dot reticle. We'll use Figure 2-17 as an example:

In Figure 2-17, we need to adjust the riflescope *down* and *right* in hopes that the next three-shot group will lie directly over the bull's-eye. Measure

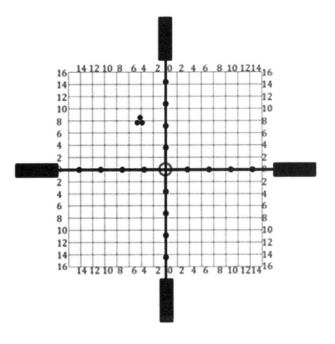

Figure 2-17.

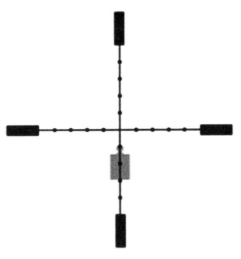

Figure 2-16.
A 7.0 MOA equals 2.07 mils.
The hold for the shot is 2.1 mils high.

how many mils down we need to adjust the riflescope, and measure how many mils right we need to adjust the riflescope. After that, convert mils to MOA, and adjust the riflescope accordingly.

The shot needs to come 2.2 mils down.
(2.2 mils)(3.375) = 7.43 MOA

The shot needs to come right 1.1 mils
(1.1 mils)(3.375) = 3.71 MOA

Adjust the riflescope 7.5 MOA down and 3.75 MOA right, and the next three-shot group should be right on the bull's-eye, provided that our riflescope has "true" and "consistent" adjustments, and our counting of the mils from the bull's-eye to the shot group was, in fact, correct.

After putting the rounds in the bull's-eye, slip the windage knob back to "0" and slip the elevation knob in accordance with the distance to the target as you would normally do, whether using a target elevation knob or a BDC elevation.

PRACTICAL EXERCISE

In order to ensure understanding of how to manipulate minutes of angle, mils, and the mil-dot reticle, get a sheet of paper and a calculator. Make sure you can answer the questions in the practical exercise using information I've provided in Figure 2-18 before proceeding. Answers for the practical exercise are provided at the end of this chapter.

Figure 2-18 provides the caliber rifle you're shooting, cartridge data, and a ballistic report for your rifle. Use this ballistic report during the practical exercise.

7mm Remington Magnum
150-grain Sierra GameKing
3,110 fps, .436 ballistic coefficient

Humidity: 78 percent relative humidity
Altitude: 0 feet above sea level
Temperature: 59 degrees F

YARDS	MOA	YARDS	MOA
25	-.32	525	5.75
50	-2.74	550	6.5
75	-3.25	575	7.25
100	-3.26	600	8.0
125	-3.0	625	9.0
150	-2.75	650	9.75
175	-2.5	675	10.75
200	-2.0	700	11.5
225	-1.5	725	12.5
250	-1.0	750	13.5
275	-.5	775	14.5
300	⊕	800	15.5
325	.5	825	16.75
350	1.25	850	17.75
375	1.75	875	19.0
400	2.5	900	20.0
425	3.0	925	21.2
450	3.75	950	22.5
475	4.25	975	24.0
500	5.0	1000	25.25

Figure 2-18.

7mm Remington Magnum
Inches of drift due to crosswind

YARDS	3 MPH	5 MPH
100	.18″	.31″
200	.8″	1.34″
300	1.87″	3.12″
400	3.44″	5.74″
500	5.63″	9.38″
600	8.38″	13.97″
700	11.97″	19.95″
800	16.41″	27.34″
900	21.64″	36.07″
1000	28.0″	46.67″

Figure 2-18.

QUESTIONS

1) The rifle is zeroed at 300 yards. How many inches low will the bullet hit if shot at 500 yards if no adjustment is made to the optic prior to the shot?

2) The rifle is zeroed at 300 yards. How many inches high will the bullet hit if shot at a 100-yard target?

3) The only target you have available is sitting at 75 yards. In order to confirm that the rifle is zeroed for 300 yards, how many inches above or below the bull's-eye should the bullets impact on the 75-yard target?

4) You're setting up for a shot at 700 yards. A 5 mph crosswind is present. The wind is coming from the immediate right, or the 3 o'clock. How many MOA up or down should you set the elevation knob? How many MOA right or left should you set the windage knob for this shot?

5) What is the correct elevation adjustment for a shot at 400 yards? What is the correct hold in mils if there is a 5-mph crosswind at the same distance?

6) What is the hold in mils for a 550-yard shot? Draw what the sight picture should look like.

7) What is the hold in mils for an 800-yard shot? Draw what the sight picture should look like.

8) What is the MOA correction for a 3-mph crosswind at 300 yards? The wind is blowing from the immediate left, or the 9 o'clock.

9) Figure 2-19 shows your sight picture after having put a three-shot group into a target at 300 yards. There are no 1-inch or 2-inch sized reference squares on the target. The target is just a large piece of white paper you bought at the convenience store nearby, with an "X" you made on the target out of red tape. In order to zero your 7mm Rem Mag for 300 yards, what adjustments do you need to make to your riflescope?

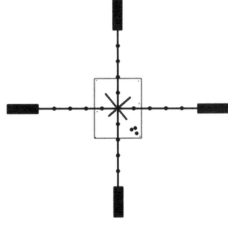

Figure 2-19.
300-yard paper target

10) Figure 2-20 shows your sight picture. Range the 40-inch-tall, man-sized silhouette in either yards or meters.

11) Figure 2-21 shows your sight picture. Range the 40-inch-tall, man-sized silhouette in either yards or meters.

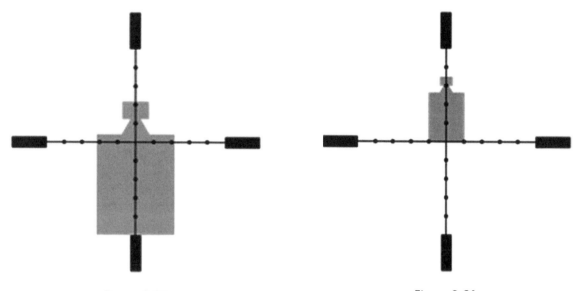

Figure 2-20.   Figure 2-21.

12) Figure 2-22 shows your sight picture. Range the 40-inch-tall, man-sized silhouette in either yards or meters.

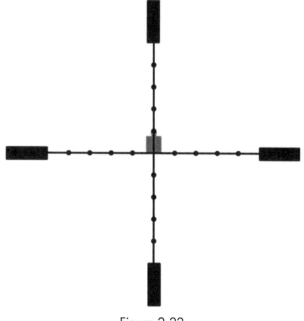

Figure 2-22.

ANSWERS

1) Convert 5 MOA at 500 yards to inches. (5 MOA)(5.00 yards)(1.047) = **26.175 inches drop @ 500 yards.**

2) Convert 3.26 MOA at 100 yards to inches. (3.26 MOA)(1.00 yards)(1.047) = **3.413 inches high @ 100 yards.**

3) Convert 3.25 MOA at 75 yards to inches. (3.25 MOA)(.75 yards)(1.047) = **2.552 inches high @ 75 yards.**

4) View the reference card to see that you need to adjust the elevation knob *up* **11.5 MOA**. Convert 19.95 inches at 700 yards to MOA to get the windage correction.
   19.95 inches / 7.00 yards / 1.047 = 2.72 MOA. We'll round that to **right 2.75 MOA.**
   Note: Be sure to wait for the wind to blow 5 mph before taking the shot.
   Don't adjust for a 5-mph crosswind, then shoot when there is no wind blowing at all.

5) View the reference card to see that at 400 yards, the adjustment required is **up 2.5 MOA**.
   Convert 5.74 inches at 400 yards to MOA, then convert that answer in MOA to mils to get the correct hold.
   5.74 inches / 4.00 yards / 1.047 = 1.37 MOA
   1.37 MOA / 3.375 = **.4 mils** is the required hold to compensate for a 5-mph full-value wind at 400 yards, as shown in Figure 2-23.

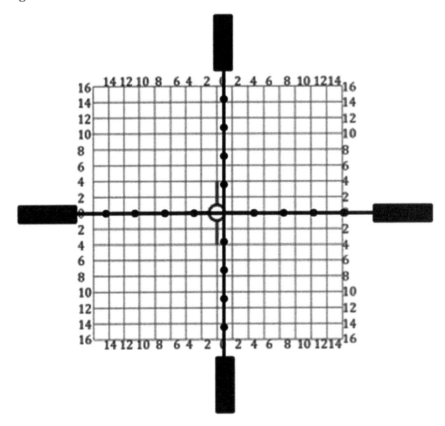

Figure 2-23.
A .4 mil hold for wind correction.

6) The MOA adjustment for a 550-yard shot is **6.5 MOA up**.
   6.5 MOA / 3.375 = **1.9 mils**
   The sight picture should look like Figure 2-24.

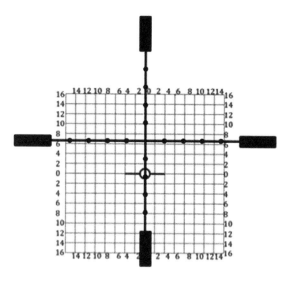

Figure 2-24.
A 1.9 mil hold for distance compensation.

7) The MOA adjustment for an 800-yard shot is **15.5 MOA up**.
   15.5 /3.375 = **4.6 mils**
   The sight picture should look like Figure 2-25.

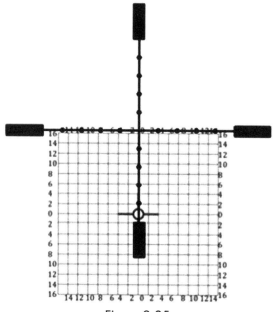

Figure 2-25.
A .6 mil hold for distance compensation

8) A 3-mph full-value wind from the 9 o'clock will take our bullet 1.87 inches at 300 yards.
1.87 inches / 3.00 yards/ 1.047 = .595 MOA
1.87 inches @ 300 yards = .595 MOA. We'll adjust the riflescope **.5 MOA left**
to compensate for a 3-mph wind that is blowing from the 9 o'clock position.

9) Based on my judgment, the center point of the three-shot group is sitting 1.4 mils low and 1 mil to the right of the point of aim. Therefore, the adjustment that needs to be made to the riflescope is:
(1.4 mils)(3.375) = 4.725 MOA, so **4.75 MOA up**
(1 mil)(3.375) = 3.375 MOA, so **3.5 MOA left**
Note: It requires a day with excellent atmospheric conditions to view bullet holes at 300 yards.

10) The 40-inch-tall target measures 7.1 mils tall.

$$\frac{(40 \text{ inches})(25.4)}{7.1 \text{ mils}} = \textbf{143 meters}$$

or

$$\frac{(40 \text{ inches})(27.94)}{7.1 \text{ mils}} = \textbf{157 yards}$$

11) The 40-inch-tall target measures 3.5 mils tall.

$$\frac{(40 \text{ inches})(25.4)}{3.5 \text{ mils}} = \textbf{290 meters}$$

or

$$\frac{(40 \text{ inches})(27.94)}{3.5 \text{ mils}} = \textbf{319 yards}$$

12) The 40-inch-tall target measures 1.0 mils tall.

$$\frac{(40 \text{ inches})(25.4)}{1.0 \text{ mils}} = \textbf{1,016 meters}$$

or

$$\frac{(40 \text{ inches})(27.94)}{1.0 \text{ mils}} = \textbf{1,118 yards}$$

Note: Attempting to precisely range targets using a mil-dot reticle proves difficult beyond 600 meters. A good rangefinder is critical to the success of your rifle and ammunition system.

You probably noticed during the practical exercise that including the number of inches the bullet drifts at each distance is pretty useless. While using ballistic software, it may be necessary to convert from inches to MOA, or from inches to mils. I just wanted to make sure that you were comfortable with converting from inches to MOA or mils. The best way I've found to set up a wind table is to have the answers in both MOA and in mils, for different wind speeds at each distance . . . but we'll get into detail about that in Chapter 5. You won't want to waste any time using a calculator while taking shots—do the math at home! An effective method I use is to organize all data into six different sections:

R Range
A Angle
W Wind
P Pressure
A Altitude
T Temperature

After determining and organizing my data, I print it onto compact-sized paper—front and back—and laminate it to resist weather, lots of use, and being stuffed in range bags or pockets. We'll cover a few different ways to set up these reference cards in Chapter 5. Here is one method you can use to organize a wind table:

WIND TABLE

.308 Winchester
175-grain HPBT
2,600 fps
.496 ballistic coefficient

Altitude: 0 feet
Temperature: 59 degrees F
Humidity: 78 percent RH
Air Pressure: 29.53 inches Hg

YARDS	3 MPH		5 MPH		8 MPH		10 MPH	
	MOA	MILS	MOA	MILS	MOA	MILS	MOA	MILS
100	0.25	0.06	0.25	0.1	0.5	0.1	0.5	0.2
200	0.5	0.1	0.75	0.2	1.25	0.33	1.5	0.4
300	0.75	0.2	1	0.3	1.75	0.5	2.25	0.7
400	1	0.3	1.5	0.4	2.5	0.7	3	0.9
500	1.25	0.4	2	0.6	3.25	0.9	4	1.2
600	1.5	0.4	2.5	0.7	4	1.2	5	1.5
700	1.75	0.5	3	0.9	4.75	1.4	6	1.8
800	2.25	0.6	3.5	1.1	5.75	1.7	7.25	2.1
900	2.5	0.7	4.25	1.2	6.75	2	8.5	2.4
1,000	3	0.9	4.75	1.4	7.75	2.2	9.75	2.8

CAPABILITIES OF DIFFERENT RIFLESCOPES AND SELECTING THE ONE FOR YOU

By now you should have a firm grasp on the minimum requirements that your riflescope must meet in order to perform correctly for you. The difference between target knobs and BDC knobs has been identified. You're familiar with both MOA and mils.

Riflescopes come in a variety of different types to fulfill the needs of different types of shooters. In this section, I'll point out the pros and the cons of each to facilitate an effective purchase for you on whichever riflescope you select. Base the choice on your needs, not on the price. Is speed on target an issue of concern for you? It isn't an issue for all shooters. Other hunters tell me that speed is critical for them. It's not for me while hunting. If I'm 300 yards plus from deer or elk, they pay attention to me but don't deviate from their normal habits or direction of travel. I have all day to take the shot. Speed is, however, an issue of concern for tactical shooters.

Vietnam-era riflescopes featured turrets having mil-dot reticles and MOA adjustments for the turrets. By utilizing these two different systems that break down fractions of a degree differently, shooters experienced issues that could've been easily avoided. Shooters would spend numerous extra man-hours during the course of their shooting experience simply converting MOA to mils and mils to MOA during the fabrication of ballistic cards for the gun, holding for wind instead of dialing in, and during the process of zeroing. In recent years, high-quality riflescope companies have addressed this issue by utilizing the same system for both the turrets and the reticle. It is truly a wonder that the transition of riflescopes having turrets and reticles that "communicate" has taken this long to hit the American market where some of the world's most demanding sportsmen and tacticians reside.

Schmidt and Bender, NightForce, U.S. Optics, and Leupold are a handful of riflescope manufacturers that provide different reticle options using the mil system coupled with elevation and windage turrets that feature .1 mil per click adjustments. The benefit of that is this: the ballistic card for whichever rifle to which this type of optic is fitted only requires a "yards/meters" column to identify the distance to the target and a "mils" column to identify the corresponding adjustment. There is no need for an additional "MOA" column. At 500 yards if my mil-hold is 3.8 mils, I can either aim 3.8 mils high using the reticle or I can dial in 3.8 mils up on the elevation turret. It's the same number. Precision shooting at close range and midrange and shooting long range can be difficult to grasp at first. Having a riflescope featuring the same scale for the turrets and the reticle will make your life much easier.

Just as there are "mil-mil" scopes, there are "minute-minute" scopes. My 5.5-22x56mm Night-Force features NightForce's MOAR reticle, which provides 1 MOA per stadia line. The odd number stadia lines are .5 MOA wide so that I can more effectively adjust my rounds center-center of the target while confirming zero or gathering ballistic data. The turrets feature 1/4 MOA per click increments. For each of my rifles that wear this optic, I only need columns identifying my distance to the target and what the MOA adjustment is for each specified range. I can either hold using the reticle or dial in the elevation adjustment. Either way, it's the same number. What I find myself doing much of the time is holding using the reticle after "dialing in the remainder." For example, if my 600-yard adjustment requires 18.75 MOA up, I dial .75 MOA up and hold 18 MOA high using the reticle. This saves time and allows me to have a perfect sight picture without guessing where to aim in space between two stadia lines.

Additionally, even the highest-grade riflescopes can occasionally track imperfectly. When dialing in a large mil or MOA adjustment, such as 25 MOA up, using the elevation turret, how do you know the scope went exactly 25 MOA up? You don't. By using the reticle and dialing in the remainder this variable is all but eliminated. I chose the "minute-minute" system over the "mil-mil" system because .25 MOA is a finer adjustment than .1 mil. A tenth of a mil is .3375 MOA. While engaging a target at the same distance for a string of 20 scored shots as an F-Class shooter, I prefer to use the turret to dial in 100 percent of my elevation adjustment to better view the mirage from one shot to the next. If holding using the reticle for double-digit MOA adjustments, your field of view below the target is smaller. In most cases, the usable mirage from which I get my wind speed and direction is located below the target. I want to see as much of the mirage as possible while shooting at any distance.

The one drawback of using my MOAR reticle is that I have four major options with which to make adjustments—none of which is ideal for tactical shooting, though the first three are very effective. I can dial in the elevation adjustment and use the reticle for the windage adjustment. I can dial in the windage adjustment (which may change when I'm ready to fire) and use the reticle for my elevation adjustment. Or I can dial in both the elevation and the windage using the turrets. None of these three options is the most effective option for engaging a target quickly with a high degree of precision. The precision is there, but the speed is not. The fourth option is to hold using the reticle for my elevation adjustment and at the same time hold for the windage adjustment as well. This will result in me aiming "in space." There will be no stadia line or crosshair laid directly over my target. The speed on target is there, but the same degree of precision is not. I avoid engaging targets using this last option at all costs. In most circumstances I'll take precision over speed.

There is a strong argument for the "mil-mil" system. For example, the H59 reticle made by Horus Vision features a reticle having .2 mils per stadia line, and instead of a crosshair with stadia lines on it, the reticle employs a grid-type system. Using my MOAR reticle on my NightForce, I have to dial in either the windage or the elevation adjustment for the maximum degree of precision. With a grid-style reticle, the shooter can apply his elevation and his windage adjustment with the reticle while still having a stadia line laid over his target. This type of reticle is the best option I've seen as of today for precision shooting without sacrificing speed as a result of dialing in adjustments.

Although the turrets of a mil-mil riflescope are .1 mil per increment, which is less precise than a .25-MOA increment, the reticle makes up for this. I mentioned that I'm a big fan of holding for the majority of the elevation adjustment and dialing the remainder. This method is both quick and gives me a precise aiming point. Let's do an example of this using a mil-mil scope featuring a Horus H59 reticle. Let's say that our 630-yard shot requires a 6.5-mil

hold. By using the reticle alone, we would have a stadia line for the 6.4-mil mark and the 6.6-mil mark and have to place our aiming point in the space between. To apply our hold and dial the remainder, all we have to do is hold 6.4 mils high and dial .1 mil up to get our 6.5 mils of elevation and use our stadia line as our aiming point. It doesn't take that much time to dial in 1 click on your scope. For tactical shooting, we're not going for the X-ring here. There isn't much space for error between the 6.4 and 6.6 mil lines. With this type of reticle, the precision is there as well as the speed.

The grid-style reticle is so effective that companies aside from Horus Vision use it in their riflescopes, including Leupold, Schmidt and Bender, and Bushnell. Do not be put off once you see a seemingly busy image of a grid-style reticle. It will not cover up your target, except with a higher amount of usable aiming points, which you would otherwise not have available.

The most difficult reticle to use is the standard mil-dot reticle. The mil-dots are spaced 3.375 MOA apart from one another—i.e., 1 mil apart. While engaging targets rapidly at different distances, the shooter has to guess where his mil hold lies if the hold ends in .2 through .8 mils. An experienced shooter is very effective at this, although he would undoubtedly be better if that mil reticle had stadia lines every .2 mils. I use a mil-dot reticle exclusively throughout this book for the images and practical exercises—not because it's the best choice for all shooters. If I teach you on the most difficult reticle, you'll have the ability to use all of the better options as well.

The benefit of a standard mil-dot reticle is that it's easier on your wallet. The fancier the reticle is, the higher the price. The least costly riflescope today featuring the H59 reticle is the Bushnell HDMR, which averages around $1,700. Despite its price, this reticle has drawbacks, just as it has some great features. Glass quality is less than that of the higher-end riflescope manufacturers. Some Bushnell HDMRs will come with glass that does just fine during a validation test, while other Bushnell HDMRs fall short. If you're willing to spend for the grid-style reticle and high glass quality, then the point is moot. Place an order for the Schmidt and Bender. If you simply don't care about using the reticle and you're excited about dialing in all your shots, a crosshair is fine. In this case, go with a .25 MOA or .125 MOA per click turret so that you have the finest adjustments available.

We've discussed a few reticle styles. The grid-style offers precision and speed for a high-dollar cost. The standard mil-dot reticle sacrifices a bit of precision while taking speedy shots, although you are still able to take speedy shots. Any nongrid-style reticle featuring stadia lines graduated in MOA or .2 mils per line offers a good compromise between speed and precision, and is likewise in the middle price range. I was very happy and successful with my 16x42mm SWFA Super Sniper for years. As mentioned, it features a standard mil-dot reticle and .25 MOA per increment turret adjustments. Although I've upgraded to the aforementioned Night-Force model that goes back and forth between multiple rifles, I continue to dedicate a 10x42mm SWFA Super Sniper to my AR-15 in order to stay proficient on the "old-school stuff."

No matter how much enjoyment I continue to get out of my NightForce, I still have fun rapidly engaging 5-inch reactive targets at odd distances up to 400 yards using my low recoil AR-15 with standard mil-dot reticle. Stapling balloons to target stands at varying target distances is great rapid-succession head shot practice for tactical shooters at very low cost. I require my students to show proficiency in this manner to demonstrate that they've effectively gathered their ballistic data and have correct adjustments for all target ranges, and that they've made their external ballistic algorithm as perfect as possible while using ballistic software to yield elevation adjustments. I avoid relying on ballistic software for elevation adjustments at close and midrange. However, getting those numbers correct while close helps us get on target once we stretch out the target range.

SCOPE TUBE DIAMETER

Why do some scopes have 1-inch-diameter tubes, and others have bigger 30mm tubes? Why do we now have 34mm and 35mm tubes as options? What is the benefit of a thicker scope tube, if any?

Your elevation and windage turrets move an erector tube within the scope body up, down, left, and right. The thicker your scope tube, the more space you have with which to move that erector tube. The thicker the scope tube, the more elevation you have to play with. A common elevation adjustment range for a riflescope featuring a 1-inch tube diameter offers around 60 MOA of available elevation. NightForce riflescopes having 30mm tubes offer 110 MOA of available elevation. Other riflescope companies commonly offer around 90 MOA of available elevation on their 30mm tubes. NightForce's 34mm tube offers 34.9 mils of available elevation (117.75 MOA).

A .308 Winchester caliber rifle with a moderately loaded 190-grain Sierra MatchKing requires around 48 MOA of elevation at 1,000 yards from a 100-yard zero. Why the heck do I need more elevation than that? There are two reasons why you may.

Extreme-Long-Range Target Engagement

If shooting at extreme long range (1,500-plus yards) with a capable caliber out of a system that keeps its shot group on target at that range, you'll need more elevation than your medium-caliber shooting counterparts at the range who stop extending their target range around 1,300 yards at best. A 300-grain Sierra MatchKing .338 Lapua Magnum bullet doesn't reach subsonic speed until around 1,800 yards. The elevation adjustment at this range for this bullet hovers around 70 MOA from a 100-yard zero. Additionally, our top match bullet manufacturing companies are always trying to design bullets that remain stable after having reached subsonic speed. Berger Bullets is one of these companies, and it claims to have succeeded with multiple calibers. A 1-inch scope tube featuring around 60 MOA of elevation just isn't going to cut it in this scenario if you want to keep a 100-yard zero as your benchmark. A 30mm tube with 90 MOA of "ups" might not cut it either for this 70 MOA requirement. How's that? I need 70 MOA, and I have 90!

Most Optics Don't Allow You to Utilize the Full Range of Elevation Adjustment

Most optics are zeroed at 100 yards somewhere in the middle of their travel when using a 0 MOA scope base. While zeroed at 100 yards, my 10x42mm SWFA Super Sniper with 30mm tube already has four baselines visible under the target knob. This tells me that I'm around 60 MOA above the bottom of my travel, giving me 30 MOA of upward available elevation. That's fine for my AR-15 that wears this scope. Most of the time, this rifle holds MOA-sized groups at 500 yards. I gathered data out to 600 yards on this rifle despite the fact that the groups are 15 inches at this distance. At 600 yards my elevation adjustment from my 100-yard benchmark is 19.5 MOA. My elevation has not topped out at this distance.

If your 100-yard benchmark is somewhere in the middle of your available adjustment travel and you need more adjustment range, you don't have to get a new scope. You can fit a 20-MOA or 40-MOA scope base under your rings as needed. This will orient the front of your scope downward, requiring you to make elevation adjustments in the down direction to reacquire your 100-yard zero. After having done so, you will have increased your available elevation by approximately the amount of MOA that your scope base boasted it provides. If you need a 20- or 40-MOA base, screw your elevation knob all the way to the bottom of its travel. Count how many MOA exist below your 100-yard zero point. If the scope base you purchase gives you more MOA than what you just counted, you will not be able to zero your optic at 100 yards using the same aiming point on the reticle. If a shooter has 30 MOA of travel below his 100-yard zero and fits a 40-MOA scope base to his rifle, he will have to deal with a 100-yard bullet impact point approximately 10 MOA above his intended impact point at 100 yards.

This issue of being zeroed at 100 yards somewhere in the middle of your available elevation travel is a non-issue if your scope features a zero-stop function. Some NightForce optics offer this option, and some do not. And NightForce isn't the only company with this feature. It's worth the extra little bit of money. You simply zero at 100 yards, pop the elevation knob off, loosen four screws as instructed in the manual, and screw your elevation all the way down. Now, on a 30mm NightForce tube, you have all 110 MOA of "ups" usable to you. Some folks insist on putting their NightForce with zero-stop function on a 20- or even 40-MOA scope base because they built their gun specifically for extreme-long-range use. These folks believe the scope base

is necessary, in addition to the zero-stop function, giving them 130 to 150 MOA of travel. Our .338 Lapua Magnum example bullet would require around 110 MOA of travel at 2,250 yards, 130 MOA at 2,450 yards, and 150 MOA of travel at 2,600 yards. If this is the type of shooting you're looking to do, the 20- or 40-MOA scope base is necessary. If your extreme-long-range shooting stops at something more reasonable, like around 2,000 yards with this type of heavy magnum caliber, you simply don't need to invest in a 20-MOA base and a riflescope with a zero-stop function. A normal 0-MOA scope base coupled with a riflescope having zero-stop will fit your needs.

FIRST FOCAL PLANE VS. SECOND FOCAL PLANE

Optics that magnify on the second focal plane feature a reticle that is "true" only on one magnification setting. If the scope is fixed power, say 10x only, this is not an issue. My 5.5-22x56mm NightForce is variable power (it magnifies the image between 5.5 and 22 times). The reticle is only true while the optic is set to 22x magnification. The MOAR reticle is 1 MOA per stadia line only at 22x. At all other magnification settings, the reticle dimensions do not represent as identified in the manual for the riflescope. My hold for a 600-yard shot is 18.75 MOA for one of my accuracy loads for my bolt-action rifle. If I apply this hold using the reticle while on the 22x magnification setting, I will hit center-center on the target. If at any other magnification setting, I will not.

First focal plane optics feature reticles that are true at all magnification settings. A 3.5-15x50mm FFP (first focal plane) NightForce will maintain its reticle dimension with respect to the target at all magnifications. If a shooter accidentally bumped his magnification to 13x and shot with a reticle hold, he would still hit center-center. You can identify a first focal plane optic versus a second focal plane optic easily. Bring the scope to you eye and focus on a target. Rotate the magnification setting from max power to low power. If the reticle gets smaller as the target gets smaller as you reduce the magnification, it's a first focal plane optic. If while you're changing the magnification setting the reticle stays the same size, the optic magnifies on the second focal plane.

Which one's better, magnifying on the first or second focal plane? It depends again on what kind of shooting you're doing. My 22x second focal plane NightForce is adequate for my needs. I can clearly focus on 50-yard targets while on max power, which is the closest I'll ever shoot with rifles that wear this optic. I only shoot in dim or well-lit conditions. I can therefore see my adjustment setting on my elevation turret if I absolutely feel the need to reduce the magnification setting.

The tactical community drifts toward the first focal plane option. In night conditions, you can't see your current elevation turret setting without taking a light source to your elevation knob. You zero it to 100 yards and leave it alone. With your night sight attached to the front of your day scope, shooting on max magnification is not going to happen. The night sight reduces your field of view, and on high magnification the digital image produced by the night sight features pixels that are just too big for the shooter to be effective. Even if a shot was taken

with this extremely tiny field of view, the shooter would spend much time trying to find his target again to verify his hit after the recoil of the rifle. The best course of action for shooting with a night sight is to reduce the magnification to 6x magnification or less. By using a first focal plane optic, the shooter can still utilize his mil or MOA holds using the reticle without ever touching his elevation turret. With a second focal plane optic the shooter would be reducing his magnification by the same amount, and the reticle would no longer be usable. So he would have to dial in his elevation adjustments in the dark, counting as he goes instead of quickly jacking the turret to the proper elevation setting for the shot as he would do in the daytime.

Do you need a true reticle on all magnification settings, or will 99 percent of your shooting be on max power? Are you going to shoot with a night sight in front of your day sight? If you're only going to use the scope on max power, a first focal plane optic probably isn't worth the extra bucks. If you shoot a lot at night, you'll get tired of clicking away on a second focal plane optic very quickly.

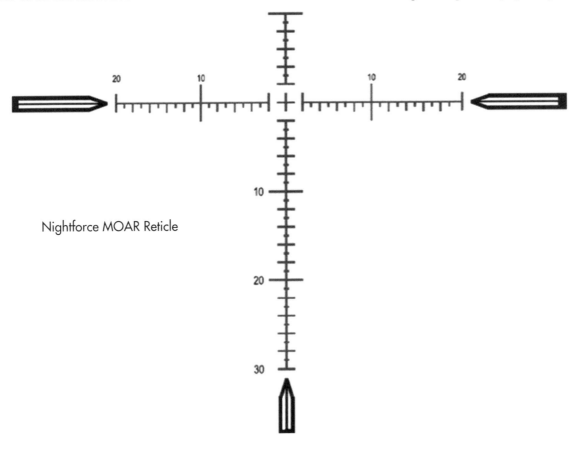

Nightforce MOAR Reticle

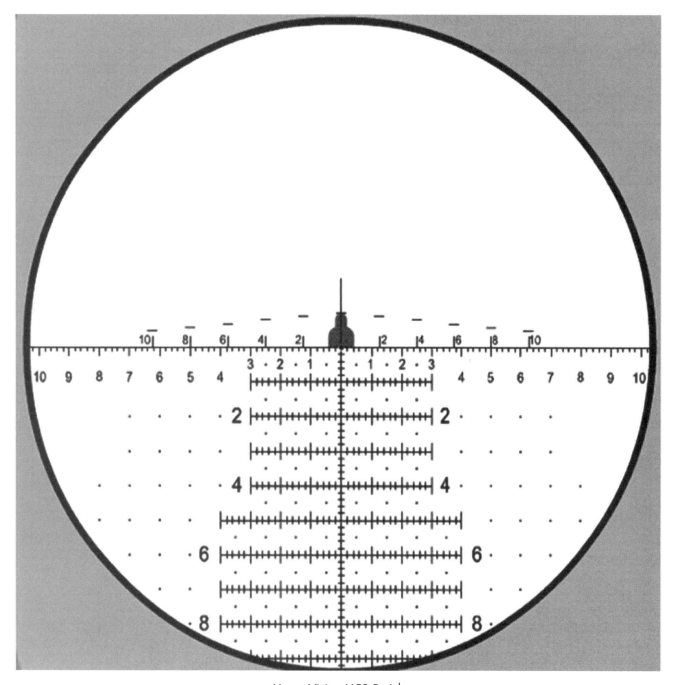

Horus Vision H59 Reticle

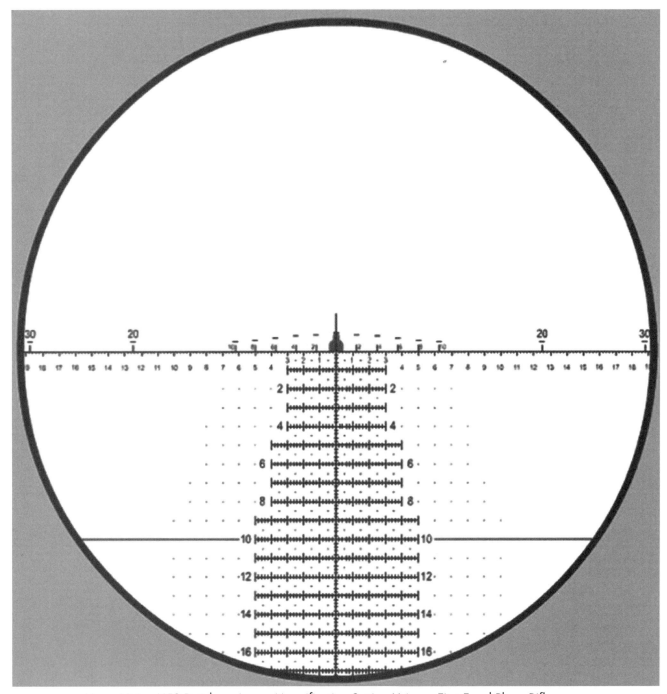

Horus Vision H59 Reticle on Lower Magnification Setting Using a First Focal Plane Riflescope.

CHAPTER THREE

GATHERING DATA, MANIPULATING BALLISTIC SOFTWARE, AND CREATING A BALLISTIC CARD

It is an awesome feeling to walk to a firing point and set up a steady firing position, knowing before I shoot that I'll hit any target I engage, up to 900 yards. When hunting, I know I can take an ethical shot on any large game animal I see within 700 yards of my location, as my shot group at that distance is 2.5 to 3.5 inches. This is not due to military training or firing a round having similar trajectory as the one I've been trained on. No, this is due to having effectively and precisely *gathered data* on my rifle. U.S. military snipers, squad-designated marksmen (if the guy running the program is worth his salt), and civilian competitive shooters alike all gather data on their rifles in one fashion or another in order to engage targets effectively at different distances. Although there are different methods to accomplish this, the intent is the same.

The importance of *gathering data* is on par with selecting a rifle, riflescope, and ammunition that together yield a sub-MOA result on a target. There are

Figure 3-1. Ranging targets with vector. Iraq.

far too many shooters who head off to the range with their sub-MOA rifles and expensive glass, shoot amazing groups at 100 or 200 yards, and leave it at that. Although that's very fulfilling, you can multiply that reward at least tenfold. Not only will I show you how to extend your shooting range, but also how to engage targets effectively at odd distances. If you're preparing for a hunting trip, I doubt the quarry you're looking for will pop up solely at the distance you used in practice.

We will follow this outline during instruction in this chapter:

1. Determine and record a rough adjustment to be on target at each distance in hundreds of yards.
2. Shoot at roughly 100, 200, 300, 400, 500, 600, 700, and 800 yards from the target.
3. Properly record the adjustment at each range, the environmental factors, and placement on the target.
4. Record the adjustment that would put you perfectly on target the next time you fire at that same range, also known as recording your *known data*.
5. Interpolate (or fill in) adjustments for the ranges in between those you've fired from.

GETTING ON PAPER AT RANGE

On the backs of some boxes of rifle ammunition is a graph or chart, such as you'll see in Figure 3-3, showing you the rough trajectory of the cartridge in inches, given a specified zero distance.

In order to get on paper at each range as in Figure 3-3, simply convert inches to either MOA or mils. Refer back to Chapter 1 if needed.

If your ammunition does not provide its rough trajectory on the back of the box, refer to the ammunition maker's website. The trajectory for most American ammunition is almost always provided there, in addition to extended ballistic references for shooting out to 500 or even 600 yards.

If shooting hand loads, or if you simply don't have a trajectory reference for your cartridges, don't just go to the range dialing in adjustments blindly, hoping to be on paper. There are plenty of ballistic software applications that are extremely effective. For example, as of this writing you can download a 30-day free trial of Remington Shoot! ballistic software from the Remington website. I've found this software to be spot on up to 750 yards if you get the ballistic coefficient and muzzle velocity correct. There is also Exbal, which you can purchase for your

Figure 3-2. Gathering data for accurized M14s up to 600 meters. Ft. Campbell, Kentucky.

100 YARDS	200 YARDS	300 YARDS	400 YARDS
⊕	-6.9 Inches	-20.7 Inches	-46.1 Inches

Figure 3-3.

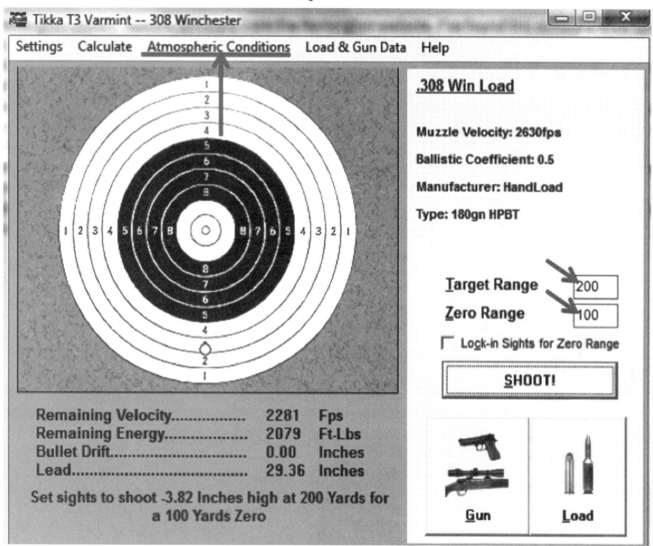

Figure 3-4. This is the main page for Remington Shoot! ballistic software.

PC or get on a Palm Pilot. There is also NightForce and ATrag. Ballistic software is extremely easy to use: you input your muzzle velocity, ballistic coefficient of the bullet, the height of your sight above the bore in inches (or *bore height),* diameter of your round in inches, environmental conditions such as altitude, temperature, and air pressure, and the distance in yards or meters that your rifle is, or will be zeroed at. After entering that information into your software, you click the "Shoot" button—if using Remington Shoot! for example—and the trajectory of your bullet will be given in inches and minutes of angle. You can also tell the ballistic software how you'd like the information given, in increments of

47

10, 25, 50, or 100 yards at a time, up to 1,000 yards or meters. In this section we'll look at how to use Remington Shoot!

The part of the ballistic software that yields the trajectory of your rifle takes the fields I've marked with arrows in Figure 3-5 into consideration. Everything else is miscellaneous information for the user to refer to later. As you can see, the user simply clicks on the cell and inputs the data as it corresponds to his rifle. The user then clicks "Apply."

In Figure 3-6, the user inputs information about his cartridge. The fields highlighted with arrows are the only ones that the ballistic software uses to calculate the trajectory of the rifle. The other fields on this page are miscellaneous data for the user's reference later. The user clicks the "Apply" box to lock in the data and go back to the "Main Page."

On the "Main Page" there is a tab labeled "Atmospheric Conditions." Be sure to fill in the fields after having clicked the "Atmospheric Conditions" tab. See Figure 3-7.

Having input all your load data, gun data, and having adjusted your atmospheric conditions to match the day during which you're shooting, simply

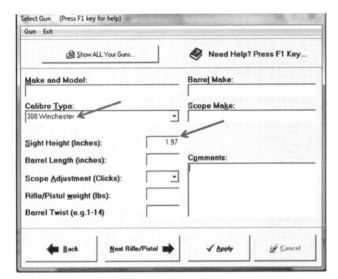

Figure 3-5. If you click on the tab marked "Gun," this screen pops up.

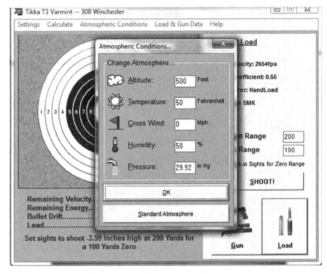

Figure 3-7. In the "Altitude" cell, make sure you input the pressure altitude, not the ground elevation.

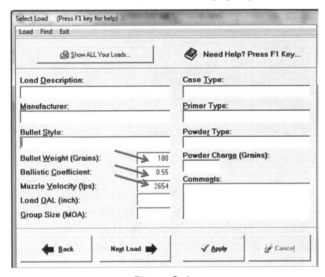

Figure 3-6.
This is the "Load" screen.

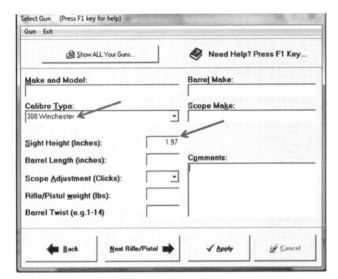

Ballistic Report

Range	Zero Adj	Path	Velocity	Energy	Drop	Drift	TOF
(Yards)	(MOA)	(Inches)	(FPS)	(FT-LBS)	(Inches)	(MOA)	(Sec)
0	0.00	-1.97	2654	2815	0.00	0.00	0.000
100	0.00	0.00	2491	2480	-2.57	0.00	0.117
200	1.72	-3.59	2334	2177	-10.70	0.00	0.241
300	4.35	-13.67	2183	1904	-25.33	0.00	0.374
400	7.40	-30.98	2037	1658	-47.17	0.00	0.516
500	10.77	-56.40	1896	1437	-77.14	0.00	0.668
600	14.64	-91.98	1763	1242	-117.26	0.00	0.833
700	18.97	-139.06	1637	1071	-168.88	0.00	1.011
800	23.66	-198.25	1518	921	-232.61	0.00	1.200
900	28.95	-272.88	1408	793	-311.78	0.00	1.405
1000	34.93	-365.83	1310	686	-409.28	0.00	1.627

100 Yards increment out to 1000 Yards

Figure 3-8.

click the "Shoot!" button, go to "Calculate" and press the "ballistics" tab, and the image shown in Figure 3-8 will appear.

As you can see in Figure 3-8, your adjustments are given in minutes of angle, and your bullet path is described in inches at each distance. The important thing is to get the muzzle velocity and ballistic coefficient of your bullet correct. Your ballistic software will yield better adjustments the closer you get to perfectly entering those two variables.

Let's do an example of how a shooter would go about gathering data using the method whereby we utilize ballistic software. In Figures 3-4 through 3-8, we have the following parameters:

Caliber	.308 Winchester
Bullet diameter	.308 inches
Bullet weight	180 grains
Ballistic coefficient	.55
Muzzle velocity	2,654 fps
Bore height	1.97 inches
Zero distance	100 yards

With this information input into my ballistic software, I would write out a chart to take to the range with me. The chart would give me good enough adjustments to get my rounds on paper as long as I was in the ballpark with the muzzle velocity and ballistic coefficient. See the chart that we'll work with in Figure 3-9.

180Gn Sierra MatchKing 2564 fps @ .55 BC

YARDS	MOA	ACTUAL IMPACT
100	0	
200	1.75	
300	4.25	
400	7.5	
500	10.75	
600	14.75	
700	19	1T + 4
800	23.75	1T + 8.75

Figure 3-9.

As you can see, I've rounded each minute-of-angle adjustment to the nearest 1/4 MOA, as my riflescope is a .25-MOA-per-click riflescope. It is not the case with all riflescopes, but my elevation turret is 15.0-MOA-per-full-rotation. As you can see in Figure 3-9, at the 700- and 800-yard lines, I have number sets off to the right. These are to help me understand the MOA adjustment more quickly. For example, look at the 700-yard adjustment of 19.0 MOA up. 1T + 4.0 MOA simply means 1 full turn—15 MOA—plus an additional 4.0 MOA.

The most important piece of the reference sheet shown in Figure 3-9 is the column on the right side of the page labeled "Actual Impact." It is very unlikely that each adjustment at each distance will yield a center-center impact on each target, as each adjustment was created by ballistic software. I find that when using ballistic software or when trusting the back of a box of ammunition, the adjustments tend to be up to 1 MOA off in either direction, but good enough to get on target to determine a precise adjustment for the next shoot. This is why we gather data on our rifle and ammunition by actually shooting these distances.

To continue the example, we're now at the range. We zero our rifle at 100 yards until our rounds are impacting center-center on the target,

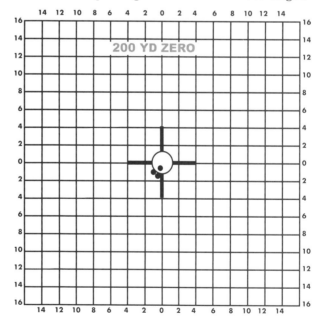

Figure 3-10.

and slip rings if necessary. We adjust our riflescope 1.75 MOA up—as our reference card suggests for a 200-yard shot—and shoot a three-round group at 200 yards. Chances are that the rounds will not impact center-center. Let's say our 200-yard target looks like the one shown in Figure 3-10.

As you can see, our rounds impacted .52 inches low with our 1.75 MOA up adjustment. Therefore, in the "Actual Impact" column on the right side of our reference card, we record ".52 inches low." We record our data in this way at every distance we shoot so that when we get home, we can record our known data and build our ballistic card.

Known data is simply the adjustment required at a given range in order to achieve a perfectly placed, center-center bullet impact on the target. In our 200-yard example, our adjustment was 1.75 MOA up, and we hit .52 inches low. At 200 yards, .52 inches equals .25 MOA. Therefore, we know that the next time we shoot at this distance, an adjustment of 2.0 MOA up at 200 yards will yield a center-center bullet impact on the target.

While gathering data, try to shoot in 100-yard or -meter increments or less. Be sure to record *all* distances you shoot at and all known data for those distances for the purpose of precise shot placement during future engagements. Although memory of your adjustments will come as you repeat shots at certain distances, do not rely on memory at all when recording known data and actual impacts on targets.

MAKING THE BALLISTIC CARD

After gathering your known data in 100-yard/-meter increments out to the farthest distance you ever intend to shoot, you can make your ballistic card. The purpose of making a ballistic card to keep with your rifle is not only to review your known data, but also to interpolate the adjustments for all ranges in between those distances for which you have known data. This allows you to engage targets at odd ranges.

There are differences between a known data sheet and a ballistic card. Figure 3-11 shows our known data sheet from the range.

Our ballistic card is shown in Figure 3-12, and I will now show you how to fill it in. You can see in Figure 3-12 that we already have our known data

180-Gn. Sierra MatchKing 2,564 fps @ .55 BC

YARDS	MOA		ACTUAL IMPACT	KNOWN DATA
100	0		0" low	0.0 UP
200	1.75		.52" low	2.0 UP
300	4.25		.79" low	4.5 UP
400	7.5		1.05" low	7.75 UP
500	10.75		1.31" low	11.0 UP
600	14.75		1.57" low	15.0 UP
700	19	1T + 4	3.66" low	1T + 4.5
800	23.75	1T + 8.75	10.47" low	1T + 10.0

Figure 3-11. Known data sheet.

inserted onto our ballistic card. I find Microsoft Excel to be an ideal program to create these. I simply copy and paste the final product of each ballistic card to PowerPoint, resize the card as small as possible, change font size if need be, print, laminate, and stick the card to the top of my buttstock, in a data book, or on a mini clipboard for the range.

As you can see, the shooter wishes to fill out his data in increments of 10 yards at a time. You may elect to draft your ballistic card in 20- or 25-yard increments depending on your preference. Look again at Figure 3-12, between 200 and 300 yards. Use the formula that follows to fill in adjustments for all ranges between 200 and 300 yards:

180-Gn. 2,564 fps @ .55 BC

YARDS	MOA	YARDS	MOA	YARDS	MOA
100		400	7.75	700	19.5
—		—		—	
—		—		—	
—		—		—	
150		450		750	
—		—		—	
—		—		—	
—		—		—	
200	2	500	11	800	25
—		—			
—		—			
—		—			
250		550			
—		—			
—		—			
—		—			
300	4.5	600	15		
—		—			
—		—			
—		—			
350		650			
—		—			
—		—			
—		—			

Figure 3-12.

(MOA adjustment at 300 yards) – (MOA adjustment at 200 yards) = Answer

$$\frac{\text{Answer}}{\text{Number of increments between the two ranges}} = \text{Answer}$$

The formula above is a bit confusing at first, but it's an easy concept after we finish this example. Let's plug in the numbers:

(4.5 MOA) – (2 MOA) = 2.5 MOA

$$\frac{2.5 \text{ MOA}}{10 \text{ increments}} = .25 \text{ MOA}$$

Now we add to our 200-yard adjustment of 2 MOA up .25 MOA at a time until we get to our 300-yard adjustment. See below:

Yards	200	210	220	230	240	250	260	270	280	290	300
MOA	2.0	2.25	2.5	2.75	3.0	3.25	3.5	3.75	4.0	4.25	4.5

Our shooter is using a 1/4-MOA-per-click riflescope. Usually we'll need to round each answer to the nearest .25 MOA. Luckily, that wasn't the case in the example above.

As you can see, there is an even spread of adjustments between the 200- and 300-yard adjustment. We can now effectively engage all targets between 200 and 300 yards, despite never having engaged a target at those distances. You would then proceed to apply the formula in the same way to interpolate the rest of your ballistic card. What you're left with is a complete ballistic card seen in Figure 3-13.

Now the shooter has a precise adjustment from 100 yards out to 800 yards in increments of 10 yards. Any target he lazes within 800 yards, he can effectively engage. On the ballistic card (Figure 3-12), the ranges to the targets are evenly spread, and the MOA adjustments follow suit. Another way you can set up your ballistic card is to have the MOA adjustment evenly spread and have the range to the target follow suit, such as in the ballistic card in Figure 3-14 that I built for my shooters carrying the M14 in RC-East Afghanistan. Notice that the riflescope is 1-MOA-per-click, and there is a range that corresponds with each increment.

Also notice in Figure 3-14 that there is a column set aside for mil holds. Refer back to Chapter 2 if you need a refresher on how to convert MOA to mils. (Hint: the magic number is 3.375.)

The end result of gathering data and fabricating

180-Gn. 2,564 fps @ .55 BC

YARDS	MOA	YARDS	MOA	YARDS	MOA
100	0	**400**	7.75	**700**	19.5
—	0.25	—	8	—	20
—	0.5	—	8.5	—	20.5
—	0.5	—	8.75	—	21.25
—	0.75	—	9	—	21.75
150	1	450	9.5	750	22.25
—	1.25	—	9.75	—	22.75
—	1.5	—	10	—	23.25
—	1.5	—	10.25	—	24
—	1.75	—	10.75	—	24.5
200	2	**500**	11	**800**	25
—	2.25	—	11.5		
—	2.5	—	11.75		
—	2.75	—	12.25		
—	3	—	12.5		
250	3.25	550	13		
—	3.5	—	13.5		
—	3.75	—	13.75		
—	4	—	14.25		
—	4.25	—	14.5		
300	4.5	**600**	15		
—	4.75	—	15.5		
—	5.25	—	16		
—	5.5	—	16.25		
—	5.75	—	16.75		
350	6.25	650	17.25		
—	6.5	—	17.75		
—	6.75	—	18.25		
—	7	—	18.5		
—	7.5	—	19		

Figure 3-13.

100-Meter Zero, M118LR
7,000 to 8,000 FT Altitude   2,494 fps @ .505BC

MILS	METERS	MOA	METERS	MOA
0	**100**	0	620	19
0.3	133	1	640	20
0.6	166	2	660	21
0.9	**200**	3	680	22
1.2	233	4	**700**	23
1.5	266	5	717	24
1.8	**300**	6	734	25
2.1	325	7	750	26
2.4	350	8	768	27
2.7	375	9	785	28
3	**400**	10	800	29
3.3	425	11	820	30
3.6	450	12	840	31
3.9	475	13	860	32
4.1	**500**	14	880	33
4.4	525	15	**900**	34
4.7	550	16	915	35
5	575	17	930	36
5.3	**600**	18	945	37
			960	38
			975	39
			990	40
			1000	41

Figure 3-14.

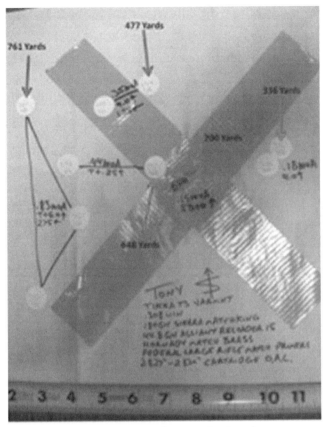

Figure 3-15. Target from gathering data.
Shows the range and my adjustment.

a ballistic card is to make the shooter capable of firing effectively at all ranges a target could possibly appear at, without ever actually having to shoot at every distance with his rifle. Naturally, it is well worth using a laser rangefinder—otherwise using data this fine-tuned is a waste. Experiment with ranging targets using the mil-dot reticle, by all means. Compare those ranges to those targets against those given by your rangefinder, and the disparity will likely disappoint you.

The next step after firing a target of the sort shown in Figure 3-15 is to measure how many inches high or low each group hit, convert inches to MOA, and record the difference into your known data for your rifle. For example, at 477 yards my adjustment was 9.0 MOA up, and the group hit 2.5 inches high (.50 MOA too high). Therefore, in my known data, I record an adjustment of 8.5 MOA up for future use, and re-interpolate the ballistic card between known data points. I mean this: I have

known data at 400 yards, 480 yards, and 500 yards, correct? So I'll keep the 400- and 500-yard adjustment the same, but now I have to change the MOA adjustments between 400 and 480 yards, as well as the ones between 480 yards and 500 yards. The changes will be small, but fine-tuning is a good thing.

SHOOTING TWO DIFFERENT TYPES OF LOADS OUT OF THE SAME GUN

Let's say we have two different types of cartridges we wish to fire out of our .308 Winchester rifle in order to serve two different purposes. For our vignette in this section, our example will be to prepare our rifle to use our 180-grain Sierra MatchKing load with one ballistic card, but we will also prepare a separate ballistic card to aid our adjustments for shooting the same 180-grain bullet, but at 950 fps, in order to be as quiet as possible while using a suppressor attached to the muzzle. Be advised: The length of the bullet you intend to shoot at subsonic speed will be safe depending upon the rate of twist of your barrel. Contact the maker of your particular suppressor to be safe. The fastest twist for the caliber you're using and heaviest bullet for the caliber you're using is a good starting point. We will use the following outline in this section:

1) Identify difference in zero between the two loads—adjust accordingly.
2) Gather data on new cartridge.
3) Fabricate new ballistic card for the new cartridge.

Figure 3-16 shows a ballistic card for our rifle's accuracy load. The MOA adjustments are slightly different, as this is the ballistic card for that same accuracy load, but fired out of a different rifle. A friend of mine was nice enough to try my ammo out in his gun and gather some data on it for me, for this comparison.

Determining Differences in Zero between Two Different Cartridges

The data for our 180-grain Sierra MatchKing in Figure 3-16 is verified, and you can see that our ballistic card is set up for a 100-yard-zero. We'll keep it simple and shoot at this distance to determine the difference in bullet impact between our two different cartridge types.

We get to the range and confirm our zero at 100 yards with our normal 180-grain Sierra MatchKing load. Our bullet impacts are shown in Figure 3-17.

180-Gn. 2,564 fps @ .55 BC

YARDS	MOA	YARDS	MOA	YARDS	MOA
100		400	8	700	20.75
110	0.25	410	8.5	710	21.25
120	0.5	420	8.75	720	22
130	0.5	430	9.25	730	22.5
140	0.75	440	9.5	740	23.25
150	1	450	10	750	23.75
160	1.25	460	10.25	760	24.5
170	1.5	470	10.75	770	25
180	1.5	480	11	780	25.5
190	1.75	490	11.5	790	26.25
200	2	500	11.75	800	26.75
210	2.25	510	12.25		
220	2.50	520	12.6		
230	2.75	530	13		
240	3	540	13.5		
250	3.5	550	14		
260	3.75	560	14.25		
270	4	570	14.75		
280	4.25	580	15.25		
290	4.5	590	15.5		
300	4.75	600	16		
310	5	610	16.5		
320	5.5	620	17		
330	5.75	630	17.5		
340	6	640	18		
350	6.5	650	18.5		
360	6.75	660	18.75		
370	7	670	19.25		
380	7.25	680	19.75		
390	7.75	690	20.25		

Figure 3-16.

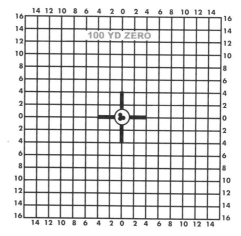

Figure 3-17.

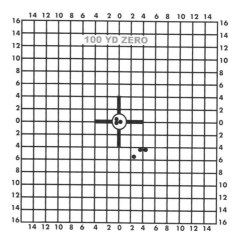

Figure 3-18.

Now we shoot our new cartridge without changing our scope adjustment. Figure 3-18 shows our result on the target. You can see that our shot group for our subsonic ammunition hit 5 MOA low (5.25 inches) and 3.25 MOA right (3.5 inches). From now on, when shooting our subsonic ammunition we adjust our riflescope 3.25 MOA left, but we do not touch our elevation adjustment. This may seem odd; I will explain why this is intelligent, shortly. Be sure to record the difference in bullet impact between the two cartridges in your data book.

We now have the following information. In Figure 3-19A is our original 180-grain SMK ballistic card; Figure 3-19B shows a shell for our subsonic load with adjustments that should be good enough to get us on target at different ranges in order to

gather further data. We generate the ballistic card shell the same as earlier this chapter, using the ballistic software and changing the muzzle velocity and ballistic coefficient. Notice I lowered the ballistic coefficient for the 950 fps load a little bit. This is because as muzzle velocity goes down, your ballistic coefficient for that same bullet goes down. Assigning the 950 fps 180-grain Sierra MatchKing a drag function of .5 ballistic coefficient was probably overly generous, but I just need to be on paper to gather data.

Gathering Data on a New Cartridge

We already know that a 5.0 MOA up adjustment at 100 yards zeroes our subsonic load to 100 yards. We'll assign our 100-yard adjustment as 5.0 MOA up so that our gun's zero shift is accounted for . . . one less thing to worry about while preparing a rifle shot. Now we shoot at 200 yards, after making a 23.75 MOA up adjustment. This is not a 23.75 MOA up adjustment from our 100-yard-zero; we're actually setting the elevation turret to exactly 23.75 MOA. We shoot, record our shot placement in our

180-Gn. 2,564 fps @ .55 BC

YARDS	MOA	YARDS	MOA	YARDS	MOA
100		400	8	700	20.75
110	0.25	410	8.5	710	21.25
120	0.5	420	8.75	720	22
130	0.5	430	9.25	730	22.5
140	0.75	440	9.5	740	23.25
150	1	450	10	750	23.75
160	1.25	460	10.25	760	24.5
170	1.5	470	10.75	770	25
180	1.5	480	11	780	25.5
190	1.75	490	11.5	790	26.25
200	2	500	11.75	800	26.75
210	2.25	510	12.25		
220	2.50	520	12.6		
230	2.75	530	13		
240	3	540	13.5		
250	3.5	550	14		
260	3.75	560	14.25		
270	4	570	14.75		
280	4.25	580	15.25		
290	4.5	590	15.5		
300	4.75	600	16		
310	5	610	16.5		
320	5.5	620	17		
330	5.75	630	17.5		
340	6	640	18		
350	6.5	650	18.5		
360	6.75	660	18.75		
370	7	670	19.25		
380	7.25	680	19.75		
390	7.75	690	20.25		

Figure 3-19A.

180-Gn. SMK 950 fps @ .5 BC

YARDS	MOA	MIL HOLD	YARDS	MOA	MIL HOLD
100	5.0 UP		300	43.96	
110			310		
120			320		
130			330		
140			340		
150			350		
160			360		
170			370		
180			380		
190			390		
200	23.75		400	65.34	
210			410		
220			420		
230			430		
240			440		
250			450	76.36	
260					
270					
280					
290		**3.25 MOA left before shooting this load**			

Figure 3-19B.

180-Gn. SMK 950 fps @ .5 BC

YARDS	MOA	MIL HOLD	YARDS	MOA	MIL HOLD
100	5.0 UP		**300**	42.75	
110			310		
120			320		
130			330		
140			340		
150			350		
160			360		
170			370		
180			380		
190			390		
200	23		**400**	64	
210			410		
220			420		
230			430		
240			440		
250			450	73.25	
260					
270					
280			**3.25 MOA left before shooting this load**		
290					

Figure 3-20.

180-Gn. SMK 950 fps @ .5 BC

YARDS	MOA	MIL HOLD	YARDS	MOA	MIL HOLD
100	**5.0 UP**		**300**	**42.75**	
110	6.75		310	44.88	
120	8.5		320	47	
130	10.5		330	49.125	
140	12.25		340	51.25	
150	14		350	53.4	
160	15.8		360	55.5	
170	17.5		370	57.63	
180	19.5		380	59.75	
190	21.25		390	61.9	
200	**23**		**400**	**64**	
210	24.9		410	65.85	
220	27		420	67.7	
230	29		430	69.55	
240	31		440	71.4	
250	33		450	**73.25**	
260	34.85				
270	36.83				
280	38.8		**3.25 MOA left before shooting this load**		
290	40.75				

Figure 3-21.

data book, and collect our known data as always. Continue to shoot and collect data at 300 and 400 yards, making your adjustments accordingly, as per the ballistic software suggestion, which will get you on paper. Figure 3-21 shows our known data that we've recorded for our subsonic ammunition. Notice our range is very limited using subsonic ammunition, and our adjustments are massive. Every target must be lased to get an exact distance in order to shoot successfully at what is considered long range for subsonic ammo.

Fabricating a Ballistic Card for a New Cartridge

Fill in the rest of the ballistic card by interpolating the data for the unknown distances that we haven't shot at yet; use the same technique we used earlier in this chapter. As long as you spread the adjustments evenly between the known data adjustments, the interpolations will be very accurate. Figure 3-21 shows the yield of our ballistic card after interpolating the unknown distance data. The bold-faced numbers are our known data.

For a refresher on interpolating data effectively, look at the adjustments depicted in bold, representing our known data. Between each set of bold numbers, the MOA adjustments are evenly spread. For example, between the 300-yard known data adjustment and our 400-yard known data adjustment, there are 2.125 MOA per 10 yards. Use the first two formulas listed below to come to this.

When we fill in the numbers the formula looks like the third and fourth line of the equation below.

(Adjustment at 400 yards) – (Adjustment at 300 yards) = Answer

Answer / Number of increments between sets of known data = MOA per 10 yards

64 MOA – 42.75 MOA = 21.25 MOA

21.25 MOA / 10 increments = 2.125 MOA per increment

Be sure to round each MOA adjustment to the nearest .25 MOA (if using a 1/4-MOA-per-click riflescope). Figure 3-22 shows the ballistic card for our 950 fps cartridge with MOA adjustments rounded to the nearest 1/4 MOA.

180-Gn. SMK 950 fps @ .5 BC

YARDS	MOA	MIL HOLD	YARDS	MOA	MIL HOLD
100	**5.0 UP**		**300**	**42.75**	
110	6.75		310	45	
120	8.5		320	47	
130	10.5		330	49.25	
140	12.25		340	51.25	
150	14		350	53.5	
160	15.75		360	55.5	
170	17.5		370	57.75	
180	19.5		380	59.75	
190	21.25		390	62	
200	**23**		**400**	**64**	
210	25		410	65.75	
220	27		420	67.77	
230	29		430	69.5	
240	31		440	71.5	
250	33		450	**73.25**	
260	34.85				
270	36.83				
280	38.75		**3.25 MOA left before shooting this load**		
290	40.75				

Figure 3-22.

180-Gn. SMK 950 fps @ .5 BC

YARDS	MOA	MIL HOLD	YARDS	MOA	MIL HOLD
100	**5.0 UP**		**300**	**30**	**3.8**
110	6.75		310	30	4.4
120	8.5		320	30	5
130	10.5		330	45	1.3
140	12.25		340	45	1.9
150	14		350	45	2.5
160	15	0.2	360	45	3.1
170	15	0.7	370	45	3.8
180	15	1.3	380	45	4.4
190	15	1.9	390	45	5
200	**15**	**2.4**	**400**	**60**	**1.2**
210	15	3	410	60	1.7
220	15	3.6	420	60	2.3
230	15	4.1	430	60	2.8
240	15	4.7	440	60	3.4
250	30	0.9	450	60	**3.9**
260	30	1.4			
270	30	2			
280	30	2.6	**3.25 MOA left before shooting this load**		
290	30	3.2			

Figure 3-23A.

Figure 3-23A shows an easier way to shoot with our 950 fps cartridge using the same data, but requiring the shooter to move the turret less for small changes in range to the target by incorporating the use of our mil-dot reticle. Figure 3-23B shows a clearer way to set up the ballistic card, taking advantage of the baseline reference on our target elevation knob.

180-Gn. SMK 950 fps @ .5 BC

YARDS	MOA	MIL HOLD	YARDS	MOA	MIL HOLD
100	**5B + 5.0**		**300**	**7B + 0.0**	**3.8**
110	5B + 6.75		310	7B + 0.0	4.4
120	5B + 8.5		320	7B + 0.0	5
130	5B + 10.5		330	8B + 0.0	1.3
140	5B + 12.25		340	8B + 0.0	1.9
150	5B + 14		350	8B + 0.0	2.5
160	6B + 0.0	0.2	360	8B + 0.0	3.1
170	6B + 0.0	0.7	370	8B + 0.0	3.8
180	6B + 0.0	1.3	380	8B + 0.0	4.4
190	16B + 0.0	1.9	390	8B + 0.0	5
200	**6B + 0.0**	**2.4**	**400**	**9B + 0.0**	**1.2**
210	6B + 0.0	3	410	9B + 0.0	1.7
220	6B + 0.0	3.6	420	9B + 0.0	2.3
230	6B + 0.0	4.1	430	9B + 0.0	2.8
240	6B + 0.0	4.7	440	9B + 0.0	3.4
250	7B + 0.0	0.9	450	9B + 0.0	**3.9**
260	7B + 0.0	1.4			
270	7B + 0.0	2			
280	7B + 0.0	2.6	**3.25 MOA left before shooting this load**		
290	7B + 0.0	3.2			

Figure 3-23B.

You already know the difference between a target knob and a BDC knob from Chapter 1. If you'll remember, on a BDC knob each number represents the range to the target. Obviously, the ballistic card in Figures 3-23A and B was built for a riflescope featuring a target elevation knob—whereby each number represents 1 MOA. You'll also remember about target knobs that every full rotation exposes another baseline. The turret depicted in Figure 3-24A is set 15 MOA above the turret in Figure 3-24B. Every full rotation (15 MOA) will expose another baseline. In Figure 3-24A, five baselines are exposed and there are 0 MOA up, so the knob is set at 5B + 0.0 MOA. In Figure 3-24B, six baselines are exposed, so the knob is set at 6B + 0.0 MOA. Having the ballistic card from Figure 3-23B will avoid confusion. Always know on what baseline your zero lies!

Adjustment:
This Represents 5B+0.0

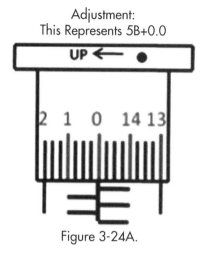

Figure 3-24A.

Adjustment:
This Represents 6B+0.0

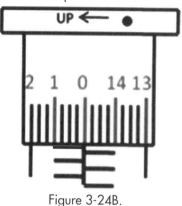

Figure 3-24B.

180-Gn. 2,564 fps @ .55 BC

YARDS	MOA	YARDS	MOA	YARDS	MOA
100		**400**	**8**	**700**	**20.75**
110	0.25	410	8.5	710	21.25
120	0.5	420	8.75	720	22
130	0.5	430	9.25	730	22.5
140	0.75	440	9.5	740	23.25
150	1	450	10	750	23.75
160	1.25	460	10.25	760	24.5
170	1.5	470	10.75	770	25
180	1.5	480	11	780	25.5
190	1.75	490	11.5	790	26.25
200	**2**	**500**	**11.75**	**800**	**26.75**
210	2.25	510	12.25		
220	2.50	520	12.6		
230	2.75	530	13		
240	3	540	13.5		
250	3.5	550	14		
260	3.75	560	14.25		
270	4	570	14.75		
280	4.25	580	15.25		
290	4.5	590	15.5		
300	**4.75**	**600**	**16**		
310	5	610	16.5		
320	5.5	620	17		
330	5.75	630	17.5		
340	6	640	18		
350	6.5	650	18.5		
360	6.75	660	18.75		
370	7	670	19.25		
380	7.25	680	19.75		
390	7.75	690	20.25		

Figure 3-25A.

180-Gn. SMK 950 fps @ .5 BC

YARDS	MOA	MIL HOLD	YARDS	MOA	MIL HOLD
100	5B + 5.0		**300**	7B + 0.0	**3.8**
110	5B + 6.75		310	7B + 0.0	4.4
120	5B + 8.5		320	7B + 0.0	5
130	5B + 10.5		330	8B + 0.0	1.3
140	5B + 12.25		340	8B + 0.0	1.9
150	5B + 14		350	8B + 0.0	2.5
160	6B + 0.0	0.2	360	8B + 0.0	3.1
170	6B + 0.0	0.7	370	8B + 0.0	3.8
180	6B + 0.0	1.3	380	8B + 0.0	4.4
190	16B + 0.0	1.9	390	8B + 0.0	5
200	6B + 0.0	**2.4**	**400**	**9B + 0.0**	**1.2**
210	6B + 0.0	3	410	9B + 0.0	1.7
220	6B + 0.0	3.6	420	9B + 0.0	2.3
230	6B + 0.0	4.1	430	9B + 0.0	2.8
240	6B + 0.0	4.7	440	9B + 0.0	3.4
250	7B + 0.0	0.9	450	9B + 0.0	**3.9**
260	7B + 0.0	1.4			
270	7B + 0.0	2			
280	7B + 0.0	2.6	**3.25 MOA left before**		
290	7B + 0.0	3.2	**shooting this load**		

Figure 3-25B.

Now that we have the two separate ballistic cards for the two different cartridges we fired out of our rifle, we can use them both at the same time, shooting both types of ammo in the same sitting if

desired. The gain from using the method I've described here is that you don't have to re-zero between different types of ammo. View our final ballistic cards in Figures 3-25A and 3-25B.

Let's say that we want to shoot a target with our 2,564 fps cartridge at 550 yards. We simply adjust to 14.0 MOA up. Now we want to engage a target at 180 yards with our subsonic round. We simply adjust to 6B + 0.0 for elevation, hold 1.3 mils high, and adjust 3.5 MOA left to compensate for the difference in zero, as we are reminded to do by the footnote at the bottom of our subsonic ballistic card. We do not slip the ring on our elevation turret to go from one cartridge to the other, because our 100-yard-zero difference in elevation between the two loads is already accounted for.

If you'll remember, our subsonic ammo for this example hits 5 MOA below and 3.5 MOA to the right of our 2,564 fps cartridge zero at 100 yards. Look at our subsonic ballistic card in Figure 3-25B at the 100-yard adjustment. The elevation is already compensated for—we just have to remember to make our 3.5 MOA left adjustment *every time* we switch from our 2,564 fps cartridge over to the subsonic cartridge we used in the example earlier.

I'll mention here that being subsonic and using a suppressor is nice in that it so greatly reduces your sound signature; however, being subsonic is bad in that it greatly reduces everything else as well. Your effective range and accuracy are greatly reduced, as is your terminal ballistic performance on fleshy targets. I support shooting suppressed— but I also support keeping the projectile at its normal muzzle velocity. Just use the same accuracy load you would use without the suppressor. Your sound signature is still greatly reduced—no muzzle blast, just the crack from the bullet moving faster than the speed of sound. After hearing muzzle blast from a rifle shot, it's fairly easy to determine the cardinal direction that the shot came from. The direction is not easy to determine, however, if a suppressor was used—even with supersonic ammunition. Ultimately, you know the application the rifle will be used for and the choice is yours.

One example I can think of for a good time to be subsonic with a suppressor involves my buddy, Roth. He currently has a couple of suppressed AR

Figure 3-26. Remington 700—Accuracy International stock with an Advanced Armament Corps Cyclone suppressor.

Figure 3-27. AR-10 Mega Machine upper and lower, with a Gemtech Sandstorm suppressor.

builds, both of which he uses with normal supersonic ammunition the majority of the time. When he hunts pigs down in Texas on his friend's property, he does build subsonic ammunition with heavy 220-grain bullets for his .300 Blackout. He uses a suppressor to avoid startling the livestock on the next farm while he shoots the pigs that are destroying his friend's crops.

Again, base the choice of whether to be subsonic or supersonic while suppressed on the application.

KEEPING AND USING A SNIPER DATA BOOK

Ideally, you don't want to record your known data on a piece of scrap paper that can get lost or thrown away. Also, it is very wise to log everything your rifle and ammunition does—in detail—

at every distance and wind speed you shoot at to allow you to better analyze the trajectory of your chosen ammunition. The best way to do this is to keep a sniper data book with the rifle. My book is always either lying in the rifle case with the gun or lying beside the gun being used while shooting is being conducted. In this section are images of each different page in the sniper data book that I created in Microsoft PowerPoint. I built this data book because I have yet to find one on the market that has everything I want in it and doesn't waste space by putting crap in it that I just don't need. When you're ready to start shooting in this manner, you can use my data book or modify it to fit your needs.

In Figures 3-33 through 3-35 you'll see examples of target cards that you will fill out at the range. It is critical that you fill these out as you

Figure 3-28. U.S. Army Sniper School instructor SGT Shriver gathering and recording data on an M107 LRSR.

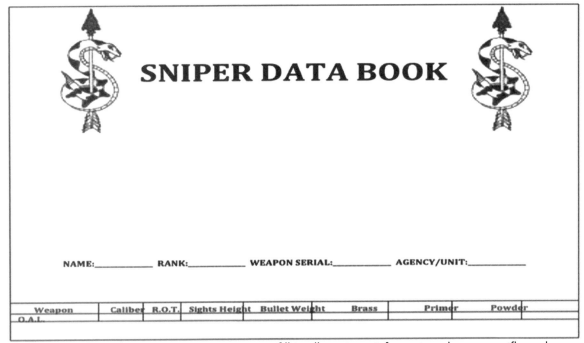

Figure 3-29. This is the cover page. Here you can fill in all pertinent information about your rifle and ammunition of choice. This is especially useful if you shoot more than one rifle so that you don't get your data books and your rifles that go along with them confused.

shoot and while you are still at the range. There are 30 "target" pages and 20 "silhouette" pages in each data book of mine. The numbers 1 through 9 represent one shot each. For each shot, you fill out the Range, Angle, Wind, Humidity, Altitude, Temperature, and Air Pressure. Be sure to circle what kind of increments you use (example: yards/meters). For each shot, jot down what your elevation setting was in MOA or mils, and what your windage adjustment was in MOA or mils, if any. Your "Call" is the last place you saw your reticle before the rifle went off, in the event you happen to pull a shot.

At the bottom of the page in the "group impact" row, you can record how many MOA or inches from your point of aim each three-round shot group was (to help you collect accurate known data). Also, for each three-round shot group you can record the group size in inches or MOA at each distance you engage targets. At the very bottom is a remarks column. I prefer to take very detailed notes, so the whole back of each 5x8 index card is left completely blank for jotting down lots of information. To the right is a representation of the target. Identify the scale of each box in inches, and place a blacked-out

dot each place a bullet strikes the target. Number each bullet accordingly, 1 through 9 on each page.

Using a sniper data book is a very effective way to go about keeping solid data; and if the data book is always with the gun, then there is no issue. Honesty time—I no longer use a sniper data book in the sense that you're familiar with. I did, however, feel it was necessary to share the idea with you so that you can consider it as an option. The reason I replaced the sniper data book with something else is that, operationally, the sniper data book is not the best choice. There are pages upon pages in the sniper data book that you're just not going to use unless in the process of gathering data. The only pages that matter while you're actually hunting— whatever your definition of that term may be—are the known data pages for your adjustment based on range to the target, and ballistic cards that you paste or tape into the book to dope the wind and account for temperature, altitude, and pressure change while shooting at long range. So why not just bring what you need?

I currently use a mini clipboard for each of my precision rifles. The information contained on the

KNOWN DATA

Yards/Meters RANGE	ADJUSTMENT	Yards/Meters RANGE	ADJUSTMENT	Yards/Meters RANGE	ADJUSTMENT
10		210		410	
20		220		420	
30		230		430	
40		240		440	
50		250		450	
60		260		460	
70		270		470	
80		280		480	
90		290		490	
100		300		500	
110		310		510	
120		320		520	
130		330		530	
140		340		540	
150		350		550	
160		360		560	
170		370		570	
180		380		580	
190		390		590	
200		400		600	

KNOWN DATA

Yards/Meters RANGE	ADJUSTMENT	Yards/Meters RANGE	ADJUSTMENT	Yards/Meters RANGE	ADJUSTMENT
610		810			
620		820			
630		830			
640		840			
650		850			
660		860			
670		870			
680		880			
690		890			
700		900			
710		910			
720		920			
730		930			
740		940			
750		950			
760		960			
770		970			
780		980			
790		990			
800		1000			

Figures 3-30 and 3-31. These are the first two pages of the data book. This is ultimately the most important part of the whole book. As you determine at ranges/shooting events your ideal MOA or mil adjustment for certain shooting distances, you fill in that data here. Fill this page (as well as all others) out in pencil. As you gather known data and fill it in, you can also use these two pages to interpolate data for shooting distances still unknown, which gets you on target better than working correctly with ballistic software. Using pencil on the page is critical. You'll find yourself erasing and writing in more precise adjustments almost every time you shoot.

ROUND COUNT

DATE	SHOTS FIRED	DATE	SHOTS FIRED	DATE	SHOTS FIRED

Figure 3-32. Immediately after the known data pages is the round count page. This simply helps you monitor your barrel life, which only really applies to competition shooters who expend around 60 to 100 rounds per match. Most non-magnum barrels have a 2,500- to 3,500-round lifespan; however, proper barrel care can greatly increase those numbers. I'm terrible at keeping an accurate round count! It is the least important thing on my mind. To mitigate this issue, I save the empty bullet boxes that my 180-grain Sierra MatchKings come in, knowing that each empty box means 500 bullets fired. Another method is to track the accuracy of your barrel. If you tuned your load to .3 MOA and your gun won't produce .5 MOA or better even as close as 100 yards anymore, then maybe it's time for a barrel change.

Figure 3-33. Target card sample.

DATE	TIME	AMMUNITION	REST TYPE
4 July 10	1400 Local	180Gn HandLoad	bipod+sand socks / sand socks / pack

SHOT NUMBER	cold/hot 1	cold/hot 2	cold/hot 3	4	5	6	7	8	9
Range Yards / Meters	300	300	300						
Angle Cosine / Degrees	0	---	---						
Wind MPH / Knots	5	3	5						
Humidity %RH	53 %	---	---						
Altitude Elev/Pressure Alt	550 ft	---	---						
Temperature F / C	74	---	---						
Pressure "Hg / MBARS	29.95	---	---						
ELEVATION	2.75 ↑								
WINDAGE	→ 1 moa	→ .5 moa	→ 1 moa						
CALL	o'clock N/A "	o'clock N/A "	2 o'clock 1.0 "	o'clock "	o'clock "	o'clock "	o'clock "	o'clock "	o'clock "
Group Impact	.25 inches from center			inches from center			inches from center		
Group Size	.2 inches / moa			inches / moa			inches / moa		
Remarks	Example of correctly filled out data card...be sure to circle "hot" or "cold" on 1st 3 shots per card.								

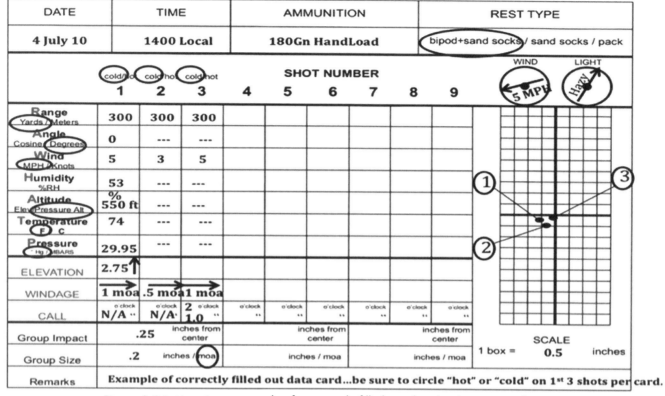

Figure 3-34. Here is an example of a properly filled out data book target card.

DATE	TIME	AMMUNITION	REST TYPE
			bipod+sand socks / sand socks / pack

SHOT NUMBER	cold/hot 1	cold/hot 2	cold/hot 3	4	5	6	7	8	9
Range Yards / Meters									
Angle Cosine / Degrees									
Wind MPH / Knots									
Humidity %RH									
Altitude Elev/Pressure Alt									
Temperature F / C									
Pressure "Hg / MBARS									
ELEVATION									
WINDAGE									
CALL	o'clock "	o'clock "	o'clock "	o'clock "	o'clock "	o'clock "	o'clock "	o'clock "	o'clock "
Group Impact	inches from center			inches from center			inches from center		
Group Size	inches / moa			inches / moa			inches / moa		
Remarks									

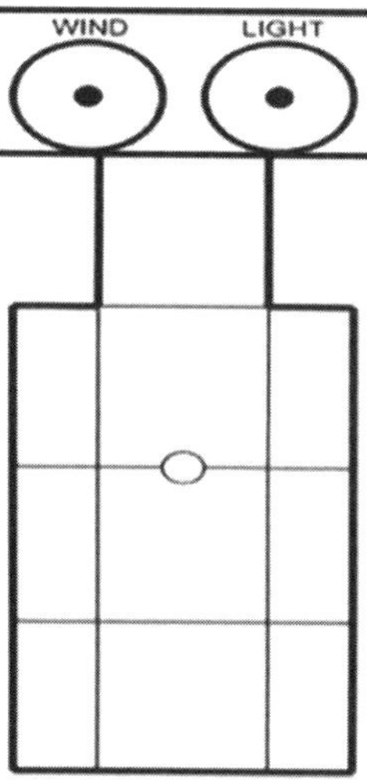

Figure 3-35. Here is what a "silhouette" target page looks like.

mini clipboard is: known data sheet (range), windage card, altitude change card, temperature change card, and pressure change card. Additionally, on the back there is a grid for gathering data that can be used in place of the sniper data book. After the gathered data is applied to the known data card, the gathered data can be erased for use next time.

In addition to being more compact than a traditional sniper data book, the known data on the mini clipboard is changeable, just like the known data page of the sniper data book, although the mini clipboard data and pages themselves are water-resistant/-proof. Even the water-resistant sniper data books become crappy to write in after they're weathered or erased upon too many times with a pencil. On the mini clipboard, each page is laminated with lamination paper or with clear packaging tape (same stuff, less expensive). Therefore, instead of using a pencil to record gathered data

and make improvements to the known data page, a fine or superfine map marker is used directly on the lamination. Figure 3-36 shows the clipboard I've got going for my .308 Win bolt-action rifle.

The front page of the clipboard contains my environmental condition ballistic cards. For any change to wind speed, altitude, temperature, or barometric pressure, I use this cover page.

Figure 3-37 shows my cold-bore shot tracker. You can see that after five cold-bore shots yielding the exact same data, I stopped keeping track of my

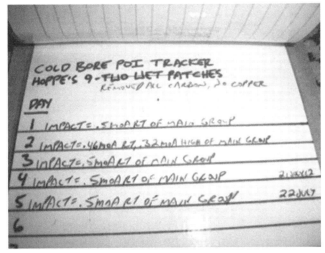

Figure 3-37.

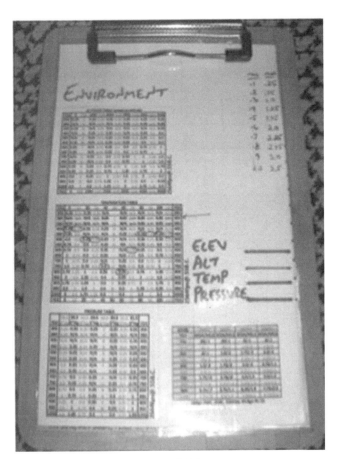

Figure 3-36.

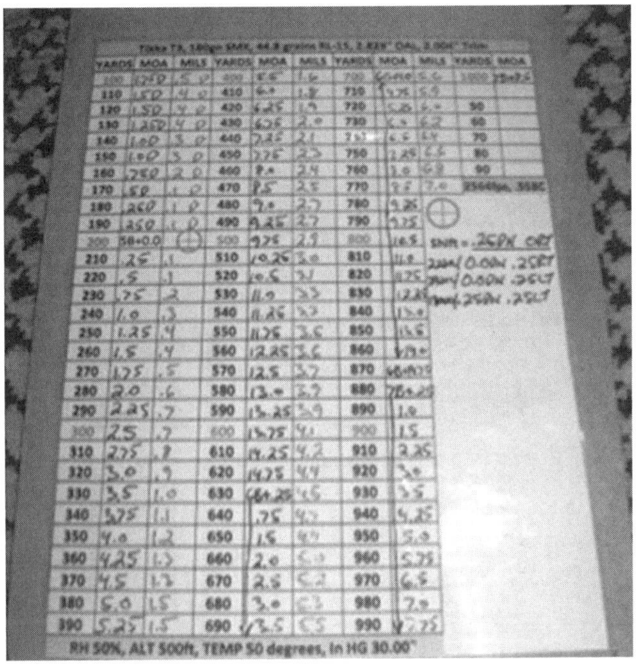

Figure 3-38. The known data page is last, but not least.

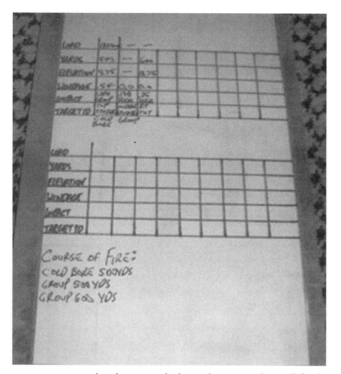

Figure 3-39. Flip the mini clipboard over and you'll find the page for gathering data. This page is laminated just like the others for use with a map marker.

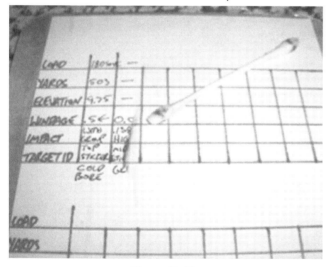

Figure 3-40.
To erase data, I simply use acetone on a cotton swab.

cold-bore shot placement. It's clear to see that I have to adjust .5 MOA to the left for each cold-bore shot after having cleaned with Hoppe's 9 at least eight hours prior to shooting.

Beneath all the laminated pages is the most important one of all—the known data page, of course. If it's the most used and most important one, why not put it on top on the front page? The answer is because each adjustment is written in permanent map marker. I'd like to protect these from getting scratched by whatever bag or cargo pocket I'm keeping the clipboard in.

The idea of using a mini clipboard in this manner as a replacement for the sniper data book was suggested to me by First Sergeant Cody Myers, HHC/1-327 IN/101 ABN DIV. I was the Sniper Section Leader for Tiger Force/1-327 IN at the time. 1sg Myers was performing spot checks on the scout platoon and mortar platoon shortly after taking over in his duty position, asking each platoon about our standard operating procedures. As my Senior Sniper Team Leader and I began describing how our crew drill goes down between the sniper and spotter, 1sg Myers got up from behind the M2010, walked into his office, and returned with a mini clipboard that looked an awful lot like what I just showed you in this section. He said, "This is what we used in my last unit at the Ranger Battalion. I'm not telling you to change to using this, but try it out and if you like it, make it yours."

It was just one of those commonsense things that made our unit a little bit better. To maintain and use this mini clipboard, all you need is a map marker that stays with the clipboard, a little bottle of acetone (for erasing), and a small Ziploc bag of cotton swabs and cotton balls (also for erasing). I just keep the acetone, swabs, and cotton balls in the D-Kit with the other tools for the gun, either back at the house (civilian rigs) or in the gun case in the arms room or sniper cage (unit rigs).

HIGH-ANGLE SHOOTING

Shooting from a high angle, such as firing down into a valley from a mountainside, yields a different trajectory than is normally observed when shooting across flat ground.

Before deploying to Afghanistan in early 2010, I spent my opportunity leave with my parents and brother in the mountains near Ten Sleep, Wyoming. The elevation we shot at was 4,000 feet, and the pressure altitude averaged 4,900 feet depending on the day—with no more than a 100-foot deviation in pressure altitude during the three-day span. The main objectives were to show my brother how to gather data, manipulate MOA and mils, and to determine whether or not the ballistic software I use properly compensates for altitude change. Until that trip, I'd only gathered data on my rifle at 500-foot ground elevation, in the Ft. Campbell area.

I went to Wyoming with my Tikka T3 Varmint .308 Win, 50 of my accuracy loads for the 180-grain Sierra MatchKing that my 1:11 rate of twist barrel likes so much, a Leupold RX-IV Rangefinder, Kestrel weather meter, sniper data book, and ACI (angle cosine indicator). I gave my brother a 10-minute class at the house on how to use MOA and mils. We then stuck the two wooden target frames we built the day prior in the back of the truck and headed to one of the many safe places to shoot on the ranch. We fired from 200

Figure 4-1. Red Reflet Ranch, Ten Sleep, Wyoming.

yards out to 900 yards in increments of 100 to 125 yards. The 200-yard zero was the exact same as it had been in Ft. Campbell, despite the altitude change. As my brother and I increased the distance between ourselves and the target, we were able to identify that the ballistic software perfectly compensated for the altitude change, which only really began to take effect beyond 450 yards. I was glad to see that my rifle maintained its .25 MOA rate of accuracy out to 625 yards and stayed within .5 MOA at distances beyond that. The accuracy of the weapon system had to have been part of what addicted my brother, John, to long-range marksmanship that day.

After gathering data on the rifle, John asked if I would leave the rifle at the house there in Wyoming while I was deployed. I agreed, based on the fact that he now knew how to properly use the weapon system, but I did give him a few conditions. "You're only allowed to shoot the hand loads that I make for the rifle (I gave him 40 loads), after those 40 shots are gone you have to clean the rifle as I specify, and you have to let me teach you how to shoot at high angle so you don't waste my hand loads on missing animals." He agreed, although that last condition gave him a confused look. What I taught him after dinner in a short class at the house surprised him. He told me, "I would've never guessed that something seeming so complicated could actually be so easy."

ADJUSTING FOR HIGH ANGLE BASED ON FLAT-GROUND DISTANCE

Observe Figure 4-2. Depicted is a shooter on a mountainside firing at a target at a lower elevation.

With your laser rangefinder, you can determine the "line of sight" distance. By simply determining this distance and adjusting for it normally, your shot will hit above your desired point of impact. But by how much? The greater the distance to the target or the steeper the angle, the more your shot will be off. The reason for this is that when you fire at a target on flat ground, gravity has the greatest effect on the bullet. When firing at an upward or downward angle, gravity has less of an effect on the bullet in flight. Therefore, the bullet will strike higher than if the shot were on flat ground.

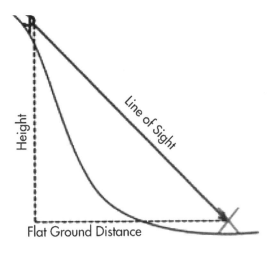

Figure 4-2.

There are a few different methods you can use. Each has its advantages and disadvantages. One method is to determine the flat-ground distance (FGD) and adjust your riflescope for that range. In Figure 4-2, the FGD is the "base" of the triangle, and is always less distance than your line of sight. All you need in order to determine the FGD is your range to the target based on your line of sight (indicated by the diagonal line in Figure 4-2), and your angle to the target given in degrees or cosine.

There are two effective methods of determining your angle to the target that we'll discuss here. One way is to make a plumb line by hanging a weighted string from a protractor. You simply aim your rifle at the target and have a buddy place the flat edge of the protractor under your barrel and read off the angle in degrees. This is the least expensive and most available method of determining angle to the target, but the sacrifice is that this system is most effective with a buddy, and you still have to convert degrees to cosine.

After you know your range to the target and your angle to the target, use the following formula to determine the FGD.

(Range to Target) (Cosine) = FGD

On a scientific calculator, you can type in your angle to the target in degrees, press the button labeled "cos," and the calculator will kick out the co-

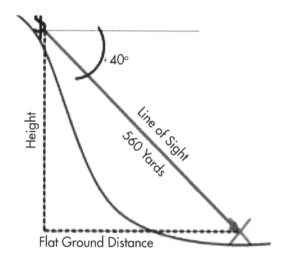

Figure 4-3.

Figure 4-4. Accurized M14, sub-MOA.

sine of that angle. For example, let's revisit Figure 4-2, but this time we'll insert a range to the target and an angle to the target to better show how this method is used to determine the FGD and adjust the riflescope accordingly.

In Figure 4-3 we can see that our shooter lased the target to be 560 yards, and he is aiming on a 40-degree downward slope. The cosine of 40 degrees is .766 (just type 40 into the calculator and press "cos" to determine that the cosine of 40 degrees = .766). Now you just plug in the numbers.

(560 yards)(.766) = 429 yards

By using this method, you would adjust your riflescope or mil hold for a 429-yard shot instead of a 560-yard shot. For example, on my riflescope I would make an adjustment of 7.25 MOA up for a 430-yard shot instead of 12.25 MOA up for a 560-yard shot. Had I not done so in this hypothetical example, my adjustment would be off by 5.0 MOA at 429 yards—a disparity of 22.46 inches!

Although this method yields the geometric flat-ground distance, it has one distinct weakness. In the last example we adjusted for a 429-yard shot, but the time of flight of the bullet is the same as that of a 560-yard shot! You'll find that using this method puts you on target effectively within about 300 to 400 yards at best.

And in the spirit of truly being long-range professionals, I'd like to show you the best method I've

found for taking precise shots at high angle—although, unfortunately, I didn't create the idea. I learned the following method as prescribed by a high-angle marksmanship school in Estes Park, Colorado. I purchased an ACI from them. Following is their recommended method of adjusting for high-angle conditions; I find their method to be hands-down most effective for accuracy.

FLAT-GROUND DISTANCE TAILORED TO YOUR BALLISTIC PROFILE

From the method shown in Figure 4-3, you can see that multiplying your range to the target by the cosine simply gives you a percentage of your line of sight as the flat-ground distance. How about instead of getting a percentage of our range to the target, we get a percentage of our original adjustment? By doing this we get an adjusted FGD based on our rifle and ammunition's ballistic profile. To put words into pictures, let's use the same example as before, but multiply the cosine by the adjustment for 560 yards instead of the range. The new formula follows:

(Normal MOA adjustment)(cosine) = New MOA adjustment

In this example, the range to the target is 560 yards. My normal adjustment for a 560-yard shot is

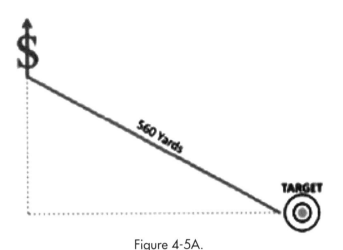

Figure 4-5A.   Figure 4-5B.

12.25 MOA up from my 200-yard zero. I punch the numbers below into the calculator and see that my new adjustment is 9.38 MOA, which I round to 9.5 MOA up for my 1/4-MOA-per-click scope.

(12.25 MOA)(.766) = 9.38 MOA

Between the two methods there is a 2.13-MOA difference at this moderate range and moderate angle. That's a 9.5-inch difference between two methods that are both accepted and taught by great precision shooters.

The more effective method for precise shooting is that of the second we've discussed, whereby you multiply your normal MOA or mil adjustment by the cosine to get your new adjustment or mil hold. I learned this more effective method of high-angle shooting from the purchase of an ACI (angle cosine indicator) from snipertools.com. The ACI is built in Estes Park, Colorado, where there also happens to be a high-angle shooting school that requires its students to come with or purchase an ACI. Upon purchasing the item, the first two methods of high-angle shooting were discussed in the instructions manual for the device. Putting their idea into prac-

tice proved more effective than simply adjusting for the FGD.

The third method of high-angle shooting is used for speed—getting on target quickly when time is an issue. Although precision suffers a bit, the following method gets the shooter on target faster—"on target" being the important part. I don't think I need to draw any picture for this one. You simply make your normal adjustment for whatever distance the target is from you and aim approximately 20 inches low. We use this method in the army. Our E-type silhouettes are 40 inches tall. If shooting that E-type silhouette from farther than 200 meters and at high angle, we simply make our normal adjustment and "hold balls," or aim at the bottom of the target.

There is one concept that I find begs clarification as per high-angle shooting. Whether shooting *upward*—say from down in a valley—or shooting *downward*—say from the top of a cliff into a low area—your bullet will hit too high. In Figures 4-5A and 4-5B, the target is 560 yards away. The adjustment is the *same* for both shots! Gravity is affecting the travel of the bullet in each example in exactly the same manner.

CHAPTER FIVE

COMPENSATING FOR CHANGING ENVIRONMENTAL CONDITIONS

Civilian long-range marksmen, law enforcement, and military snipers alike would be wise to compensate for range, angle, wind, pressure, altitude, and temperature—or RAWPAT. We've already covered how to compensate for range to the target by familiarizing you with ballistic software and gathering data in Chapter 3, and you're tracking how to compensate for the change in trajectory while taking a shot at high or low angle. We will now cover the environmental factors: wind, barometric pressure, pressure altitude, and temperature. We will be using our ballistic software program for this. Be sure to refer to Chapter 3 if you're not already familiar with using ballistic software. This is the primary purpose for which I use ballistic software: creating windage, altitude change, temperature change, and pressure change cards yielding adjustments in minutes of angle.

Figure 5-1. Sniper section, HHC Scouts, 1-327 Infantry, 101st Assault, Iraq.

COMPENSATING FOR WINDAGE

Wind speed is the only environmental condition that you're better off learning to accurately determine on your own, without the aid of an electronic device. After the factor of range to the target, wind is the factor that affects a bullet's trajectory the most.

When we talk about compensating for crosswinds, we will refer to "value." If you imagine your shooting position as sitting in the center of a clock face and your rifle aimed at the 12, wind coming from the 12 and 6 o'clock is zero value—you don't adjust for it at all. Wind coming from the 1, 5, 7, and 11 o'-clock is a half-value wind, so you'd adjust your rifle-scope half its normal adjustment. Wind coming from the 2, 3, 4, 8, 9, and 10 o'clock is a full-value wind.

In my experience, the easiest cartridge for which to compensate windage is the M118LR cartridge that the army makes for the M110 SASS, the accurized M14, and the SR-25. Its ease of use directly translates to the fact that the shooter does not need to refer to a wind-speed table in order to adjust the riflescope prior to a shot. The formula is simple enough to do in one's head quickly—in less time even than it would take to refer to a chart. Following is that formula:

$$\frac{(\text{wind in mph})(\text{range in hundreds})}{10} = \text{minutes of angle}$$

For example, let's say you're setting up for a shot with the M118LR cartridge at 600 meters with an 8-mph full-value crosswind. The formula would look like this:

$$\frac{(8 \text{ mph})(6.00 \text{ meters})}{10} = 4.8 \text{ minutes of angle}$$

Above you can see that 8 times 6 equals 48, and 48 divided by 10 is 4.8 MOA. Therefore, you would adjust your riflescope 4.75 MOA into the direction of the wind if using a 1/4-MOA-per-click scope, or 5.0 MOA into the wind for a 1/2-MOA-per-click scope. As you can see, it is very easy to compensate for trajectory due to wind when using the M118LR cartridge, if you estimate the wind speed accurately.

This formula only applies to a bullet moving approximately 2,650 fps, with a .308-inch diameter, having a ballistic coefficient of .505. Of course, most bullets don't have those parameters. Therefore, you would most likely not be dividing by the constant of 10. I would challenge anyone to divide any number by a goofy constant like 9.56. It's just not happening. So, if not shooting this cartridge, you really can't get a reliable windage adjustment by doing a formula in your head. This is where creating an easy-to-read wind table comes into play—because reading the answer from a table would be faster than using the formula and inputting the numbers on a calculator, then dividing by a different denominator than "10." Figure 5-2 shows an example of one effective way to set up a wind chart.

WIND 2,564 fps @ .55 BC

	MOA/MILS	MOA/MILS	MOA/MILS	MOA/MILS	
YARDS	3 MPH	5 MPH	8 MPH	10 MPH	YARDS
100	.25/.1	.25/.1	.5/.1	.5/.1	100
200	.5/.1	.75/.2	1.0/.3	1.5/.4	200
300	.5/.1	1.0/.3	1.75/.5	2.0/.6	300
400	.75/.2	1.5/.4	2.25/.7	2.75/.8	400
500	1.0/.3	1.75/.5	3.0/.9	3.75/1.1	500
600	1.5/.4	2.25/.7	3.75/1.1	4.5/1.3	600
700	1.75/.5	2.75/.8	4.5/1.3	5.5/1.6	700
800	2.0/.6	3.35/1.0	5.25/1.6	6.5/1.9	800
900	2.25/.7	3.75/1.1	6.25/1.9	7.75/2.3	900
1,000	2.75/.8	4.5/1.3	7.0/2.1	8.75/2.6	1,000

Figure 5-2.

The table shown in Figure 5-2 is for a .308 Winchester cartridge, moving 2,564 fps at the muzzle, having a ballistic coefficient of .55 BC. If you do the math, you'll notice that the trajectory as it is affected by wind is similar enough to the M118LR cartridge that if the shooter were to use the formula for the M118LR, he would be on target at close range and midrange, getting more and more off target as the range to the target increases. Figure 5-2 shows the best way I've found to set up wind tables—with the distance to the target in hundreds or even every 50 meters along the left column going down, the wind speed across the top, and the adjustment in both MOA and mils given as the data. Therefore, this is the kind of wind chart that I will demonstrate how to set up in this chapter. But first, we have to discuss how to read wind speed.

Judging Wind Speed

It is fairly easy to tell what 3-, 5-, 8-, and 10-mph winds look like. There are many different methods to determine wind speed. I use mirage at the target and the appearance of plant life and lightweight manmade objects around the target, if present. Only concern yourself with wind at the target.

If you've ever been driving on a hot day and seen what appears to be water on the road in the distance ahead of you, you've seen mirage with the naked eye. For shooting applications, when using an optic having 14x magnification or more, and quality lenses, mirage can be identified whether the day is hot or not. I can still focus on very usable mirage with my fixed 16x Super Sniper riflescope on a cold 25-degree Fahrenheit day. This is because with an optic, you're looking through a large amount of atmosphere and viewing the movement of the air mass as a whole.

To view mirage, focus your optic onto the target. Then, back off your focus by 5-to-10 yards closer to your position; you'll then view heat waves crossing the target or boiling up into it. This is the most effective method of getting a good wind-speed reading. If the mirage appears to be moving across the target at the speed of a person walking slowly, the wind is 3 mph. If it's the speed of a person walking normally, it's 5 mph. If the mirage is moving the speed of a person jogging, it's 8 mph, and if it's the speed of a person running, the wind speed is 10 mph. If the mirage is boiling straight up into the target, the wind speed is zero—for the time being. Many long-range shooters will not shoot into a boiling mirage, knowing that the wind will most likely kick up during the bullet's flight. They'll dial in for a light wind, wait for the wind to kick up to that speed and direction, then fire.

If the ground is relatively flat from you to the target, you should observe mirage despite the temperature that day. When shooting across dead space, such as from across a valley from terrain feature to terrain feature, you'll need a higher temperature to view mirage.

While I strongly recommend using mirage as the primary tool with which to obtain a wind speed at the target, foliage, such as leaves or tall grass, can be an excellent aid to help with your wind call.

There are many different approaches to reading wind from plant life. I simply think about what 3, 5, 8, or 10 mph winds would do to whatever kind of plant I'm looking at. Don't go too high into the air to observe plant life, though. The only wind you care about for shooting up to about 600 or 700 yards yards/meters is the wind speed at the target. The higher above the target you go, the faster the wind will be. For example, if a 10- to 15-foot-tall tree near the target has leaves that are in constant motion (a good indicator of an 8-mph wind), the wind speed at the target will most likely be only 3 or 5 mph—but definitely less than 8 mph. Take your wind read at ground level, not high above it.

Wind Direction

Let's say you're shooting a 500-yard target with a .308 Winchester. You cannot observe mirage at the target despite your best efforts, although 3-foot-tall grass around the target is leaning 45 degrees to the left due to a crosswind, which appears to be crossing the target from right to left at the speed of a person jogging. You adjust for an 8-mph crosswind, 3 MOA to the right, using the wind chart shown in Figure 5-3.

WIND 2,564 fps @ .55 BC

YARDS	MOA/MILS 3 MPH	MOA/MILS 5 MPH	MOA/MILS 8 MPH	MOA/MILS 10 MPH	YARDS
100	.25/.1	.25/.1	.5/.1	.5/.1	100
200	.5/.1	.75/.2	1.0/.3	1.5/.4	200
300	.5/.1	1.0/.3	1.75/.5	2.0/.6	300
400	.75/.2	1.5/.4	2.25/.7	2.75/.8	400
500	1.0/.3	1.75/.5	3.0/.9	3.75/1.1	500
600	1.5/.4	2.25/.7	3.75/1.1	4.5/1.3	600
700	1.75/.5	2.75/.8	4.5/1.3	5.5/1.6	700
800	2.0/.6	3.35/1.0	5.25/1.6	6.5/1.9	800
900	2.25/.7	3.75/1.1	6.25/1.9	7.75/2.3	900
1,000	2.75/.8	4.5/1.3	7.0/2.1	8.75/2.6	1,000

Figure 5-3.

You recover the target and find that you compensated too much for the wind, and your group is sitting 7.85 inches off to the right of the bull's-eye. How could this have happened? You may have adjusted for a full-value wind instead of a half-value wind. View the "wind direction aid" diagram in Figure 5-4.

Adjusting for wind coming from different directions is not difficult to understand. Take the example where we adjusted for an 8-mph wind blowing

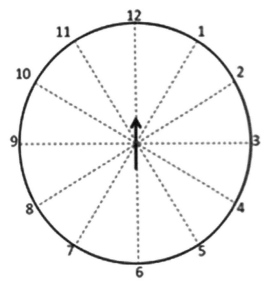

Figure 5-4.

WIND 2,564 ps @ .55 BC

YARDS	MOA/MILS 3 MPH	MOA/MILS 5 MPH	MOA/MILS 8 MPH	MOA/MILS 10 MPH	YARDS
100	.25/.1	.25/.1	.5/.1	.5/.1	100
200	.5/.1	.75/.2	1.0/.3	1.5/.4	200
300	.5/.1	1.0/.3	1.75/.5	2.0/.6	300
400	.75/.2	1.5/.4	2.25/.7	2.75/.8	400
500	1.0/.3	1.75/.5	3.0/.9	3.75/1.1	500
600	1.5/.4	2.25/.7	3.75/1.1	4.5/1.3	600
700	1.75/.5	2.75/.8	4.5/1.3	5.5/1.6	700
800	2.0/.6	3.35/1.0	5.25/1.6	6.5/1.9	800
900	2.25/.7	3.75/1.1	6.25/1.9	7.75/2.3	900
1,000	2.75/.8	4.5/1.3	7.0/2.1	8.75/2.6	1,000

Figure 5-5.

from right to left. By looking at the chart, we found that our adjustment should be 3 MOA to the right. This is only correct if the wind is coming from the 2, 3, or 4 o'clock. If the wind is coming from the 1 or 5 o'clock, you must adjust for a half-value wind. In this case, the adjustment would be 1.5 MOA to the right for a half-value wind instead of 3 MOA.

As stated earlier, wind coming from the 12 and 6 o'clock is zero value and requires no adjustment. Wind coming from the 1, 5, 7, and 11 o'clock is a half-value wind, requiring that you adjust your riflescope half its normal adjustment. Wind coming from the 2, 3, 4, 8, 9, and 10 o'clock is a full-value wind. If it looks like 5 mph, for example, adjust for 5 mph. Let's do four examples with the same wind chart we've been

using for .308 Winchester, shown in Figure 5-5, in order to ensure 100 percent understanding.

1) The target is 300 yards away, and the mirage is moving to the right from the 9 o'clock at the speed of a person walking slowly. So, we adjust our riflescope .5 MOA to the left (into the wind) to compensate for a 3-mph full-value wind.
2) The target is 700 yards away, and the mirage is moving to the left from the 5 o'clock at the speed of a person jogging. For that 8-mph full-value wind, we would normally dial in 4.5 MOA to the right, but wind from the 5 o'clock only affects our bullet at half value. Therefore, we take half the value of our adjustment: 2.25 MOA to the right (into the wind) instead of 4.5 MOA.
3) The target is 650 yards away, and the mirage is moving to the left from the 3 o'clock at the speed of a person walking at a normal pace. So 5 mph at 600 yards would be 2.25 MOA right, and 5 mph at 700 yards would be 2.75 MOA right, therefore we split the difference and adjust 2.5 MOA right for a 5 mph full-value wind.
4) The target is 800 yards away. A stiff 10-mph wind is coming from the 12 o'clock. Because that is a zero-value wind, we make no adjustment, despite the high wind speed.

In essence, if the wind is approaching the target from a full-value direction, make the normal adjustment according to the wind chart. If the wind is approaching the target from a half-value direction, make half the adjustment you would have made for a full-value wind. And if the wind is approaching the target from the 12 or 6 o'clock, make no wind adjustment. Now let's identify how to make a custom wind chart for your particular rifle and favorite cartridge. Again, revisit the chapter on manipulating ballistic software and gathering data if you are unfamiliar with ballistic software, as we are about to use it.

FABRICATING A CUSTOM WIND CHART

This may appear to be a bit much, but in the world of long-range precision marksmanship, properly correcting for wind speed is what separates a very good shooter from the new guy who just has good data on his rifle to correct for range to the target.

First we need to determine the muzzle velocity and ballistic coefficient of your bullet. By determining these two factors, our ballistic software will yield for us the effect of different wind speeds at different distances. We will follow this outline to fabricate our wind chart:

1) Gather data at the range.
2) Determine muzzle velocity and ballistic coefficient.
3) Fabricate wind chart and fill in windage adjustments in MOA and mils.

For the following scenario, we will be using an AR-15 chambered in .223 Remington, firing 55-grain Hornady FMJ-BT ammunition. I've found this combination to yield sub-MOA shot groups up to 400 yards.

Gathering Data at the Range

We head off to the range with the goal of determining the muzzle velocity and ballistic coefficient of our bullet. All we need to do at the range is zero and record the zero distance, then shoot at three other distances and record the drop or rise of the bullet in inches. For this caliber bullet, a 500-yard maximum target distance would provide more perfect ballistic truing. For all cartridges that have MOA group size potential beyond 500 yards, true your ballistics at the farthest effective range available. Below are our results from the range. All of the following information is data actually gathered at the range—nothing hypothetical.

Determining Muzzle Velocity and Ballistic Coefficient—"Truing"

We now return home with the information that we've gathered from the range about our rifle and ammunition. In our ballistic software, we insert our environmental conditions, gun data, and load data. As a benchmark, we'll use the muzzle velocity of 2,970 fps and the ballistic coefficient of .34 to see if that gets us close to the correct trajectory. This is reportedly the muzzle velocity (MV) and ballistic coefficient (BC) of the 5.56mm U.S. Army ball ammo, the projectile weighing 62 grains.

As you can see in Figure 5-6, we set our rifle zero on our software to 51 yards, our target range to the farthest target we shot at today, and insert our tentative MV and BC.

Fill in muzzle velocity and ballistic coefficient by clicking on "Load," as in Figure 5-7.

Fill in gun profile. Be correct on "Caliber Type" and "Sight Height." See Figure 5-8.

Fill in the "Atmospheric Conditions" *of the day* during which you shot. Click "OK." See Figure 5-9.

We now press the "Shoot!" button on our software with a zero range of 51 yards and a target range of 304 yards (the farthest distance we gathered data at today). We proceed to adjust the muzzle velocity in the "load" portion of our software until our software yields 4.43 inches low for a 304-yard shot, given our 51-yard zero range. Our ultimate goal here is to make our ballistic profile on the software mirror our rifle's trajectory at the range.

ENVIRONMENTAL CONDITIONS

Pressure Altitude:	550 feet (Remember, this is not ground elevation)
Temperature:	75 degrees F
Wind:	0 mph
Humidity:	50 percent
Pressure:	29.92 inches Hg

DATA GATHERED

YARDS	MOA	ACTUAL IMPACT (INCHES)	KNOWN DATA
51	0.0 up	0 high—zeroed	
100	0.0 up	1.2 high	
200	0.0 up	.80 high	
304	0.0 up	4.43 low	

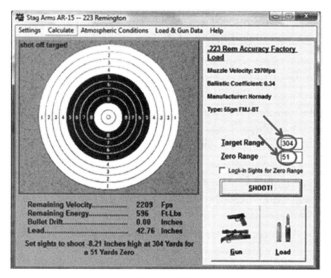

Figure 5-6.

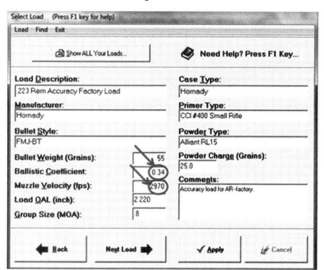

Figure 5-7.

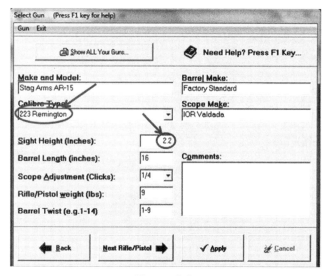

Figure 5-8.

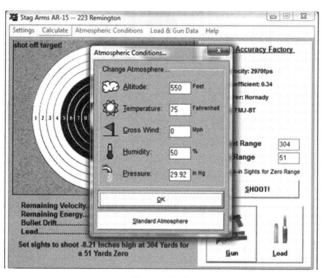

Figure 5-9.

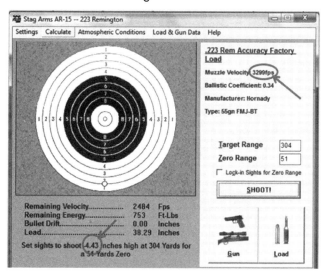

Figure 5-10.

Figure 5-11.

As you can see in Figure 5-6, the software did not yield a 4.43-inches drop at 304 yards. Our benchmark bullet is hitting too low (8.21 inches low), and, therefore, is too slow. We will now speed up the muzzle velocity until the drop yielded by our software is 4.43 inches low.

As you can see in Figure 5-10, we had to bump the muzzle velocity up to 3,299 fps for our software to yield a 4.43-inches drop at 304 yards, given a 51-yard zero. Next we'll see how 3,299 fps at .34 BC looks at the next farthest range we gathered data at: 200 yards.

You can see in Figure 5-11 that our software yielded .88-inch high, but we're shooting for .80-inch high. We adjust the BC and muzzle velocity a little bit to get as close to .80-inch high at 200 yards as possible.

Figure 5-12 shows that we've adjusted the muzzle velocity and BC.

Figure 5-13 shows that we raised the ballistic coefficient to .40 BC and lowered the muzzle velocity to 3,240 fps, which yielded a .82-inch high impact at 200 yards, very close to what we saw at the range. Next, let's look at Figure 5-14 to see how that effected our impact at 304 yards on our software. Is it still 4.43-inches low?

The new yield at 304 yards is 4.46 inches low, which is very close to perfect. Most of the time, no matter how much you manipulate the muzzle velocity and ballistic coefficient, your software will not yield "perfect" results. Ballistic software is only so perfect, but it is a very important tool when it comes to shooting at this level. If you mess with the software some more, you'll see that you cannot get any closer to our actual gathered data than the trajectory created from a muzzle velocity of 3,240 fps at .40 BC—so this is the MV and BC that we'll roll with to create the wind chart and all other atmospheric conditions charts. Before we continue making the wind chart, take a look at Figure 5-15 to begin examining an excellent feature of our ballistic software. From the screen shown in Figure 5-15, you can go to "Calculate" and "Ballistic Report" to reach the screen shown in Figure 5-16.

You can see in Figure 5-16 that, as a result of having our muzzle velocity and ballistic coefficient, we can now extrapolate data for ranges we haven't shot at yet. If we have our MV and BC close to perfect, the adjustments for each given range shown by the software should not only get us on paper at these ranges, but impact within about 1 MOA above or below the

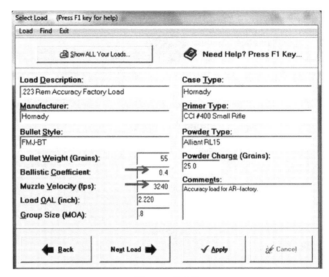

Figure 5-12.

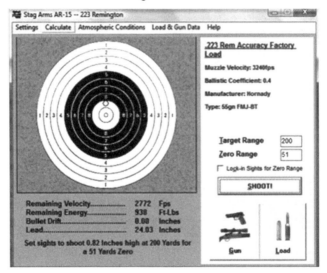

Figure 5-13.

Figure 5-14.

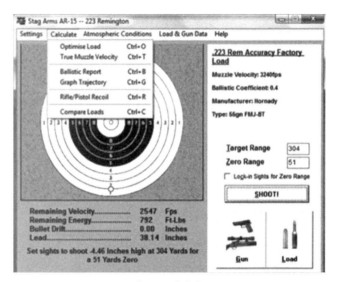

Figure 5-15.

Ballistic Report

Range	Velocity	Energy	Path	Drop	Drift	TOF	Zero Adj
(Yards)	(FPS)	(FT-LBS)	(Inches)	(Inches)	(MOA)	(Sec)	(MOA)
300	2555	797	-4.16	-17.51	0.00	0.313	1.33
310	2534	784	-4.93	-18.79	0.00	0.325	1.52
320	2513	771	-5.75	-20.13	0.00	0.337	1.72
330	2492	758	-6.65	-21.56	0.00	0.349	1.93
340	2471	746	-7.57	-23.00	0.00	0.361	2.13
350	2450	733	-8.55	-24.49	0.00	0.373	2.34
360	2430	721	-9.60	-26.05	0.00	0.385	2.55
370	2409	709	-10.70	-27.68	0.00	0.397	2.76
380	2389	697	-11.87	-29.36	0.00	0.410	2.99
390	2369	685	-13.10	-31.11	0.00	0.422	3.21
400	2348	673	-14.40	-32.93	0.00	0.435	3.44

10 Yards increment out to 500 Yards

Figure 5-18.

Ballistic Report

Range	Zero Adj	Path	Velocity	Energy	Drop	Drift	TOF
(Yards)	(MOA)	(Inches)	(FPS)	(FT-LBS)	(Inches)	(MOA)	(Sec)
0	0.00	-2.20	3240	1282	0.00	0.00	0.000
100	-1.17	1.24	2999	1099	-1.75	0.00	0.096
200	-0.39	0.82	2772	938	-7.35	0.00	0.200
300	1.33	-4.16	2555	797	-17.51	0.00	0.313
400	3.44	-14.40	2348	673	-32.93	0.00	0.435
500	5.94	-31.10	2152	565	-54.81	0.00	0.569
600	8.78	-55.13	1964	471	-84.03	0.00	0.715
700	12.03	-88.19	1787	390	-122.27	0.00	0.875
800	15.84	-132.72	1623	322	-171.98	0.00	1.052
900	20.13	-189.72	1471	264	-234.17	0.00	1.245
1000	25.17	-263.52	1337	218	-313.15	0.00	1.460

100 Yards increment out to 1000 Yards

Figure 5-16.

point of aim—in my experience, up to 750 yards if you also account for the other environmental conditions. We can use this ballistic shell later to gather data at more distant ranges. This also is the most effective way for military and law enforcement snipers to extrapolate adjustments for shots beyond those which they've ever taken. The process I've just walked you through is called "truing."

The next step is to go to "Range Increment" and select "10 Metre/Yard," as shown in Figure 5-17.

You can reduce your range increments to 10 yards at a time instead of 100 yards at a time. (See Figure 5-18) This is much more useful for gathering data on an unknown distance range, whereby you have to range the target—which will most likely not be on a yard-line divisible by hundreds.

Fabricate Wind Chart and Fill In Windage Adjustments in MOA and Mils

Let's fabricate a custom wind chart for our rifle now. First, set the atmospheric conditions to a more useable baseline. (Figure 5-19) You'll want to set up your atmospheric baseline with nice round numbers like these, so that compensating for other environmental changes later in this chapter will be easier.

Figure 5-20 shows the shell of our wind chart. Let's start with the 3-mph column and plug 3 mph into the "Atmospheric Conditions" tab of your software. (Figure 5-21)

Range Increment		Report Options	Save Report...			
10 Metre/Yard	▶	Maximum Report Range			Drift	TOF
25 Metre/Yard	▶	100 Metre/Yard			(MOA)	(Sec)
50 Metre/Yard	▶	250 Metre/Yard		0	0.00	0.000
100 Metre/Yard	▶	500 Metre/Yard		75	0.00	0.096
Print Preview		750 Metre/Yard		35	0.00	0.200
Exit		1000 Metre/Yard				
300	1.33	-4.16	2555	797	-17.51	0.00	0.313
400	3.44	-14.40	2348	673	-32.93	0.00	0.435
500	5.94	-31.10	2152	565	-54.81	0.00	0.569
600	8.78	-55.13	1964	471	-84.03	0.00	0.715
700	12.03	-88.19	1787	390	-122.27	0.00	0.875
800	15.84	-132.72	1623	322	-171.98	0.00	1.052
900	20.13	-189.72	1471	264	-234.17	0.00	1.245
1000	25.17	-263.52	1337	218	-313.15	0.00	1.460

100 Yards increment out to 1000 Yards

Figure 5-17.

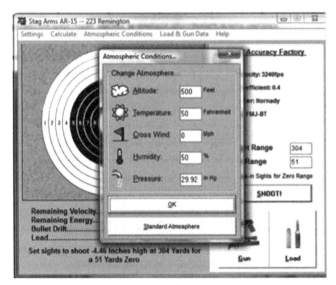

Figure 5-19.

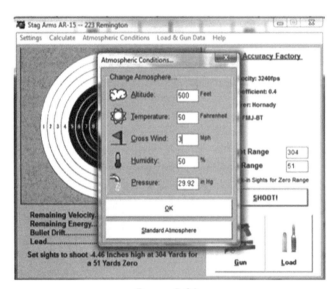

Figure 5-21.

WIND

	MOA/MILS	MOA/MILS	MOA/MILS	MOA/MILS	
YARDS	3 MPH	5 MPH	8 MPH	10 MPH	YARDS
100					100
200					**200**
300					300
400					**400**
500					500
600					**600**
700					700
800					**800**

Figure 5-20. .223 Rem, 3,240 fps at .40 BC.

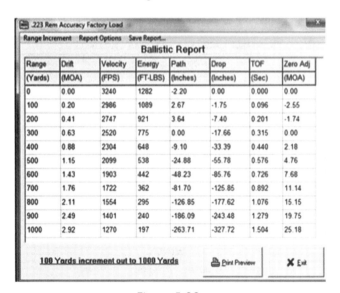

Figure 5-22.

Figure 5-22 shows how easy it is. Look at the column labeled "Drift." This column tells us what a full-value 3-mph wind at each of these ranges will require the windage adjustment shown in MOA. Let's fill these into our wind chart under our 3-mph column, rounding to the nearest .25 MOA for our 1/4-MOA-per-click riflescope. (Figure 5-23.)

Now, using the screen shown in Figure 5-24, change the wind speed in the "Atmospheric Conditions" tab to 5 mph and fill out your wind chart (Figure 5-25) in the same way.

Fill out the rest of the columns in the same manner, as seen in Figure 5-26.

Now convert all MOA answers above into mils and add the mils answers to the chart (Figure 5-27) so that later, you can use either one you'd like—

WIND

	MOA/MILS	MOA/MILS	MOA/MILS	MOA/MILS	
YARDS	3 MPH	5 MPH	8 MPH	10 MPH	YARDS
100	0.25				100
200	**0.5**				**200**
300	0.75				300
400	**1**				**400**
500	1.25				500
600	**1.5**				**600**
700	1.75				700
800	**2**				**800**

Figure 5-23.

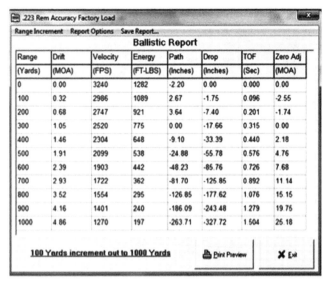

Figure 5-24.

WIND

YARDS	MOA/MILS 3 MPH	MOA/MILS 5 MPH	MOA/MILS 8 MPH	MOA/MILS 10 MPH	YARDS
100	0.25	0.25			100
200	**0.5**	**0.75**			**200**
300	0.75	1			300
400	**1**	**1.5**			**400**
500	1.25	2			500
600	**1.5**	**2.5**			**600**
700	1.75	3			700
800	**2**	**3.5**			**800**

Figure 5-25.

WIND

YARDS	MOA/MILS 3 MPH	MOA/MILS 5 MPH	MOA/MILS 8 MPH	MOA/MILS 10 MPH	YARDS
100	0.25	0.25	0.5	0.75	100
200	**0.5**	**0.75**	**1**	**1.25**	**200**
300	0.75	1	1.75	2	300
400	**1**	**1.5**	**2.25**	**3**	**400**
500	1.25	2	3	3.75	500
600	**1.5**	**2.5**	**3.75**	**4.75**	**600**
700	1.75	3	4.75	5.75	700
800	**2**	**3.5**	**5.75**	**7**	**800**

Figure 5-26.

WIND

YARDS	MOA/MILS 3 MPH	MOA/MILS 5 MPH	MOA/MILS 8 MPH	MOA/MILS 10 MPH	YARDS
100	0.25/.1	0.25/.1	0.5/.1	0.75/.2	100
200	**0.5/.1**	**0.75/.2**	**1/.3**	**1.25/.4**	**200**
300	0.75/.2	1/.3	1.75/.5	2/.6	300
400	**1/.3**	**1.5/.4**	**2.25/.7**	**3/.9**	**400**
500	1.25/.4	2/.6	3/.9	3.75/1.1	500
600	**1.5/.4**	**2.5/.7**	**3.75/1.1**	**4.75/1.4**	**600**
700	1.75/.5	3/.9	4.75/1.4	5.75/1.7	700
800	**2/.6**	**3.5/1.0**	**5.75/1.7**	**7/2.1**	**800**

.223 Rem, 3240 fps @ .40 BC

Figure 5-26.

MOA adjustment on your turret or a mil hold with your reticle.

Always describe your type of ammunition, muzzle velocity, and ballistic coefficient on the bottom or beside each wind chart, ballistic card, or atmospheric adjustment card you create. You wouldn't want to do all this work just to forget which rifle or ammunition one of your charts matches. You can see in the final product of our wind chart (Figure 5-27) that the numbers can be confusing at first. You do not have to insert windage adjustments in both MOA and mils if you don't want to, of course—that falls under shooter's preference. You may elect to insert just one type of adjustment or the other. As long as you have a wind chart for your rifle and your ammunition—and you use it—you're golden. Now you just need to practice observing wind speed at the target and wind direction correctly, which takes lots of practice. In addition, if you dial in or use a mil hold for a specific wind speed, be sure to only break the shot at that wind speed. It sounds like common sense, but it's another step to add to the anatomy of your rifle shot.

COMPENSATING FOR TEMPERATURE

We create a temperature chart to compensate for changes to the air temperature from our baseline. If you remember from the "Compensating for Wind" section prior to this, our baseline is as shown in Figure 5-28.

Our ballistic card for the trajectory of our rifle

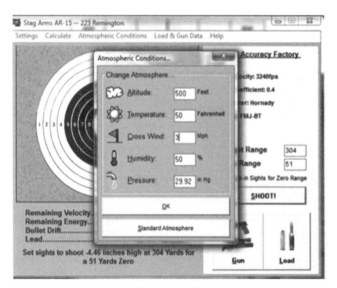

Figure 5-28.

is built based on this baseline, so if we're taking a shot at long range and the temperature is 50 degrees F, there is no need to make any adjustment to compensate for temperature change. But if the temperature is 20 degrees Fahrenheit or more in either direction, the change in the trajectory of our bullet at long range is absolutely worth compensating for. Let's go step by step together on how to make a temperature chart for our rifle. We will follow this outline:

1) Create a temperature chart shell.
2) Fill in ballistics under the baseline column.
3) Use ballistic software to complete the temperature chart.

Create a Temperature Chart Shell

We'll begin the process by using the shell shown in Figure 5-29.

Fill in Ballistics under the Baseline Column

Our baseline column is 50 degrees F, as the ballistic card for compensating for range to the target will be generated at 50 degrees F on our ballistic software. Use the ballistic software to determine our adjustments at each range in hundreds, at 50 degrees F, zeroed at let's say . . . 200 yards, since a 200-yard zero is only .36 MOA away from a 51-yard zero for the ammunition we're using.

The data in Figure 5-30 is produced with the ballistic baseline temperature of 50 degrees F.

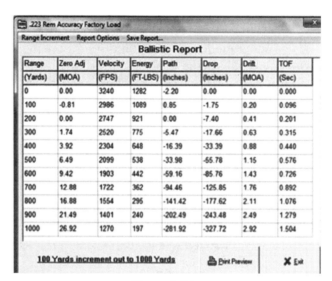

Figure 5-30.

YARDS	10	20	30	40	50	60	70	80	90	100	YARDS
100											100
200											**200**
300											300
400											**400**
500											500
600											**600**
700											700
800											**800**

.223 Rem, 3240 fps @ .40 BC

Figure 5-29.

TEMPERATURE

YARDS	10	20	30	40	50	60	70	80	90	100	YARDS
100					-0.75						100
200					**0**						**200**
300					1.75						300
400					**4**						**400**
500					6.5						500
600					**9.5**						**600**
700					13						700
800					**17**						**800**

.223 Rem, 3240 fps @ .40 BC

Figure 5-31.

Round each adjustment in MOA to the nearest .25 MOA and insert under the 50 degrees F column. At this stage, your chart should look like Figure 5-31.

The adjustments shown in Figure 5-31 are in MOA, as you can see on the ballistic software. Now, use the ballistic software to determine what the adjustments would be at 100 degrees F, given our 200-yard zero.

Use Ballistic Software to Complete the Temperature Chart

Go to "Atmospheric Conditions" and change the temperature from 50 degrees F to 100 degrees F, as shown in Figure 5-32.

Now go to "Calculate" and "Ballistic Report," as in Figure 5-33, to view what our MOA adjustments would need to be to shoot in 100-degree-Fahrenheit weather.

Use this information to fill out the 100-degrees-Fahrenheit column.

As you can see in Figure 5-34, there is a 1 MOA difference at 700 yards between a shot at 50 degrees F and 100 degrees F. This is a difference of 7.33 inches on the target. The difference on the target at 800 yards would be 10.47 inches if the temperature change goes uncompensated for. Fill out the rest of the temperature chart in the same manner, recording in each column the required MOA adjustment for each range and temperature, given our 200-yard zero.

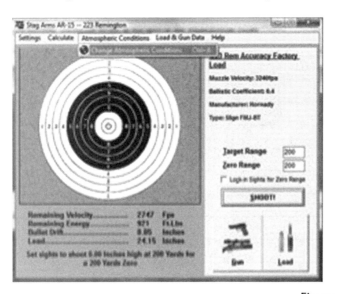
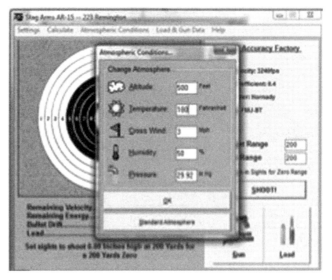

Figure 5-32.

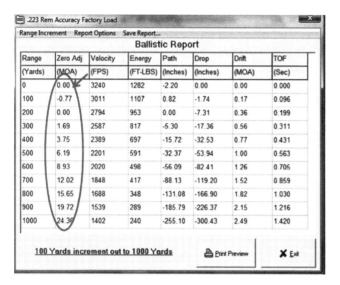

Figure 5-33.

In Figure 5-35, you can already see that, with the ammunition we're using, we don't need to worry about temperature change affecting our trajectory when shooting less than 400 yards—so let's modify our chart to the data shown in Figure 5-36.

If you were to continue filling out the temperature chart, you would get the results seen in Figure 5-37.

Now, to make this chart (Figure 5-37) useful when shooting, we'll change our chart data. Right now, our chart is telling us what our MOA adjustment should be at different temperatures and distances. We will change it to show us the difference in MOA from our baseline temperature.

With the chart shown in Figure 5-38, we can more easily compensate for temperature changes from our baseline. If the temperature drops, the air mass that the bullet has to pass through will be

TEMPERATURE

YARDS	10	20	30	40	50	60	70	80	90	100	YARDS
100					-0.75					-0.75	100
200					0					0	**200**
300					1.75					1.75	300
400					4					3.75	**400**
500					6.5					6.25	500
600					9.5					9	**600**
700					13					12	700
800					17					15.75	**800**

.223 Rem, 3240 fps @ .40 BC

Figure 5-34.

TEMPERATURE

YARDS	10	20	30	40	50	60	70	80	90	100	YARDS
100	-0.75				-0.75					-0.75	100
200	0				0					0	**200**
300	1.75				1.75					1.75	300
400	4				4					3.75	**400**
500	6.75				6.5					6.25	500
600	10				9.5					9	**600**
700	13.75				13					12	700
800	18				17					15.75	**800**

.223 Rem, 3240 fps @ .40 BC

Figure 5-35.

83

TEMPERATURE

YARDS	10	20	30	40	50	60	70	80	90	100	YARDS
400	4				4					3.75	400
500	6.75				6.5					6.25	500
600	10				9.5					9	600
700	13.75				13					12	700
800	18				17					15.75	800

.223 Rem, 3240 fps @ .40 BC

Figure 5-36.

TEMPERATURE

YARDS	10	20	30	40	50	60	70	80	90	100	YARDS
400	4	4	4	4	4	4	3.75	3.75	3.75	3.75	400
500	6.75	6.75	6.5	6.5	6.5	6.5	6.5	6.25	6.25	6.25	500
600	10	9.75	9.75	9.5	9.5	9.25	9.25	9.25	9	9	600
700	13.75	13.5	13.25	13	13	12.75	12.5	12.25	12.25	12	700
800	18	17.75	17.5	17.25	17	16.75	16.5	16.25	16	15.75	800

.223 Rem, 3240 fps @ .40 BC

Figure 5-37.

TEMPERATURE

YARDS	10	20	30	40	50	60	70	80	90	100	YARDS
400	0	0	0	0	B	0	0.25	0.25	0.25	0.25	400
500	0.25	0.25	0	0	A	0	0	0.25	0.25	0.25	500
600	0.5	0.25	0.25	0	S	0.25	0.25	0.25	0.5	0.5	600
700	0.75	0.5	0.25	0	E	0.25	0.5	0.75	0.75	1	700
800	1	0.75	0.5	0.25	LINE	0.25	0.5	.75	1	1.25	800

.223 Rem, 3240 fps @ .40 BC

Figure 5-38.

denser, and therefore the bullet will have a lower point of impact on the target than normal. If the temperature is hotter than our baseline, the air mass is thinner, and therefore the bullet will hit higher than normal. Remember, 50 degrees Fahrenheit is our baseline data. If the temperature you're shooting in is 50 degrees F, just use the adjustments from your known data page or from your ballistic card.

Remember the following:

If the temperature goes down, the scope goes up (adjust up)
If the temperature goes up, the scope goes down (adjust down)

We'll use the chart shown in Figure 5-38 for the following example. Let's say we have a target at 800 yards and the temperature is 20 degrees F. We therefore adjust .75 MOA *up* from our normal adjustment at 800 yards (a 6.28-inch difference on the target).

For an 800-yard shot at 90 degrees F, we would adjust our scope *down* 1.0 MOA (8.38-inch difference on the target). Always be sure to adjust your riflescope in the correct direction! Think before you shoot. I promise you that you'll adjust the wrong direction for windage once or twice if you adjust for wind with the turret instead of using a mil hold with the reticle. This is common, although embarrassing, for new long-range shooters, even if no one else sees. You'll retrieve your target and think to yourself, "Wow—rookie mistake." Fortunately, after you adjust the wrong direction a couple times, you'll never do it again.

COMPENSATING FOR ALTITUDE

As stated at the beginning of the chapter, ignore ground elevation—as per use in ballistic software. Here, we're adjusting for pressure altitude. The only thing we need ground elevation for is to calibrate the device from which we determine pressure altitude. I use a Kestrel weather meter to get the barometric pressure, pressure altitude, and temperature readings when I shoot. Our ballistic software works off of pressure altitude, as does the Kestrel weather meter or like device. Whatever device you choose to measure environmental conditions, just be sure to purchase a model with all of those fea-

tures. I've tried a wristwatch that measures the same things, but I did not find it to read accurately enough, especially when I came to measuring temperature. On my wrist, it would read 115 degrees Fahrenheit on an 85-degree day.

Building an altitude chart to compensate for a change in altitude from our baseline is going to be almost the same process we used to build the temperature chart. We'll start with our blank shell, Figure 5-39, then we'll fill in our baseline elevation column of 500-feet altitude as we set up our ballistic card using 500 feet as our baseline. I chose that number only because that's the normal pressure altitude in the Ft. Campbell, KY, area, where I live and do most of my shooting.

After setting up our software, we generate data for our baseline MOA adjustments, as shown in Figure 5-41.

PRESSURE ALTITUDE

YARDS	500	1K	2K	3K	4K	5K	6K	7K	8K
300									
400									
500									
600									
700									
800									

Figure 5-39.

Figure 5-40.

PRESSURE ALTITUDE

YARDS	500	1K	2K	3K	4K	5K	6K	7K	8K
300	1.75								
400	4								
500	6.5								
600	9.5								
700	13								
800	17								

Figure 5-41.

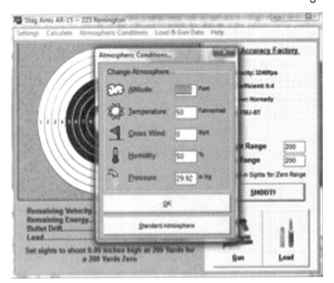 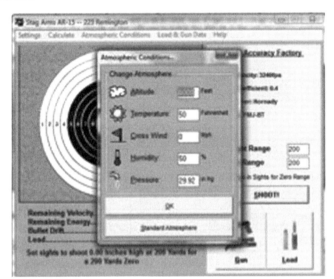

Figure 5-42.

PRESSURE ALTITUDE

YARDS	500	1K	2K	3K	4K	5K	6K	7K	8K
300	1.75								1.5
400	4								3.5
500	6.5								5.75
600	9.5								8.25
700	13								11
800	17								14

Figure 5-43.

PRESSURE ALTITUDE

YARDS	500	1K	2K	3K	4K	5K	6K	7K	8K
300	1.75	1.75	1.75	1.75	1.75	1.75	1.75	1.75	1.5
400	4	4	3.75	3.75	3.75	3.75	3.75	3.5	3.5
500	6.5	6.5	6.25	6.25	6.25	6	6	5.75	5.75
600	9.5	9.5	9.25	9	8.75	8.75	8.5	8.5	8.25
700	13	12.75	12.5	12.25	12	11.75	11.5	11.25	11
800	17	16.75	16.25	15.75	15.5	15	14.75	14.5	14

Figure 5-44.

PRESSURE ALTITUDE

YARDS	500	1K	2K	3K	4K	5K	6K	7K	8K
300	B	0	0	0	0	0	0	0	0.25
400	A	0	0.25	0.25	0.25	0.25	0.25	0.5	0.5
500	S	0	0.52	0.25	0.25	0.5	0.5	0.75	0.75
600	E	0	0.25	0.5	0.75	0.75	1	1	1.25
700	-	0.25	0.5	0.75	1	1.25	1.5	1.75	②️
800	LINE	0.25	0.75	1.25	1.5	2	2.25	2.5	3

.223 Rem, 3240 fps @ .40 BC

Figure 5-45.

We now fill in the rest of our MOA adjustments by manipulating our ballistic software in the same exact way that we used the software to determine how temperature change would affect our shot. Simply change the altitude on the software to match the altitude in the column you're working on, and fill in the MOA adjustments.

In the second image in Figure 5-42, we adjusted our altitude to 8,000 feet. Now we go to "Calculate" and "Ballistic Report" as we did earlier this chapter for windage and temperature change, and yield the results shown in Figure 5-43.

Fill in the rest of the columns from 1,000-feet altitude to 7,000-feet altitude using the same method. The completed chart should look like Figure 5-44.

As we did with the temperature chart, we now count the MOA required from the baseline to any new elevation and draft a new altitude chart. For example, a 700-yard shot taken at 500-foot altitude required a 13 MOA up adjustment, but at 8,000- foot altitude would require only an 11 MOA up adjustment. Therefore, the difference is 2 MOA. (See Figure 5-45)

Make sure to trim any useless data from your charts. As you can see, I do not have a 100- or 200- yard line listed in this chart. This is because there is no adjustment required for ranges that close. Also, there is no column for 0-foot altitude—as there is no adjustment needed from the baseline, even at 800 yards.

As you travel to higher altitudes, the air becomes thinner. Therefore, your bullet will strike higher than expected. So *as the altitude goes up, your scope adjustment goes down.* For example, our normal adjustment under our baseline environmental conditions for a 600-yard shot would be 9.5 MOA up. If we go to a mountainous area at a 5,000-foot altitude, we would adjust our riflescope .75 MOA down from that—setting our adjustment at 8.75 MOA up, a difference of 4.7 inches on our target.

COMPENSATING FOR BAROMETRIC PRESSURE

Lastly, we compensate for barometric pressure. This, like temperature and altitude, can be measured using a Kestrel weather meter. Barometric pressure is measured in either inches of mercury (Hg) or millibars. Since we live in America, I use inches Hg. The baseline for the cartridge we've been using this whole chapter has been 29.92 inches Hg, which is standard atmospheric pressure. Before and during poor weather the barometric pressure may rise or fall. We build our barometric pressure chart the same way we built our temperature and altitude charts earlier this chapter.

Start out with the shell.

	BAROMETRIC PRESSURE					
Yards	**28.00" Hg**	**29.00" Hg**	**29.92" Hg**	**31.00" Hg**	**32.00" Hg**	**Yards**
300						300
400						400
500						500
600						600
700						700
800						800

Fill in your baseline MOA adjustments.

	BAROMETRIC PRESSURE					
Yards	**28.00" Hg**	**29.00" Hg**	**29.92" Hg**	**31.00" Hg**	**32.00" Hg**	**Yards**
300			1.75			300
400			4			400
500			6.5			500
600			9.5			600
700			13			700
800			17			800

Go to "Atmospheric Conditions," change 29.92 inches Hg to 31.00 inches Hg and record the MOA adjustments for that column. (See Figure 5-46)

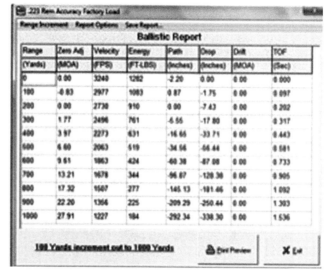

Figure 5-46. Fill in the rest of the chart using this method.

			BAROMETRIC PRESSURE			
Yards	**28.00″ Hg**	**29.00″ Hg**	**29.92″ Hg**	**31.00″ Hg**	**32.00″ Hg**	**Yards**
300	1.75	1.75	1.75	1.75	1.75	300
400	3.75	4	4	4	4	400
500	6.25	6.5	6.5	6.5	6.75	500
600	9.25	9.25	9.5	9.5	9.75	600
700	12.25	12.5	13	13.25	13.5	700
800	16	16.25	17	17.25	17.75	800

As with the temperature and altitude tables, determine how many MOA away each column is from the baseline. For example, an 800-yard shot at 29.00 inches Hg would require a .75 MOA down adjustment.

			BAROMETRIC PRESSURE			
Yards	**28.00″ Hg**	**29.00″ Hg**	**29.92″ Hg**	**31.00″ Hg**	**32.00″ = Hg**	**Yards**
400	0.25	0	B	0	0	400
500	0.25	0	A	0	0.25	500
600	0.25	0.25	S	0	0.25	600
700	0.75	0.5	E	0.25	0.5	700
800	1	0.75	LINE	0.25	0.75	800
		.223 Rem., 3,240 fps @ .40 BC				

As you can see, we've again shaved off the useless portion of the chart. At 300 yards, no matter what the air pressure is, no adjustment is needed; therefore, we get rid of that whole column. As always, we label each chart we make with the ammunition, muzzle velocity, and ballistic coefficient. The more perfect you were at determining your muzzle velocity and ballistic coefficient for your load of choice, the more perfect your pressure altitude, temperature, and barometric change charts will be.

A QUICK WORD ABOUT HUMIDITY

You may be wondering if humidity affects a bullet's trajectory; it does to a very small extent. By setting your baseline to 50 percent humidity in the "Atmospheric Conditions" tab of the software, the humidity can only change by 50 percent in either direction—to 0 percent or 100 percent. At 1,000 yards, a 50 percent change in humidity affects our .223 Remington cartridge by only half an inch—one click on a 1/4-MOA-per-click riflescope at 1,000 yards moves the impact of the bullet 2.62 inches. We cannot compensate for half an inch at 1,000 yards—let alone even *see* half an inch at that range. Even if we could, a very respectable group size at 1,000 yards is 8 inches large. If we were shooting, say, a .308 Winchester rifle with 180-grain Sierra MatchKing bullets at 1,000 yards, a 50 percent humidity change would only affect our shot by .44 inches—still only half an inch difference despite the slower bullet and wider diameter of the round. As you can see, humidity just doesn't matter when shooting up to 1,000 yards/meters, which is precisely why compensating for humidity change was dropped from the course at the US Army Sniper School in Ft. Benning, Georgia.

PRACTICAL EXERCISE

As usual, in order to ensure understanding, determine the elevation and windage adjustments in MOA (minutes of angle) for each set of environmental conditions below. Use the Practical Exercise Charts: ballistic card, wind chart, altitude chart, temperature chart, and barometric pressure chart. Answers can be found at the end of this chapter

PRACTICAL EXERCISE CHARTS

BALLISTIC CARD

YARDS	MOA		YARDS	MOA
25	4.25 UP		425	4.5
50	.5 UP		450	5.25
75	-0.5		475	5.75
100	-0.75		500	6.5
125	-0.75		525	7.25
150	-0.5		550	8
175	-0.5		575	8.75
200	5B + 0.0		600	9.5
225	0.5		625	10.25
250	0.75		650	11
275	1.25		675	12
300	1.75		700	13
325	2.25		725	13.75
350	2.75		750	14.75
375	3.25		775	15.75
400	4		800	17

.223 Rem. 3,240 fps @ .40 BC

WIND

	MOA/MILS	MOA/MILS	MOA/MILS	MOA/MILS	
YARDS	3 MPH	5 MPH	8 MPH	10 MPH	YARDS
100	.25/.1	.25/.1	.5/.1	.75/.2	100
200	.5/.1	.75/.2	1.0/.3	1.25/.4	200
300	.75/.1	1.0/.3	1.75/.5	2.0/.6	300
400	1.0/.3	1.5/.4	2.25/.7	3/.9	400
500	1.25/.4	2.0/.6	3.0/.9	3.75/1.1	500
600	1.5/.4	2.5/.7	3.75/1.1	4.75/1.4	600
700	1.75/.5	3.0/.9	4.75/1.4	5.75/1.7	700
800	2.0/.6	3.5/1.0	5.75/1.7	7.0/2.1	800

.223 Rem. 3,240 fps @ .40 BC

PRACTICAL EXERCISE CHARTS

PRESSURE ALTITUDE

YARDS	500	1K	2K	3K	4K	5K	6K	7K	8K
300	B	0	0	0	0	0	0	0	0.25
400	A	0	0.25	0.25	0.25	0.25	0.25	0.5	0.5
500	S	0	0.52	0.25	0.25	0.5	0.5	0.75	0.75
600	E	0	0.25	0.5	0.75	0.75	1	1	1.25
700	-	0.25	0.5	0.75	1	1.25	1.5	1.75	2
800	LINE	0.25	0.75	1.25	1.5	2	2.25	2.5	3

.223 Rem. 3,240 fps @ .40 BC

TEMPERATURE

YARDS	10	20	30	40	50	60	70	80	90	100	YARDS
400	0	0	0	0	B	0	0.25	0.25	0.25	0.25	400
500	0.25	0.25	0	0	A	0	0	0.25	0.25	0.256	500
600	0.5	0.25	0.25	0	S	0.25	0.25	0.25	0.5	0.5	600
700	0.75	0.5	0.25	0	E	0.25	0.5	0.75	0.75	1	700
800	1	0.75	0.5	0.25	LINE	0.25	0.5	0.75	1	1.25	800

BAROMETRIC PRESSURE

Yards	28.00" Hg	29.00" Hg	29.92" Hg	31.00" Hg	32.00" Hg	Yards
400	0.25	0	B	0	0	400
500	0.25	0	A	0	0.25	500
600	0.25	0.25	S	0	0.25	600
700	0.75	0.5	E	0.25	0.5	700
800	1	0.75	LINE	0.25	0.75	800

.223 Rem., 3,240 fps @ .40 BC

After building your altitude, temperature, and pressure change charts, continue to make improvements to your known data page but be careful. You need to refer to these charts before changing known data for target ranges beyond 400 yards. For example, one of my 60-grain .223 Remington loads should require a 7.5-MOA adjustment for a 400-yard shot from my 100-yard zero. This is only at my 50 degrees Fahrenheit benchmark! A 20-degree Fahrenheit temperature shift in either direction from my baseline requires a .25-MOA adjustment in elevation. So if it's 70 degrees Fahrenheit, I'll put 7.25 MOA on the gun instead of 7.5 MOA. If I'm low or high on the target, then I'll adjust my known data . . . not the temperature chart. If it's 70 degrees Fahrenheit and I put 7.5 MOA on the gun for that 400-yard shot and hit .25-MOA high on the target, I'll refer to my temperature chart before changing my known data. As soon as I see that I should have come down .25 MOA on the gun due to the temperature, I'll know not to change my known data—because I messed up at the range and my data is fine. Had I referred to the temperature chart prior to shooting, I would've put the right D.O.P.E. on the gun in the first place. Refer to your environmental charts before changing your known data.

QUESTIONS

1) RANGE **525 yards**
   WIND **3 mph full value** from 3 o'clock

   ALTITUDE 500 feet
   TEMPERATURE 50 degrees F
   PRESSURE Standard (29.92 inches Hg)

2) RANGE **375 yards**
   WIND **8 mph full value** from 8 o'clock

   ALTITUDE 500 feet
   TEMPERATURE 50 degrees F
   PRESSURE Standard (29.92 inches Hg)

3) RANGE **700 yards**
   WIND **10 mph** from 6 o'clock

   ALTITUDE 500 feet
   TEMPERATURE 25 degrees F
   PRESSURE Standard (29.92 inches Hg)

4) RANGE **775 yards**
   WIND **5 mph half value** from 5 o'clock

   ALTITUDE 6,000 feet
   TEMPERATURE 80 degrees F
   PRESSURE Standard (31.00 inches Hg)

5) RANGE **425 yards**
   WIND **10 mph half value** from 11 o'clock

   ALTITUDE 5,000 feet
   TEMPERATURE 30 degrees F
   PRESSURE Standard (29.92 inches Hg)

6) RANGE **650 yards**
   WIND **5 mph full value** from 9 o'clock
   ALTITUDE 500 feet
   TEMPERATURE 90 degrees F
   PRESSURE Standard (32.00 inches Hg)

ANSWERS

1) RANGE   **525 yards   7.25 MOA up**
   WIND   **3 mph Full Value** from 3 o'clock   **1.25 MOA right** or .4 mils right

   ALTITUDE   500 feet   N/A
   TEMPERATURE   50 degrees F   N/A
   PRESSURE   Standard (29.92 inches Hg)   N/A

2) RANGE   **375 yards   3.25 MOA up**
   WIND   **8 mph full value** from 8 o'clock   **2.25 MOA left** or .7 mils left

   ALTITUDE   500 feet   N/A
   TEMPERATURE   50 degrees F   N/A
   PRESSURE   Standard (29.92 inches Hg)   N/A

3) RANGE   **700 yards   13 MOA up**
   WIND   **10 mph** from 6 o'clock   **N/A**

   ALTITUDE   500 feet   N/A
   TEMPERATURE   25 degrees F   .25 or .5 MOA up
   PRESSURE   Standard (29.92 inches Hg)   N/A

4) RANGE   **775 yards   15.75 MOA up**
   WIND   **5 mph half value** from 5 o'clock   **1.75 MOA right** or .5 mils right

   ALTITUDE   6,000 feet   2.25 MOA down
   TEMPERATURE   80 degrees F   .75 MOA down
   PRESSURE   31.00 inches Hg   .25 MOA up

5) RANGE   **425 yards   5.5 MOA up**
   WIND   **10 mph half value** from 11 o'clock   **1.5 MOA left** or .4 mils left

   ALTITUDE   5,000 feet   .25 MOA down
   TEMPERATURE   30 degrees F   N/A
   PRESSURE   Standard (29.92 inches Hg)   N/A

6) RANGE   **650 yards   11 MOA up**
   WIND   **5 mph full value** from 9 o'clock   **2.5 or 3.0 MOA left** or .8 mils left

   ALTITUDE   500 feet   N/A
   TEMPERATURE   90 degrees F   .5 or .75 MOA down
   PRESSURE   Standard (32.00 inches Hg)   .25 or .5 up

CHAPTER SIX

SHOOTING OVER OR UNDER OBSTRUCTIONS

Between your firing position and the target are power lines and a bridge that is no longer used for travel. Just by eyeballing the shot, you're unsure whether or not your bullet will strike the obstructions in your way. Can you take the shot or not?

The knowledge in this chapter lies more in the realm of tactical marksmanship. Shooting over or under possible bullet obstructions is a rare event, even for law enforcement and military marksmen. Although you'll almost never need this information, I've decided to include it in this book because knowing how to shoot in the presence of obstructions furthers your understanding of the trajectory of your rifle. Believe it or not, you already possess the knowledge in order to facilitate obstacle shooting—as long as you have read and understood the material prior to this chapter. You know how to create a ballistic card for your rifle with the data represented in MOA. You know how to use that ballistic card to create a separate card, having data represented in mils. And you know how to use mil holds for shots instead of dialing in a MOA adjustment.

Figure 6-1A shows a ballistic card representing the trajectory of an M118LR cartridge fired out of a .308 Winchester caliber rifle. This is perfectly safe for the gun, as the 7.62x51mm NATO round can safely be fired out of a rifle chambered in .308 Winchester (but not always vice versa due to the lower chamber pressure tolerances of the 7.62x51mm chamber). The ballistic card in Figure 6-1A is set up for MOA adjustments rounded to the nearest .25 MOA. In Figure 6-1B, we see a ballistic card representing the same trajectory, but expressed in mils instead of MOA. To create the ballistic card in mils, simply convert each MOA adjustment from MOA to mils using the formula below:

MOA/3.375=mils

We will use the ballistic card labeled Figure 6-1B, expressing adjustments in mils, for the duration of this chapter.

Figure 6-2 is a representation of a mil-dot reticle. On it I've placed different yardages based on our mil-hold chart in order to refamiliarize you with how to use mil holds. Look at our ballistic card expressed in mils and double check that I've placed the reference marks correctly on the reticle, based on what you know. We will leave these reference marks on the reticle image to help facilitate our first example.

As a reminder before we get started, it is important to remember that each mil dot is .2 mils tall; thus half a mil dot is .1 mil tall. As you can see in Figure 6-2, the hold for a 500-yard shot with our 200-yard zero is 2.9 mils. If shooting at 500 yards, the bullet should strike the top edge of the third mil dot down from the crosshair.

We'll take the same image—still utilizing the reference marks for simplicity's sake—and add a target this time. Figure 6-3 shows our mil dot reticle with a 40-inch-tall, E-type military silhouette. We range the target, finding its range to be 500 yards. For realism, I tried to make the target in the picture as close to 2.2 mils tall as I could, since 2.2 mils tall is an accurate height representation for a 500-yard, 40-inch tall target.

After ranging the target, look at your ballistic card with the data given in mils. Prepare to set up your

M118LR

YARDS	MOA	YARDS	MOA	YARDS	MOA	YARDS	MOA
10	12.75	310	3	610	14.5	910	2T + .75
20	3.75	320	3.5	620	T + 0.0	920	2T + 1.25
30	0.75	330	3.75	630	T + .25	930	2T + 2.0
40	0.5D	340	4	640	T + .75	940	2T + 2.5
50	1.25D	350	4.25	650	T + 1.25	950	2T + 3.25
60	1.75D	360	4.75	660	T + 1.75	960	2T + 4.0
70	1.75D	370	5	670	T + 2.25	970	2T + 4.5
80	2D	380	5.5	680	T + 2.75	980	2T + 5.25
90	2D	390	5.75	690	T = 3.25	990	2T + 6.0
100	**1.75D**	**400**	**6**	**700**	**T + 3.75**	**1000**	**2T + 6.75**
110	1.75D	410	6.5	710	T + 4.25	2,611 fps @ 505 BC	
120	1.75D	420	6.75	720	T + 4.75		
130	1.5D	430	7	730	T + 5.25		
140	1.25D	440	7.5	740	T + 5.75		
150	1.25D	450	7.75	750	T + 6.25		
160	1D	460	8.25	760	T + 6.75		
170	.75D	470	8.5	770	T + 7.25		
180	.5D	480	9	780	T + 7.75		
190	.25D	490	9.25	790	T + 8.50		
200	**5B + 0.0**	**500**	**9.75**	**800**	**T + 9.0**		
210	0.25	510	10.25	810	T + 9.5		
220	0.5	520	10.5	820	T + 10.0		
230	0.75	530	11	830	T + 10.75		
240	1	540	11.5	840	T + 11.25		
250	1.25	550	11.75	850	T + 12.0		
260	1.5	560	12.25	860	T + 12.25		
270	2	570	12.75	870	T + 13.0		
280	2.25	580	13	880	T + 13.75		
290	2.5	590	13.5	890	T + 14.25		
300	**2.75**	**600**	**14**	**900**	**2T + 0.0**		

Figure 6-1A.

M118LR

YARDS	MILS	YARDS	MILS	YARDS	MILS
10	3.8	310	0.9	610	4.3
20	1.1	320	1	620	4.4
30	0.2	330	1.1	630	4.5
40	-0.1	340	1.2	640	4.7
50	-0.4	350	1.3	650	4.8
60	-0.5	360	1.4	660	5
70	-0.5	370	1.5	2,611 fps @ 505 BC	
80	-0.6	380	1.6		
90	-0.6	390	1.7		
100	**-0.5**	**400**	**1.8**		
110	-0.5	410	1.9		
120	-0.5	420	2		
130	-0.4	430	2.1		
140	-0.4	440	2.2		
150	-0.4	450	2.3		
160	-0.3	460	2.4		
170	-0.2	470	2.5		
180	-0.1	480	2.7		
190	-0.1	490	2.7		
200	**0**	**500**	**2.9**		
210	0.1	510	3		
220	0.1	520	3.1		
230	0.75	530	3.3		
240	1	540	3.4		
250	0.4	550	3.5		
260	1.5	560	3.6		
270	0.6	570	3.8		
280	0.7	580	3.9		
290	0.7	590	4		
300	**0.8**	**600**	**4.1**		

Figure 6-1B.

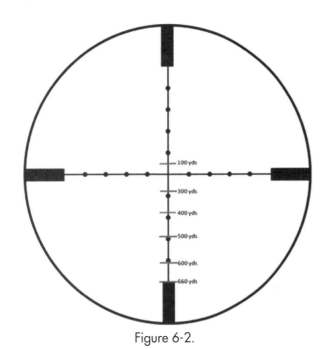

Figure 6-2.

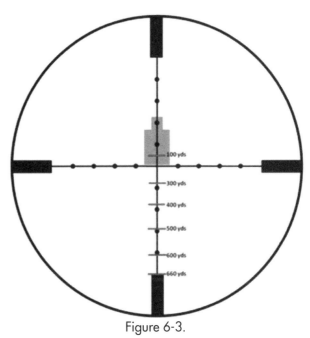

Figure 6-3.

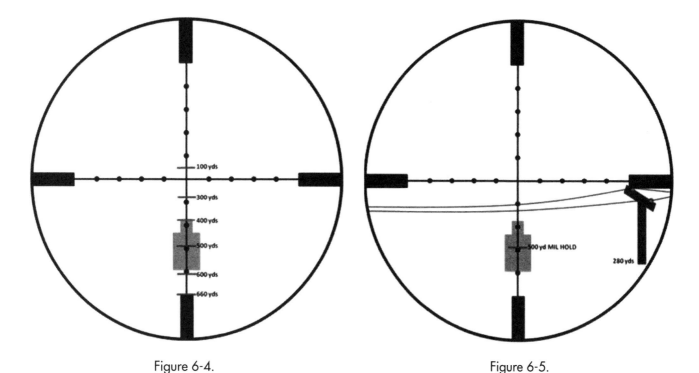

Figure 6-4.

Figure 6-5.

shot using a mil hold. We double-check that our rifle is zeroed for a 200-yard shot (0.0 MOA up, and five baselines readable). We then place our target in the reticle as if we're about to take a 500-yard shot on our target, which is 500 yards away. Our mil hold for a 500-yard shot is 2.9 mils up. You can see that in Figure 6-4, we have properly placed our target in the reticle for a shot using a mil hold of 2.9 mils up. With the rifle zeroed at 200 yards, and given this mil hold, the shot would be on target if no obstacles were present.

In Figure 6-5, you can see that we've still got our 500-yard target, we've still got our 2.9 mil hold, but now we've added power lines between our position and the target. The power lines themselves are too thin to range, so we've ranged the wooden pole, which appears to be the same distance as the power lines. The power lines are 280 yards away. Given the placement of our target in the reticle, if we were to squeeze off our shot, would it strike the power lines? You don't have to eyeball it to know.

The power lines are 280 yards away, correct? Where is the bullet going to strike at 280 yards? Well, what's the mil hold for a 280-yard shot?

Based on the data expressed in our ballistic

card, the mil hold for a 280-yard shot is .7 mils up. In Figure 6-6, I've placed a reference mark at the .7 mils up point on our reticle. You know that our rifle is zeroed at 200 yards. When the bullet hits the 200-yard mark, its elevation will be at the reticle. When the bullet hits the 280-yard mark, its elevation will be at the .7 mils up point (or at the reference mark labeled "280 yd MIL HOLD"). By now, it should be pretty clear that our bullet should pass unobstructed over the top of the power lines and hit our 500-yard target. If the shot is unobstructed, such as in this scenario, you have the option to either engage the target with a mil hold *or* by dialing in an adjustment of 9.75 MOA up with your elevation knob, and aiming center-center on the target using the crosshair.

Let's do an example now with the same range to the target, but a different range to the power lines. In Figure 6-7, we still have our 500-yard target properly placed in the reticle. Now the power lines are 330 yards away. Look at our ballistic card that is set up in mils. Our mil hold for a 330-yard shot is 1.1 mils up. It definitely appears as though our bullet may strike the power lines if we take this shot—but that doesn't mean we can't take the shot.

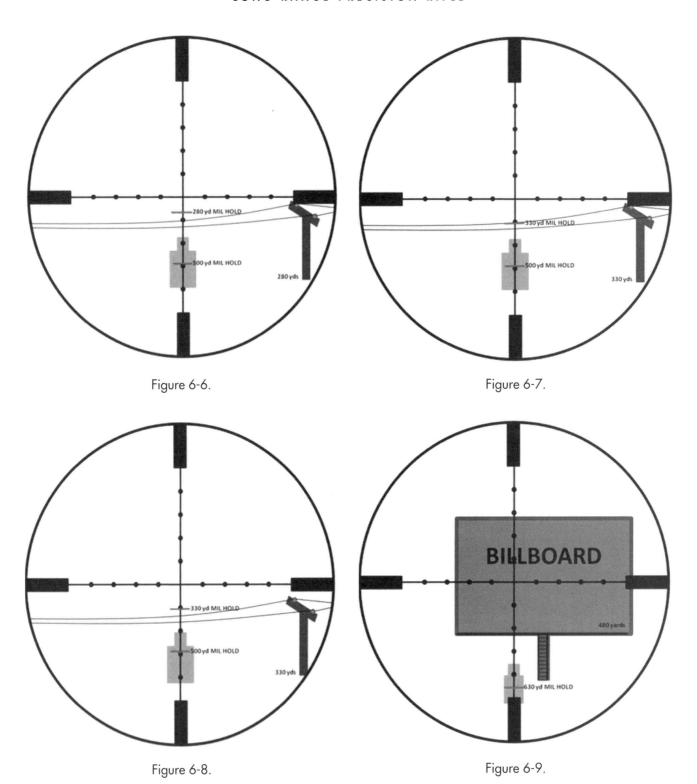

Figure 6-6.

Figure 6-7.

Figure 6-8.

Figure 6-9.

If you look in the image shown in Figure 6-8, our shot is now clear to pass above the power lines. All we've done is aimed higher on the target. We know that at the 330-yard point, the bullet will pass 1.1 mils below our crosshair. By aiming for the top quarter of our target, our bullet should still hit the target while missing the power lines. Another option would be to wait for the target to move farther away or closer to our position. As soon as the shot would go over or under the obstruction, the shot can be taken. Let's do one more example for good measure. This time though, you'll have to determine yourself whether or not the shot is clear or will be obstructed.

PRACTICAL EXERCISE

Figure 6-9 shows a 630-yard target—a 40-inch E-type military training silhouette. There is a 7- to 8-foot-tall billboard providing a possible obstruction. The range to the billboard is 480 yards. Continue to use the ballistic card that we've been using this entire chapter to complete the questions pertaining to this scenario.

QUESTIONS

1) What is the mil hold for a 630-yard shot?
2) Is the E-type silhouette properly placed in the sight picture to put a shot on a 630-yard target?
3) What is the mil hold for a 480-yard shot?
4) Will our bullet go above the billboard, under the billboard, or strike the billboard?

ANSWERS

1) What is the mil hold for a 630-yard shot?
4.5 mils
2) Is the E-type silhouette properly placed in the sight picture to put a shot on a 630-yard target?
Yes
3) What is the mil hold for a 480-yard shot?
2.7
4) Will our bullet go above the billboard, under the billboard, or strike the billboard?
The bullet will go under the billboard, unobstructed.

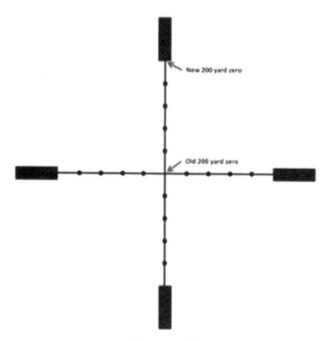

Figure 6-10.

Before concluding this chapter, I'd like to leave you with one more concept related to shooting over/under obstructions. You may have felt as though we were limited by the ballistics of our rifle and cartridge combination by only having the ability to shoot up to 660 yards using mil holds and could, therefore, only engage targets with possible obstruction up to 660 yards. This is not the case. To extend our shooting range using mil holds beyond 660 yards, all we have to do is imagine our 200-yard rifle zero is at the 5.0 mils down point on our reticle, as in the image labeled Figure 6-10.

By using this visual method, we now have 10 mils below our 200-yard zero to work with instead of only 5 mils. Ten mils equals 33.75 MOA. Look at the ballistic card we converted to mils at the beginning of this chapter. Note the adjustment at 950 yards—2T + 3.25 MOA. One full turn of our target knob yields a 15 MOA up adjustment, therefore 2T + 3.25 MOA (two full turns plus 3.25 MOA) equals 33.25 MOA. We can now use the same method as prescribed in this chapter to engage targets with possible obstructions out to 950 yards. Should we actually zero our rifle to the top of the baseline at 200 yards, we can also shoot using mil holds out to 950 yards, should we choose to do this.

CHAPTER SEVEN

HAND LOADING FOR PRECISION RIFLES

PERFORMANCE ANALYSIS:
FACTORY MATCH-GRADE AMMUNITION VS. QUALITY HAND LOADS

My Tikka T3 with heavy varmint barrel was the first sub-MOA guaranteed rifle I purchased; this was seven years ago. As we've discussed in Chapter 1: Rifle and Ammunition Selection, a sub-MOA guarantee is a statement from the company that built the rifle saying that at 100 yards, the rifle will print less than a 1.047-inch shot group. Using factory match-grade ammunition—168-grain Federal Gold Medal Match—my rifle consistently shot .8-MOA groups at 100 yards. I began hand loading the .308 Winchester caliber for which my new rifle was chambered. After five or six days of shooting in order to find the most accurate powder and powder weight for my barrel, my rifle was consistently printing .25-MOA groups at 100 yards and .25-MOA to .35-MOA groups at 200 yards. When shooting out to 800 yards, the shot groups hovered around .5 and .6 MOA.

Sitting in a gun case waiting for me to get back to the States from my last deployment was my Stag Arms AR-15, which is chambered in 5.56x45mm. I purchased it a couple years prior. It had a traditional M4-style collapsible buttstock, a 1913 rail above the receiver, a short hand guard, and a chrome-lined 16-inch barrel with a 1:9 twist rate. The rifle was obviously intended to be a close-quarters type rifle, especially due to the presence of the chrome-lined barrel—a sacrifice in accuracy done by many manufacturers in order to increase reliability and barrel longevity, despite being exposed to a high volume of fire. I mounted an EOTech sight to the rifle and consistently shot groups hovering right at 1 MOA with factory 55-grain Hornady FMJ ammunition at 50 and 100 yards.

While deployed in Afghanistan, I had only one firearm-related project in my head for when I returned home: I would change my AR-15 from a CQB setup to a precision rifle setup, and I'd keep that setup if the rifle performed favorably. The goal of this project was to see how much accuracy I could get out of a chrome-lined AR-15 barrel by using hand loads.

The changes I made to the accessories of the gun were more a function of mitigating human error during the act of firing: I replaced the traditional M4-style buttstock with a Magpul PRS buttstock, which would give me a flat surface to set on a sand sock for a steadier firing position. I replaced the short hand guard with a 12.5-inch PRI Mounts hand guard. This would allow me to attach a bipod closer to the muzzle. The more distance a shooter can create between his rear rest (sand sock, for example) and his front rest (bipod, for example), the steadier his firing position will be. If you've heard the expression "wider is better" as it pertains to stability, then by the same theory, longer is also better than shorter.

As my optic choice, I selected a 10x42mm SWFA Super Sniper riflescope. I became a huge fan of the 16x42mm Super Sniper that lives on my .308 Winchester to this day, so it just made sense to go with a company that I already trusted due to hundreds of spent cartridges and successful shooting events. I fired using this new rifle setup for a couple weekends and felt the need to replace the heavy and gritty stock trigger with a Chip McCormick 3-pound single-stage trigger. This did not increase the accuracy of the rifle itself, although I no longer had to fight the trigger. Therefore, the new trigger reduces the likelihood of human error on my part and makes for more enjoyable shooting events.

As I pointed out above, I was able to tune the accuracy of my .308 Winchester down to .55 MOA more accurate at 100 yards using hand loads as opposed to using factory match ammunition. I was able to tune the accuracy of my AR-15 down to .6 MOA more accurate. Let's crunch some numbers: If a shooter consistently shoots 3.5-inch groups at 400 yards, his group size in minutes of angle is .84 MOA. If he is only able to tighten up his shot group by .5 MOA by using hand loads, his new group size is .34 MOA. His group size in inches at 400 yards is now 1.42 inches versus 3.5 inches. The farther away this shooter puts shot groups on paper the more noticeable the accuracy of his hand loads are in comparison to the more expensive factory match ammunition.

I, of course, ended up being very happy with the result I was able to create for my AR-15. I now have a semiautomatic rifle that consistently fires sub-MOA groups out to 400 yards. The accuracy at 500 yards is right at 1 MOA. I was surprised to get those accuracy results from an "off the rack" rifle with a 16-inch chrome-lined barrel. The overall result is that I've put together a sub-MOA rifle for short and midrange use on an easily wieldable, short, low-recoil platform. The rifle is capable of placing a first-round hit on a 25-pound or larger varmint, or in the vitals of medium to large game given midrange and short-range target engagement conditions—provided I have *time* and opportunity to establish a steady firing position and get a good range in yards to the target. If needed, a quick follow-up shot is available due the semiautomatic nature of the design. The rifle is low recoil enough that upon firing the target does not "jump" out of the field of view of the riflescope. I can see the reaction of the target without the aid of a spotter. The low recoil is simply a function of the caliber type (5.56x45mm), the semiautomatic nature of the design, and the heavier overall weight of the rifle. I shoot paper most of the time—of course—to gather data and practice, but trips to the ranch should be fun from here on out. I'll still use my Tikka T3 for game animals out there, but I can keep the AR-15 by the sliding glass door on a bipod or in a truck with a rangefinder next to it for targets of opportunity on coyotes and foxes.

As you can see here, you can significantly increase the accuracy of a rifle by properly building hand loads—even a rifle without a sub-MOA guarantee, such as my Stag Arms AR-15 (Figure 7-1).

After building up a rifle as far as I'm going to build it, determining an accuracy load through hand

Figure 7-1. My Stag Arms AR-15 after modification.

Figure 7-2. From the top, a Mega Machine upper and lower AR-15,
a Mega Machine upper and lower AR-10, and a Stag Arms AR-15.

loading, and gathering data at extended range, if the rifle and ammunition combination yield sub-MOA shot groups, I am satisfied. The rule I have for myself is that the rifle can only look as good as it performs. My AR-15 (the bottom rifle in Figure 7-2) earned its paint after yielding sub-MOA shot groups at 500 yards with 55-grain Hornady V-Max bullets. A benefit of paint is that when rained on, clean-up is easy and the paint works as a rust preventative. In my Sniper Section, we would use Krylon Camouflage spray paint. It dries quickly and is flat in tone (doesn't shine). The Krylon, however, creates a rough finish and needs to be touched up occasionally due to wear. I now use automotive paint for durability. There are many advantages to using automotive paint: I can purchase the colors by the pint, I'm not limited on color choice, and running the auto paint through an airbrush gun gives me a smaller spray pattern so that I can produce finer lines and detail. The result is a more durable finish and, in my opinion, a more professional-looking final product. It does require more time, however. It takes about seven hours as opposed to one or two hours with the Krylon Camouflage spray paint.

Cost Comparison

Not only does the *correct* act of hand loading dramatically increase the accuracy of your rifle, it is also more cost effective. Let's crunch some more numbers. We'll even get the more expensive, well-made components that I love so much.

PRODUCT	COMPONENT COUNT OR WEIGHT	PRICE
.308 Winchester, Hornady Match rifle cases #8661	50 count	$33.10
.308 caliber, 180-grain Sierra MatchKing HPBT bullets	500 count	$155.16
Alliant Reloder 15 rifle powder	Two 5-pound jugs	$199.60
Federal large rifle primers, match	1,000 count	$35.22

Each piece of brass can be fired between five and seven times if the shooter chooses to do a full resize every time (we'll talk about neck sizing later in this chapter), so we'll be generous and say that we'll only fire each piece of brass five times. With 50 pieces of brass (see chart above) costing $33.10, we can build 250 cartridges. Therefore, we will only be using half the number of bullets. The cost of 250 of the 180-grain Sierra MatchKing bullets is $77.58. We will only use one-fourth the number of available primers for these first 250 hand loads. The cost of that is $8.81. There are 7,000 grains in one pound. At 44.8 grains of powder per cartridge (near maximum safe load, reportedly), 250 hand loads requires 11,200 grains of powder. To build 250 hand loads, we will use $159.68 of our 10 pounds of available rifle powder. In total, to build 250 hand loads using the above excellent components, the cost is $279.17.

Compare this to the cost of Federal Gold Medal rifle cartridges in the caliber of .308 Winchester. I consider these cartridges to be among the best compared to other factory match-grade ammunition. The cost of 20 rounds of Federal Gold Medal Match comes to $36.19. Therefore, 250 rounds of the same ammunition costs $452.38. Every 250 cartridges you shoot by hand loading with some of the best components available, you save $173.21. Not only that, but the performance of your rifle and ammunition should be at least .5 MOA more accurate. In addition, you have components remaining. Below is a breakdown of the cost effectiveness we've just covered above, excluding the fact that we have components remaining:

Cost of firing 250 hand loads, using Match Brass and Sierra MatchKing bullets: $279.17

Cost of firing 250 cartridges of Federal Gold Medal Match (.308 Winchester): $452.38

Cost of one hand-loaded cartridge, using Match Brass and Sierra MatchKing bullets: $1.12

Cost of one cartridge of Federal Gold Medal Match (.308 Winchester): $1.81

As you can see, hand loading is more cost-effective, although certainly more noticeable in the long term. Hand loading is also much more accurate when compared to shooting factory match-grade ammunition in both rifles that I hand load for. The real cost to you is *time*. It takes time to build your own rifle cartridges. I generally press out 30 cartridges in one hour or less, taking my time on my single-stage press, giving attention to each load at each step of its development.

I wanted to be clear on the accuracy increase you can expect by hand loading and the cost effectiveness of hand loading in order to motivate you to begin doing so if you haven't already. Now that I've (hopefully) made a good sale to you as to the merit of the procedure, we can finally get to the important part—how to create match-grade rifle cartridges.

BUILDING PRECISION CARTRIDGES

Every piece of reloading equipment that you buy will come with clear "how-to" directions, and anything that you find to be unclear in those instructions can be explained by searching the Internet. (YouTube.com is a surprisingly good source for instructional videos.) I will, therefore, not bore you with the specifics of how to operate each little tool/device that comes with the package. Rather, in the rest of this chapter, I will outline my exact process. There are a few steps I take for accuracy that only other serious shooters and competition shooters seem to take. Most hand loaders do not take all of these steps, as many hand loaders make their loads for semiautomatic, high-volume-of-fire-type rifles and pistols. I will identify for you all steps I take that are "Above the Rest," as it were.

We'll use a .308 Winchester bolt-action rifle with a 1:11 rate of twist as our example rifle for the first part of this chapter. The Greenhill Formula we used in Chapter 1 yields a 1.294-inch bullet length as stable for our 1:11 rate of twist barrel.

We decide we'd like to use Sierra MatchKing bullets due to all the success stories we hear about them. Competition shooters we know have had success with them, and the U.S. Army uses the 175-grain Sierra MatchKing in its M118LR rifle cartridges for the M110 SASS, the late and great M24, the SR-25, and accurized EBR M14. So we'll

$$\frac{(\text{bullet diameter})(\text{bullet diameter}) \times 150}{\text{rate of twist}} = \text{stable bullet length in inches}$$

$$\frac{(.308)(.308) \times 150}{11} = 1.294 \text{ inches long}$$

try these bullets first. With a quick call to Sierra Bullets, one of the bullet smiths tells us that the .308 caliber bullet having an average length closest to 1.294 inches long is the 180-grain Sierra MatchKing. We order these online. (I religiously order components from Midsouth Shooter's Supply in Tennessee, as their selection is great and their business is so close to my house.) The information from the bullet smith made perfect sense. My reasoning was this: The U.S. Army's M24 had a 1:11.25 twist rate. They've matched that with a 175-grain bullet for long-range stability. Our 1:11 rate of twist would need a slightly longer bullet, so the 180-grain bullet made by the same company and of the same hollow-point boattail style makes sense so far.

Upon viewing Sierra's reloading manual, we see that they've already tested many different rifle powders from different manufacturers while shooting the 180-grain Sierra MatchKing .308 caliber bullet. There is an asterisk next to Alliant Reloder 15, identifying it as the powder they found to be most accurate in their test rifle. It's got to be a sign, so we buy one pound of Reloder 15 online. We only buy a pound just in case we don't get amazing results. The maximum safe load reported by Sierra's reloading manual is 45.0 grains of powder per cartridge. We'll make sure not to exceed that, even if we don't identify any pressure problems after shooting loads containing 45.0 grains of Alliant Reloder 15. You will not blow up your rifle action by exceeding your maximum safe load by too much, as some will tell you. If using *rifle* powder in your rifle cartridge, exceeding your safe load by too much raises the risk of accelerated throat erosion, decreased brass life, and possible case head separation of brass (when the brass splits in half). I've seen only one shooter blow up his rifle action. He built a compressed load for a rifle using *pistol* powder for a 5.56x45mm rifle cartridge. Pistol powder burns much faster than rifle powder. This guy blew up his action, but I've seen a pistol shooter blow his revolver in half by making loads with too *little* powder. The bullet was so slow, one of them didn't exit the muzzle and became stuck in the barrel. The next bullet sent down the barrel blew the firearm in half, only to be still connected by a small piece of metal. The point is to stay within the safe powder-charge spectrum for each powder and bullet combination, and only use recommended powders for your caliber and bullet weight. If you follow the rules, you won't damage your expensive equipment.

DETERMINING YOUR ACCURACY LOAD

Every rifle and barrel is different. Once we have all the components and we need to start hand loading, we're not just going to build a bunch of cartridges with the same powder charge and hope they shoot well. Every rifle barrel is different! You may go to very helpful websites such as Handloads.com and find that some guy reported that 45.0 grains of Alliant Reloder 15 consistently shoots .2-MOA groups at 100 yards with the 180-grain Sierra MatchKing. That's excellent for him, but our rifle is different, even if our rifle is the same make and model as his, having the same barrel length and twist rate. What we'll do is build the 15 loads for our safe powder-charge range. To ensure that each powder charge below has a "fair shake" compared to the others, we'll make sure to use the same brass weight for each set of three loads. For example, if all three loads containing 44.2 grains of powder are built using 152.6-grain brass, all three loads containing 44.4 grains of powder are built using 152.7-grain brass, and all three loads containing 44.6 grains of powder are built using 152.8-grain brass, then each powder weight that we're testing has an equal opportunity to perform well and beat out the others tested. I'll identify the importance of matching brass weights later.

Number of loads	3	3	3	3	3
Powder weight in grains	44.2	44.4	44.6	44.8	45.0

Given our particular bullet and rifle powder combination, somewhere between 44.2 grains and 45.0 grains of Alliant Reloder 15 is the most accurate powder charge for our rifle. When we get to the range, we'll confirm zero with some factory ammunition to make sure that our hand loads are on paper. The hand loads are usually within 1 MOA of the point of impact of normal factory or factory-match ammunition. After having zeroed, we very patiently and very slowly fire the three loads containing 44.2 grains of Reloder 15. We record in our data book where that specific group is on our target. Very patiently and slowly, shooting as accurately as possible by applying all fundamentals of marksmanship, we fire the three loads containing 44.4 grains of Reloder 15 at a different target (same distance) and record where that shot group is in our data book. We do this with all 15 of our hand loads. One of our groups of three hand loads will be obviously tighter and more accurate than the rest—and one, some of, or most of the other groups will be just terrible, depending on the rifle powder you're using. In our case, we achieve the following results:

Powder weight	Group size at 100 yards
44.2 grains	.55 inches
44.4 grains	1.62 inches
44.6 grains	.84 inches
44.8 grains	.24 inches
45.0 grains	.33 inches

So far, our best group is .24 inches at 100 yards, using 44.8 grains of Alliant Reloder 15. But we're not done. It's clear to see that a 44.7-grain powder weight or a 44.9-grain powder weight may be able to get us even more accuracy. We build the following hand loads for the next day that we shoot, this time dedicating five cartridges per powder weight instead of three cartridges in order to give us a more conclusive idea of which powder weight is truly best in our rifle.

Number of loads	5	5	5
Powder weight in grains	44.7	44.8	44.9

Our results after our next shoot are as follows:

Powder weight	Group size at 100 yards
44.7 grains	.39 inches
44.8 grains	.30 inches
44.9 grains	.21 inches

A QUICK WORD ON VELOCITY

Based on the data we've gathered, it is fair to say that our accuracy load is 44.9 grains of Alliant Reloder 15, when using the 180-grain Sierra MatchKing bullet. You may be asking yourself why we wouldn't want to use the 45.0-grain load? It produces a faster bullet and, while the shot groups are not as good as our accuracy load, they're still well under 1 MOA. Wouldn't we want more velocity for shooting long range? The answer is, no.

Earlier in this book, you learned about riflescope mechanics and how to effectively gather external ballistic data. In short, if you know how to dial-in a minute of angle adjustment or mil hold to put your shots center-center on your target, you'll want those shots to be as close together as possible. There is very little gain in the maximum distance your rifle will be able to shoot—called the maximum effective range—by adding .1 grain, .2 grains, or even .3 grains of powder. The muzzle velocity is actually very comparative. The *type* of powder would have more of an effect on changing the muzzle velocity—because a different type of powder would have a faster or slower burn rate. If you find that your accuracy load is not pushing out to your desired target distance—but that it's close—try another rifle powder, get a longer barrel, or change the caliber. Ideally, you'll do the research so that you make the right choice first. The .308 Winchester bolt-action rifle that we're using in the example for this chapter will shoot better groups at 800 yards all day with our accuracy load of 44.9 grains of Reloder 15, as opposed to loads with 45.0 grains of the same powder. After finding our accuracy load, we can build a bunch of them and gather data in increments of 100 yards/meters out to as far as possible—see Chapter 3 for more on this.

The above process is the best way I've found to determine the accuracy load for any rifle. Now that you know the big-picture goal—which is to determine the accuracy load for your rifle and gather data—we'll get into the finer details of the actual process of hand loading.

CASE PREP: RESIZING, DEPRIMING, AND CLEANING

As you fire a cartridge in your rifle, the pressure and heat cause the brass to expand within the chamber. I used to fully resize each fired casing of mine. As you can see in Figure 7-3, I have the 20 cartridges that I've fired at the range during my last shoot. We'll use .223 Remington casings to describe this process.

All casings have resizing lubricant from the base of the case to the case shoulder. We also lube the inside and outside of the case neck. Try not to let any resize lube get on the case shoulder (the angled part). Note that, depending on your dies and size of your brass, you may not need to lube *every* case. For .223 Remington brass, I leave every fifth casing dry (without lube) to prevent buildup in the resizing die. Also for this caliber, I do not lube the inside of the case neck of every fifth casing. Though

Figure 7-4. This is the resizing die that I use. I find that I need to skip the resize lube on every fifth casing to prevent buildup.

I don't have to lube the inside of every case neck for .223 Remington or .308 Winchester, I *do* have to lube the inside of every case neck for .338 Lapua Magnum. It just depends on your dies and your brass. Figure 7-4 shows my resizing die.

Running a piece of brass into the resizing die will return the external dimensions to their pre-firing condition. Note the decapping pin sticking out of the bottom of the die. This will knock out our spent primer as we resize the casing.

Each resized casing has lubricant on it. To clean this off, I put my casings in a brass tumbler. (See Figure 7-5.) This also cleans carbon from the inside of the case and primer pocket, and resizing lubricant from the inside of the neck and outside of the case. Some hand loaders tumble their casings before resizing to remove carbon, sand, and grit in order to keep their sizing die as clean as possible. Then they wipe the lube off the brass or simply tumble again after resizing to remove the case lubricant. I've found no issue with a bit of carbon

Figure 7-3. Lubricated casings to be resized.

Figure 7-5. Rifle casings are sent
into the brass tumbler after the resizing process.

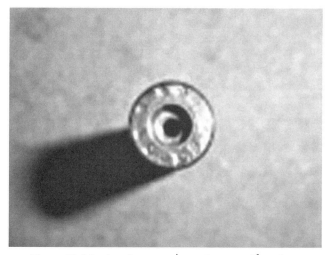

Figure 7-6A. A primer pocket prior to uniforming.

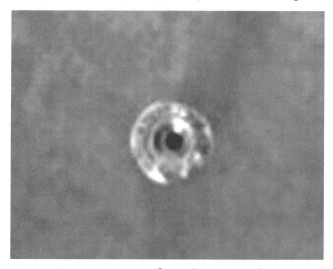

Figure 7-6B. A uniformed primer pocket.

damaging any resizing dies. I tumble the brass fired from my AR-15 before resizing because they hit the ground and have the chance of picking up dirt or sand. I don't tumble my .308 Winchester brass after firing as none of my .308 Winchester brass ever goes into sand or dirt. I take them from the chamber and put them straight back into their cartridge box. After sizing the .308 Winchester brass, however, I tumble to remove the case lubricant. I don't want my rifle powder exposed to any compound or mixture, such as the case lube left behind on the inside of the case mouth. I don't want to risk fouling the rifle powder or even adding a new variable that I'm unsure about or haven't tested yet. Be sure to clean each resizing die after use.

Primer Pocket Uniforming and Case Trimming

Using Hornady Match Brass for my .308 Winchester, I simply don't need to uniform the primer pockets after each firing—only the first time when the brass is brand new. Using Lapua Match Brass and Hornady brass for my 5.56x45mm AR-15, I don't have to uniform my primer pockets after firing, either. But when firing Lake City Brass through my AR-15, I have to uniform the primer pocket after every firing, which is why I don't fire Lake City brass anymore. During the firing process, a bulge is sometimes created inside the primer pocket. If you choose not to uniform a primer pocket that needs

it, upon seating the new primer, you'll notice that the casing wobbles when stood upon a flat surface. The primer is supposed to be level with the base of the casing or slightly sunken in beyond the depth of the base of the casing. If the primer sticks out too far, you may risk a slam fire if you are shooting the cartridge out of a semiautomatic rifle. Also, you want all of your primers to be seated to the same depth. Consistency translates to accuracy.

To uniform a primer pocket, insert your primer pocket uniformer into a drill. Please don't waste your time attempting this process by hand; you would easily spend 10 minutes on one casing. Squeeze the trigger on the drill. The primer pocket uniformer will allow itself to go only so deep. When

Figure 7-7. The case trimmer is adjusted to fit a piece of brass with the desired length.

the primer pocket uniformer can cut no deeper, you're done. Each casing should take no more than 10 seconds. Again, do this procedure for new brass and never again on the same brass piece. If you're using high-quality brass, no bulge will be produced in the primer pocket as a result of firing. Look into your primer pocket after uniforming and you'll notice that the remaining freshly cut brass appears to be very clean and the surface is flat.

We started out with 20 casings. They've been resized, deprimed, and tumbled for cleanliness for about eight hours. Let's say that all of our 5.56mm casings were 1.748-inches long before they were fired. Now that they've been fired and fully resized, each casing should be longer than 1.748 inches. Any casing that *did not* grow .003-inch longer upon resizing, I throw away. When a casing does not grow upon full resizing, this tells me that the brass has had enough firings, and further firings could result in a case-head separation. Each casing that grew longer than its original pre-firing length (1.748 inches) must now be trimmed back to that length. This process should be done before a new primer is seated into the case.

To trim the case, first set up your trimmer by inserting a case that is already 1.748 inches long. Gently touch the cutter to the case mouth and adjust the stopper to prevent any case from being trimmed shorter than 1.748 inches long. Put casings that require trimming into the trimmer one at a time, and rotate the handle until it sounds and feels like the cutter is no longer cutting any material. Remove the casing and check the length with your micrometer. Is the case 1.748-inches long? If it is still too long, trim it some more. But if the case is only long or short by .001 inch, that's fine; this won't have a negative affect on shot placement or accuracy. Of course, as with everything else in hand loading, try to get it perfect, though.

After your case is trimmed to the desired length, chamfer the inside and outside of the case mouth. This will remove the 90-degree angle produced during the cutting process and burrs. See Figure 7-8 to view the difference between a chamfered and an unchamfered case mouth. Leaving a case mouth unchamfered will likely cause a failure to feed in your rifle and damage the bullet upon seating the new round into the unchamfered case mouth.

Figure 7-8. A freshly trimmed case mouth (left) shown next to a chamfered case mouth (right).

Be sure to research the minimum and maximum safe case lengths before trimming. I can tell you right now that case length does not affect accuracy much at all unless the case length is too long. If the case length is too short, accelerated throat erosion can occur. We'll describe these two issues in detail later in this chapter. Stay within the case-length specifications for your caliber and try to trim each casing to the same length.

When my brass is new (unfired), some of the case mouths are imperfect. They are either not circular or have varying internal diameter. Therefore, I neck-size all new brass, then tumble to remove case lubricant. Upon pulling the casings out of the tumbler I measure the length of each case. My shortest Hornady Match .308 Winchester brass is usually 2.002-inches long when it's brand new, then neck-sized. As a result, I trim all new brass that I've just neck-sized to 2.002-inches long (to match the shortest of the bunch).

Let's say I shoot 50 rounds at the range, go home, and resize all the fired casings. Some are 2.004-inches long, most are 2.006-inches long, and some up to 2.010-inches long. The shortest of the bunch are 2.004-inches long, so I trim that entire batch of brass to 2.004-inches long so they're all the same for next time. Be sure not to trim to a case length that will result in the case mouth impacting the throat of your rifle. Again, stay within spec as per case length. After finding your accuracy load—i.e., the ideal powder type and powder weight for the brass you're using and bullet combination—you may choose to experiment with different case lengths in order to produce more accuracy. However, I've found this to be a waste of time. "Just stay within specification" would be my advice on case length, but keep all brass of the same lot at the same length to be consistent. There are other details to be concerned with that have more of an effect on accuracy.

LOT YOUR BRASS BY WEIGHT!

After uniforming the primer pocket and trimming and chamfering the case, you are done removing brass. Therefore, it is now time to separate the brass casings into lots by weight. *Every successful hand loader certainly doesn't do this, but it is a very common practice among competitive shooters.* A "lot" is simply a collection of items that are all as close to identical to one another as possible. In this scenario, each lot will have brass of the same length to the nearest .001-inch, and will have brass the same weight to the nearest .1 grain. Weigh each piece of brass, and organize them into lots as I've done in Figure 7-9.

Each column of brass in Figure 7-9 has the same weight. The entire left column of three casings weighs 91.7 grains. The three pieces of brass in the next column to the right all weigh 91.8 grains, and so on. For maximum accuracy, I'll shoot each column of ammunition in the same grouping at the same target. At the range, the three loads featuring 91.7-grain brass will be shot at the 100-yard target. The three loads featuring 91.8-grain brass will be fired at the 200-yard target, and so on.

Why lot brass by weight? The external dimensions of each piece of resized brass will be the same. Therefore, if one piece of brass weighs 97.0 grains, and another piece weighs 96.0 grains, the 97.0-grain piece of brass will have less internal case volume.

Figure 7-9. Each column of three pieces of brass has the same weight.

With less room for powder, this will likely create slightly more muzzle velocity, given the same seating depth of the bullet. This will not change our zero at 100 yards if all cases are built by the same company, but vastly different brass weight will have enough effect on the path of our bullet to noticeably affect group size. As a matter of fact, in my AR-15, I use Hornady brass (not match). The lightest cases have up to a .5-MOA difference in trajectory starting at 250 yards than the heaviest cases.

Another issue to be tracking as per brass weight is that if you reload brass made by *different* companies, the difference in brass weight is often such that your accuracy load—powder weight—will be different between the two different companies, and your zero will be different even though you're using the same bullet. To keep it simple, I'd recommend sticking with one specific brand of brass. Otherwise, you'll have to build an accuracy load for each different brass type that you use.

While gathering data, I note the case weight of each lot that I shoot. If my bullets were to impact higher with heavier brass than I'm used to using, I would not change my known data. I simply make another, completely separate known data card for that new, heavier brass weight. You'll have to either apply this method, or just identify a different accuracy load for your casings that have a very different case weight. For example, most of my Lapua Match casings (.223 Rem) weigh between 96 and 97.3 grains. Most of my Lake City casings (5.56x45mm)

weigh between 91.5 and 94 grains. The Lapua Match casings have less internal case volume because they are much heavier than the Lake City casings. I could have approached this problem two different ways:

Option 1: Determine accuracy load with one type of brass, then load brass from the other company with that same powder weight and bullet recipe. From there, create separate known data cards and ballistic cards for the Lapua Match and Lake City brass.

I used this course of action instead:

Option 2: Determine the accuracy load for the Lake City brass. My most accurate powder charge was 25.0 grains of Alliant Reloder 15. Determine the accuracy load for the Lapua Match brass. My most accurate powder charge was 24.9 grains. From there, create separate known data cards and ballistic cards for the Lapua Match and Lake City brass. I have not yet needed to create anything separate for the two different brass types, because 24.9 grains of powder out of the Lapua Match case is producing the same muzzle velocity as 25.0 grains of powder out of the Lake City case. This is likely due to the fact that the Lapua Match case has less internal case volume, and will therefore produce more muzzle velocity with the same amount of powder.

Priming the Cases

When I started hand loading, I lotted my primers by weight for my .308 Winchester. One lot of primers weighed 5.1 grains, the next 5.2 grains,

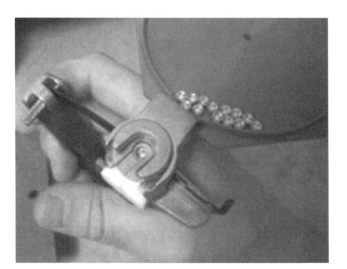

Figure 7-10. Squeezing the handle raises the primer. Not much more to say than that.

and the next 5.3 grains. I found this to be a waste of time with this particular rifle, as this work did not increase accuracy. After you've decided which brass weights you will use for your next shoot, and you've put them into their lots, prime each piece of brass while keeping the brass in their lots by weight.

WEIGHING A POWDER CHARGE

After all casings are primed, they are ready to accept the powder charge. It is very important to use your scale correctly. *I would not recommend* loading your rifle cartridges by volume, as this reduces accuracy. By weighing each charge separately, you know they're all the same and none are exceeding the maximum safe load by mistake. Use a digital scale that weighs down to the nearest tenth of a grain (.1 grain). Let's say that I already have my accuracy load—25.0 grains of powder using Lake City Brass. I set up my powder silo to kick out about 24.5 to 24.8 grains of powder. This device would be used alone if we were loading by volume.

I turn on the scale and calibrate it as per the directions for that scale. I zero out the weight of the scale with my powder saucer on the scale. My scale now reads all zeroes before adding powder. Upon adding powder, I see that I currently have less than 25.0 grains of powder, as in Figure 7-11. This is good. Now I trickle more powder into the saucer until I have 24.9 grains of powder on the scale. After there are 24.9 grains of powder on the scale, I trickle one flake of rifle powder per three seconds at a time. The moment my scale tips over to 25.0 grains, I'm done.

Upon removing my saucer, I can see that my scale reads -95.7 grains. This is perfect, because the weight of my empty saucer is 95.7 grains. If the scale reads any weight besides -95.7 grains—which it does on occasion—I would dump the powder back into the powder silo, re-zero the scale, and start over. If your scale loses zero often, move the scale more than 12 inches away from all ferrous metal objects and turn off all electronic devices in the room, and that problem of your scale losing its zero should be taken care of. As a related note, leave your cell phone in another room. If you simply weigh your powder charges during daylight hours, you can weigh your powder charges with the lights

Figure 7-11. The powder silo (top) would be used alone if loading by volume. For greater accuracy, I use a digital scale that weighs to the tenth of a grain.

off in the room that you're weighing your powder in. This seems excessive and some of it sounds like witchcraft, but active electronics affect electronic scales. Turning off electronics saves time. The proximity to ferrous metal objects will corrupt the proper functioning of the scale much more than electronic devices.

SEATING THE BULLET

Just as there is a most accurate powder charge, powder type, and bullet length for your rifle barrel, there is also a most accurate cartridge overall length (OAL or COAL). Each rifle is different and each type of bullet is different. Some bullets will be more accurate if the COAL is as long as it possibly can be without the bullet touching the lands of the bore when the cartridge is chambered. Other bullets will be most accurate with the bullet engaging the lands upon the cartridge being chambered. After determining your most accurate powder weight using a bullet weight and length that is stabilized in your rifle at long range, you then must determine the most accurate cartridge overall length.

Be aware that the deeper you seat the bullet into the case, the more powder you can safely use. The deeper-seated bullet will produce less muzzle velocity. This sounds backward, I know. With more pressure condensing the powder from a more deeply seated bullet, wouldn't the pressure in the chamber be higher while firing? No. The gases expand more freely with a more deeply seated bullet because there is nothing to prevent the initial forward movement of the bullet. A bullet close to or touching the lands requires more pressure buildup to produce initial movement down the bore.

I absolutely recommend using a competition die set for the kind of hand loading we're doing. I would also recommend using a single-stage press instead of a rotary press, so that you can give 100 percent of your attention to the cartridge you're working on. Before seating a bullet, ensure that all casings to be seated with a bullet have a primer, your desired powder charge, the proper case length, and that the case mouths have been chamfered. Now it's time to screw our bullet-seating die into our press. Notice the increments on the top of the bullet-seating die in Figure 7-13. Each tick mark represents .001 inch of length. Using a micrometer, we'll measure the cartridge overall length of a round that we are attempting to imitate, or that we know is the correct length. For my 5.56x45mm AR-15, I'm looking for a COAL of 2.220 inches. Therefore, I verify the length of an already built 5.56mm cartridge as having that same length, insert the cartridge onto the shell holder of my press, and significantly back off the bullet-seater by rotating counter-clockwise on the turret knob, almost all the way up.

We then run the cartridge all the way up into the press, making sure we don't seat the bullet any

Figure 7-13. This bullet seating die's turret knob is set as high as it goes.

Figure 7-12. This cartridge overall length is 2.221 inches.

113

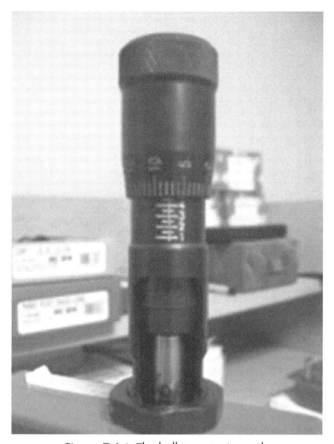

Figure 7-14. The bullet seater is gently touching the bullet at this stage.

deeper. Insert the cartridge having the proper overall length into the press and raise the arm to the top of its stroke. Now we screw the bullet-seater down just until it gently touches our bullet, as in Figure 7-14. This is our starting point. Lower the press arm, remove the cartridge, and back off (loosen) the turret .015 to .020 inches.

Again, be sure to separate all of your bullets by length and weight, as is the practice of many competitive shooters. If separating 5.56mm (.224 caliber) bullets, a pill calendar is a good way to separate them by length, as each compartment can hold about 15 projectiles. For .308 caliber bullets, I use recycled handgun ammunition trays, as in Figure 7-16.

Each bullet in Figure 7-16 is lotted by length. Each vertical column contains bullets of the same length. My lots increase by .001-inch per column. For example, if that center column contains bullets measuring .684 inches from bullet base to ogive, then the column to its immediate right contains bullets measuring .685 inches, and so on.

After the bullets are in separate lots by length, select one lot to use. Let's say that for our next shoot, we'll only use 55-grain V-MAX bullets that measure .818-inch long from bullet base to bullet tip. Take all of the .818-inch long bullets and weigh them one at a time. Put the bullets in lots by weight, in columns in the same manner we lotted our brass earlier this chapter. The lightest bullets are usually 54.7 grains, the heaviest ones usually 55.1 grains and, of course, the majority of bullets are 54.8 to 55.0 grains.

Take a look at your casings on your loading tray that are filled with powder. Each row has a different

Figure 7-15. Pill calendars can be used for lotting bullets by length.

Figure 7-16. Bullets lotted by length.

brass weight, therefore each column with the same weight brass should be fired at the same target distance for maximum accuracy. We'll use the first column to shoot and confirm zero at 50 yards, the second row for 100 yards, the third for 200 yards, and so on. The casings in each row are the same so far, so let's keep them that way. We'll use .818-inch long bullets in all columns of equal weighted casings, but in column one, we'll seat the 54.8-grain bullets, in column two we'll seat the 54.9-grain bullets, and so on. By the end of the process, the lots within each row will be identical and there will only be very small variation between each lot. This will keep our shot groups as tight as possible at each target distance as per the performance of the rifle itself. We—the shooters—still have to do our part. Essentially, all cartridges shot at each target distance will be identical.

You can see on the turret in Figure 7-17 that we backed it off a little more than 15 thousandths of an

inch so that we don't risk seating the bullet too deep. Place a casing containing powder on the shell holder. Run it up into the press until the case mouth engages the bullet guide.

Drop the bullet to be seated into the bullet window. Gently run the cartridge up into the press until it stops. Do not use force. Remove the cartridge and measure the overall length with a micrometer.

The current COAL should be longer than desired, which in this example it is. In our example

Figure 7-18. The bullet is dropped into the bullet guide.

Figure 7-17. Case mouth is touching the bullet guide.

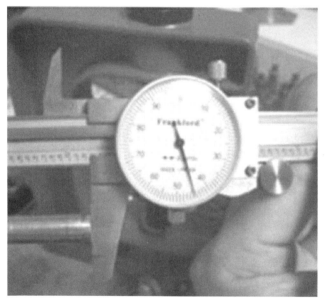

Figure 7-19. The load is raised into the press, then measured for length.

Figure 7-20. This turret adjustment
yielded 2.245 inches COAL.

Figure 7-21. This turret adjustment
yielded 2.220 inches COAL.

shown in Figures 7-18 and 7-19, our overall length is currently 2.245-inches long. Our desired COAL is 2.220-inches long. Using the turret on the die, tightening another .025 inches (or 25 tick marks) should yield our desired COAL. We'll tighten .024 inches so we don't seat the bullet too deeply. We can always add another .001 inches and raise the cartridge into the press again if needed.

We adjust our turret .024 inches tighter, as in Figure 7-21, and raise the cartridge back up into the bullet-seating die.

Don't seat the rest of your bullets with the final turret adjustment shown in Figure 7-22! That adjustment yielded 2.220 inches for that bullet and that piece of brass, but will more than likely not yield the same COAL for subsequent attempts.

We can seat the bullet deeper, but we can't pull it out without putting a bullet-pulling die into our press. To prevent seating the bullet too far, be sure to back off the turret .005 to .010 inches before

Figure 7-22. Final COAL after second bullet seating.

seating each new bullet to each new casing with powder and primer. Seat a new bullet to a new powdered case with the seater die backed off .005 to .010 inches, look on the micrometer how many inches deeper you need to seat the bullet, adjust the seater die, and continue just like we did for this first cartridge. Follow this procedure until all cartridges are seated to the same depth. If you do this perfectly, each cartridge will have been run up into the press twice: once to initially seat the bullet yielding a COAL that is a little too long, and a second time to seat the bullet to its perfect depth in the casing after having made a precise adjustment to the seating die. After all bullets are seated, you are finished, unless you desire to crimp the bullet. If these loads are going into a semiautomatic rifle, some hand loaders advocate that you should crimp the necks. Some bullets need crimping. Others just flat-out don't. I'll explain.

CRIMPING THE BULLET

Crimping is an extremely quick process. Screw the crimping die into your press, and lower the handle until the arm is at its highest point. Screw in the crimping die until the bottom of the die engages the shell holder at the shell holder's highest point. Raise your press handle, which will lower the arm. Screw the crimping die down into the press an additional 1.5 turns, and set the die in place with the lock ring. The farther down you screw the crimping die, the tighter the crimp will be on the bullet. Put a cartridge on the shell holder and raise the cartridge into the crimping die. If you look into the top of the die, you'll see the collet close around the case mouth. These are the instructions that accompany my crimping die. I need to use this die for one type of bullet that I run in my AR-15, but I don't need to crimp the other one.

When I crimp my bullets that require it, I apply an additional 1.5 turns of the crimping die for loads fired from my AR-15. Thankfully, I found the process of crimping to be a waste of time when loading with 55-grain Hornady V-MAX bullets for my 5.56x45mm AR-15. Accuracy, consistency, and trajectory results were identical in bullets that I crimped and bullets that I did not crimp. Some people believe a semiautomatic bolt slams a cartridge with an uncrimped bullet into the chamber with such force that the bullet will move deeper into or come slightly out of the casing upon chambering. If this occurs, it's easy to identify.

I took one cartridge with a crimped bullet, measured the overall length, chambered it into my AR-15 allowing the bolt to slam forward with full force, extracted the round, and re-measured the COAL (Cartridge Overall Length). The COAL was still the same, which is good. I carried out the same process with a cartridge made with identical components—everything the same, except that this cartridge had no crimp. After extracting the un-crimped cartridge from the chamber, I found no change to the overall length. I verified this with multiple uncrimped cartridges using the 55-grain Hornady V-MAX bullet. Yet, when using 62-grain Barnes TSX bullets, my COAL *grows* .005 inches upon every chambering! I *have to* crimp my loads when using this bullet. The 62-grain Barnes TSX has less surface area in contact between the inside of the case mouth and the bullet due to the rings that are cut out on this particular bullet. This is the reason why the bullet slightly dislodges upon the chambering of the round. My 62-grain Barnes TSX bullets dislodge upon chambering to the point that the bullet impacts the lands of the bore. I suppose that by observing this, I accidentally determined the headspace of my AR-15 and found that, with my current COAL, my bullet are .005 inches away from the lands. Test the final product of your work by chambering the load, extracting it, and re-measuring it. If the COAL is different, you have to crimp. If the COAL is unchanged, then don't waste your time, as crimping the case mouth will accomplish nothing for you.

If you have to crimp, be sure to crimp each cartridge exactly the same amount every time. If you use a 1.5-turn crimp, stay consistent. It may make sense that the tighter the crimp, the more pressure will occur inside the casing upon firing and, therefore, more muzzle velocity will be noticed. You'll have to figure this out for yourself if you choose to crimp your rounds. If you change your muzzle velocity though, that would likely change your accuracy powder charge. Whatever crimp you choose, stay consistent. As a note, my AR-15 experienced identical muzzle velocity with crimped and un-crimped 55-grain Hornady V-MAX bullets.

I hope I've sold you on the worthiness of the process of hand loading. The act is worthwhile for the accuracy gain and monetary savings. The primary cost to you is in *time*. As mentioned before in this chapter, I generally take an hour to press out 30 match-grade rounds. I did not identify here the setup or complete manipulation of each reloading tool. Each tool comes with specific and easy directions. Rather, my intent by adding this chapter was to show the difference in performance between factory match-grade ammunition and *well-made* hand loads. I did my best to illustrate my specific process—everything that I do that you just won't find in the instructions that accompany each reloading tool. Reloading precision ammunition for a precision rifle goes beyond building rounds that will successfully exit the muzzle. Determine your accuracy load with the proper bullet length for the rate of twist of your rifle, lot your bullets and brass by weight, and keep your COAL identical on every cartridge. That's your starting point for precision hand loading. Keep learning and build upon those techniques I've shared with you. I hope the tips and tricks in this chapter yield amazing results for you!

HAND LOADING FOR THE .338 LAPUA MAGNUM

Support continues to grow in the United States for rifles that are capable of achieving a first-round hit beyond 1,000 meters. Rifles calibers such as .338 Lapua Magnum, .408 Cheytac, and .50 BMG are a few calibers that were built for the heavy sniping community, though they are also available to civilians for sport and hunting. The .338 Lapua Magnum is one caliber that, on a sub-MOA platform (such as the Sako TRG 42), consistently yields first-round

hits out to 1,500 meters—provided the shooter properly compensates for range, angle, wind, altitude, temperature, and air pressure.

However, there are a couple drawbacks for most shooters that keep them from buying such rifles. One is that people don't want to pay the cost of ammunition. The average price for .338 Lapua Magnum is $117.00 for a box of 20 rounds. The other drawback is that most shooters do not possess the knowledge to make this cartridge worth $5 every time they squeeze the trigger. If you only know how to put rounds on paper out to 200 yards, you're probably not going to get your money's worth from a .338 Lap Mag.

Jon Burson, a friend of mine, recently asked if we could develop some reloads for his Sako TRG 42, chambered in .338 Lapua Magnum. I, of course, said yes, as I was very curious as to how finely we could tune the accuracy of his rifle. And besides, how can you say "no" to a friend? We proceeded to use the exact same process as I outlined earlier in this chapter. Components included .338 Lapua Magnum brass, GM215M Federal Large Magnum Primers, 250-grain Lapua HPBT bullets, and Hodgdon Retumbo rifle powder. Jon told me that for his powder and bullet combination, the powder charge window that he wanted to experiment with was 97.0 grains to 100.0 grains of Hodgdon Retumbo powder. All brass was lotted by weight after it was sized and trimmed. We built three rounds of each different powder charge, increasing each powder charge by .5 grains. All shot groups were printed at 200 yards. Here are the results:

CASE TRIM: 2.712 INCHES

Powder weight	Group Size in MOA	Group impact from point of aim
97.0 grains	.65 MOA	.84 MOA high
97.5 grains	.55 MOA	.65 MOA high
98.0 grains	.36 MOA	.32 MOA high
98.5 grains	.18 MOA	.71 MOA high
99.0 grains	1.05 MOA	1.13 MOA high
99.5 grains	.112 MOA	.61 MOA high
100.0 grains	.98 MOA	.98 MOA high

As you can see on the previous page, the most accurate load was produced using 99.5 grains of Hodgdon Retumbo rifle powder. We're, of course, not finished. Our most accurate load may be sitting right next to 99.5 grains of powder. So now we built loads ranging from 99.2 grains to 99.8 grains of powder. Below are the results from that day.

As you can see below, 99.5 grains of Hodgdon Retumbo is still our accuracy load. The next step, as usual, is to zero the riflescope for the accuracy load and slip rings as necessary, build all future cartridges using 99.5 grains of that type of powder, gather data, build a ballistic card, and determine the muzzle velocity (MV) and ballistic coefficient

CASE TRIM: 2.712 INCHES

Powder weight	Group size in MOA	Group impact	Case weight
99.2 grains	.33 MOA	.30 MOA high	324.9 grain, 325.7 grain, 325.9 grain
99.3 grains	.55 MOA	.43 MOA low	326.1 grain, 326.2 grain, 326.3 grain
99.4 grains	.78 MOA	0.0 MOA high or low	326.4 grain, 326.6 grain, 326.6 grain
99.5 grains	.31 MOA	.61 MOA high	326.5 grain, 326.5 grain, 326.5 grain
99.6 grains	.95 MOA	.54 MOA high	326.7 grain, 327.0 grain, 327.0 grain
99.7 grains	.36 MOA	.44 MOA high	327.4 grain, 327.4 grain, 327.4 grain
99.8 grains	.81 MOA	.54 MOA high	327.5 grain, 327.6 grain, 328.2 grain

Figure 7-23. Jon Burson and his Sako TRG 42.

(BC). If you'll remember, finding the MV and BC allows us to create environmental ballistic cards to help us account for wind speed, pressure altitude, temperature, and barometric pressure (see Chapters 3 and 5).

Jon was pleased with the results: lots of money saved through hand loading, and more accuracy produced. His average group size at 200 yards is .27 MOA . . . not too shabby. If he wanted to try to yield more accuracy, Jon would have to experiment with different cartridge overall lengths, putting the bullets into the lands by different amounts, or by backing the bullets off the lands by other amounts. Or to build a better accuracy load, he could start from scratch with a completely different rifle powder. I personally don't think he'll tighten it up much more, but he looks pretty content to me with his shot groups hovering around a quarter minute of angle.

For anyone considering hand loading for the .338 Lapua Magnum, I've added this piece to both motivate you and get you to a starting point. Remember though, even with the same make and model as the rifle pictured here (Figure 7-23), your accuracy load will likely not be exactly the same. Ultimately, you have to do the work for yourself—which is part of the fun.

Some time has passed since drafting this portion of the hand-loading chapter. I'll share with you now that Jon developed an accuracy load using the same powder, but changed his bullet to the 300-grain Berger OTM. He reports his accuracy at midrange in minutes of angle is identical to his 250-grain bullet accuracy recipe, but he is getting better long-range stability out of his 300-grain Berger OTM loads at 1,000 yards and beyond. The length of the 300-grain Berger OTM appears to match his 1:10 rate of twist better than the length of his 250-grainers. Regardless of your caliber, develop a different accuracy load if you change the bullet you're using. After building a different accuracy load for that new bullet, test it against your previous accuracy load and compare them next to each other at long range. If the bullet weights are different between those two loads and the accuracy is similar at 100, 200, or 300 yards, you are likely to find that one of those bullet weights performs better at long range due to having more stability in flight.

When Jon still lived in the Fort Campbell, KY,

area we would hit Rock Castle Shooting Center about once a month with a small group of friends in order to have access to a 1,000-yard range. Jon would achieve the same groups out to 800 yards with his .338 Lap Mag as I achieved with my .308 Winchester, although he easily outperformed me from 950 yards and beyond every time. This frustrated him a bit, as normally he only shoots between 300 and 800 yards with his rifle due to the type of rifle ranges he has immediate access to. For this reason he built a Remington rifle chambered in .308 Winchester for use out to 800 yards in order to be more cost-effective, while at the same time getting similar performance in accuracy.

Jon is a great shooter, and I think other shooters can learn a thing or two from him. If you're not shooting at target distances that allow you to take advantage of the .338 Lapua Magnum ballistics, then why have that rifle or any other heavy magnum for that matter? If someone expresses no interest in learning how to shoot at long range, then again, why have this type of rifle? However, if you intend to learn or already know how to shoot long range and have access to these types of ranges, then I would absolutely look into a heavy magnum caliber rifle as a viable option.

MORE HAND-LOADING TECHNIQUES

Lotting Brass and Tracking the Number of Firings

There are a number of reasons why a shooter would want to track how many times a piece of brass has been fired. Back when I used to fully resize my .308 Winchester brass every time, I noticed that my most accurate groups were yielded using once-fired brass that weighed around 152.5 grains. This happened to be the brass weight that I found my accuracy load with during load development. After I started neck sizing, I noticed that my most accurate groups were achieved using twice-fired brass with no full resizings. Another reason to track the number of firings of a piece of brass is that one method to determine when to throw brass away is to just count the number of full resizings done to the brass; some shooters chuck 'em after five full resizings. Yet another reason is to just be as consis-

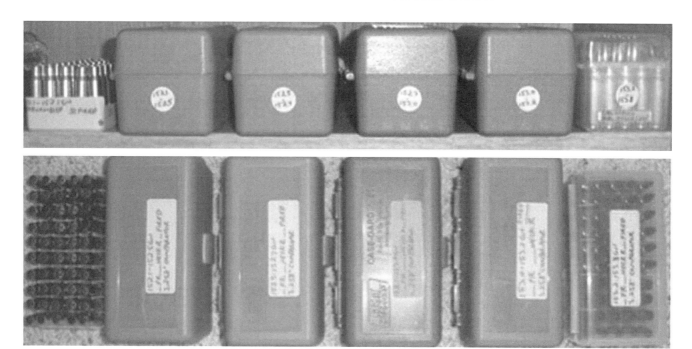

Figure 7-24. These ammo boxes are an important part of my organization system.

tent as possible. Since I do my best to perform well next to extremely experienced shooters during F-Class T/R competition, I make sure that during the competition I'm using brass that's been fully re-sized once (or twice-fired neck-sized brass) for optimal accuracy in my gun.

When I started hand loading, I tried to track the number of firings each piece of brass had and tried to keep them in the proper batches, but I failed epically in that regard. I'd fire at the range, come home, resize, and tumble the brass. After trimming back down to the desired length and deburring, I'd simply weigh the brass and put the brass into Ziploc bags that were lotted by weight. Each bag had brass of identical weight but a mixture of different number of firings from one piece to the next. In order to mitigate this, I started an organization plan.

The ammo boxes shown in Figures 7-24 and 7-25 each contain 50 Hornady Match .308 Winchester casings. All cases are trimmed to 2.002 inches (to ensure the weighing process would be as true as possible). Each piece of brass was weighed and placed in its respective lot. You can see that among a total of 300 Hornady Match cases, the lightest ones I got were 151.1 grains and the heaviest ones were 153.8 grains. There were two boxes that among 50 pieces of brass had only a .2-grain weight

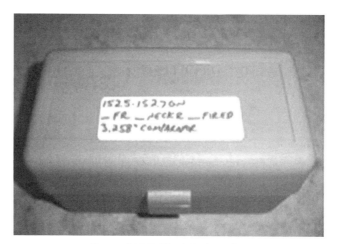

Figure 7-25. The label on this box is the brass life indicator.

deviation, which is pretty exceptional. This would likely *never* happen by measuring a fresh box of 50 Hornady Match casings, but when you weigh and lot 300 pieces, the specs on each box you build will, of course, be much tighter. As we've discussed, your most accurate groups are going to be achieved by using brass of equal weight on the same target—all other cartridge specs being equal, such as overall cartridge length, rifle powder weight, bullet weight, and bullet length.

Figures 7-26 and 7-27 depict the specific

method I use to track the number of full resizings, neck sizings, and total shots fired per lot of brass.

Brass pieces within each lot are organized from lightest to heaviest, in the order in which they are fired. The lightest piece of brass in Figure 7-26 weighs 152.5 grains. The heaviest piece weighs 152.7 grains. In the order they are fired, each piece is either identical in weight to the piece prior or is slightly heavier than the piece prior. This ensures that from one fired round to the next, there is as minimal difference in brass weight change as possible.

Figure 7-27 shows the order in which I fire each round. Were I to build cartridges for the entire box of 50 rounds, I would prime and powder each case, grab 50 bullets of all identical length, weigh all bullets, and organize the bullets from lightest to heaviest. The lightest bullet would be the first shot fired; the heaviest would be the 50th shot fired. Each bullet would be identical in weight to the bullet prior, or slightly heavier than the bullet prior. Again, this is to ensure minimal specification difference from one cartridge to the next in order to produce the best group size on target. Let me put pictures to this idea to clarify.

For a 28 July, 2012, F-Class T/R competition held at Memphis Sportsman Shooting Association, I needed to build 40 additional cartridges to add to the 30 cartridges that I had already prepared. To the left of the press in Figure 7-28, I have 40 primed and powdered cases, organized from light to heavy. The lightest case is the bottom left case; the heaviest is the top right case. To the right side of the press I have 40 bullets. All bullets are 180-grain Sierra MatchKings, and all bullets measure the same length. The left column of bullets weighs 179.7 grains, the middle column weighs 179.8 grains, and the right column weighs 179.9 grains. Figure 7-29 shows which bullet is to be seated in which piece of brass.

Following the bullet-seating process, as the brass weight increases, so does the bullet weight. This ensures that from one cartridge to the next, there is zero or minimal specification change from one shot to the next.

Figure 7-28.

Figure 7-26.

Figure 7-27.

Figure 7-29.

In most of my ammo boxes are fired cases, fully prepared cartridges, and unfired cases. I *do not* fully resize or neck size any case until all 50 cases are fired from the ammo box. This is done to accurately track the brass life. You can see in Figure 7-30 that the brass life indicator inside the case reads that the brass cases contained within that ammo box have had zero full resizings (FR) and zero neck resizings (Neck R) applied to them. After all casings are fired, I'll neck size all 50 cases, tumble, trim, and chamfer all cases, keeping them together for the entire process. I won't tumble them with any piece of brass from any other lot. After the brass prep is complete, I'll reweigh the brass and re-sort the empty brass in the ammo case in order by weight—from light to heavy, in the order they'll be fired once again. I won't change the weights on the brass life indicator, even though as I trim, the casings will become lighter and lighter with more firings. After all casings are returned to the case, I'll write in pencil on the brass life indicator "1 Neck Re-Size" and "1 Fired."

In Figure 7-31 you can see a small, round sticker indicating that, when the brass was fresh, it weighed 153.0 to 153.2 grains depending on the piece. After neck sizing the brass, each piece grew an average of .004 inches. All brass was then trimmed to 2.004-inches long, then reweighed. In the left column of brass shown, all pieces of brass weigh 152.8 grains. Each column after weighs .1 grain more, so the far right column weighs 153.2 grains. Despite this, I will not change the brass weight indicator on the ammo box, and I'll keep all 50 pieces in the same lot throughout their lifetime. I will likely find that with my accuracy load, a certain weight of this Hornady Match brass will out perform the other lots, if only by a little. For competition shooting, this small difference will be worth knowing.

If I can time everything perfectly between practice shooting events and competitions, I'll have 60 fired casings available for the competition—those casings having two neck sizings done to them since the last full resizing. Those are the ones I'll compete with for score, as my rifle performs most accurately with that number of neck sizings after a full resize.

In addition to tracking your brass life, you should also keep records of what group sizes in minutes of angle or inches you're getting out of

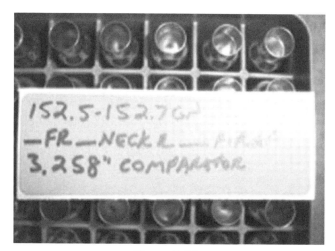

Figure 7-30.

Figure 7-31. Fired once, neck sized, tumbled, trimmed, and chamfered.

each lot of brass and what distances you are shooting. For my .308, my most accurate brass weight with my accuracy load is 152.5 grains. Again, this is the brass weight with which I found my most accurate powder charge during load development . . . probably not a coincidence. To conclude this section, my current plan is to neck size four times, then perform a full resize; neck size another four times, then a full resize. By the time I'm about to perform the fifth full resize, the brass life will be likely nearing its end. But by then, each piece of brass will have had 24 firings. Again, neck sizing increases brass life as opposed to full resizing; this is because

Figure 7-32. Once-fired 153.0-grain brass.

Figure 7-33. Unfired lightweight 152.1-grain brass.

full resizing works the brass more. Neck sizing only works the neck, squeezing it back down to spec after each firing. During the lifetime of each lot of brass, not only will I track the accuracy in minutes of angle of this lot of brass, but I'll also track the accuracy in MOA based on how many firings the brass has. For all I know, on the ninth firing I may get .19 MOA accuracy consistently. We'll just have to wait and see.

TRAJECTORY DIFFERENCE BETWEEN FIRED AND UNFIRED BRASS

At medium and long range, there is a small but noticeable difference in trajectory between fired and unfired rifle brass. I've noted earlier in this section

the range of brass weight I've found in Hornady Match .308 Winchester brass. After observing the difference in weight, I wondered if the lightest unfired brass would yield a lower muzzle velocity than the heavier, unfired brass as a result of having more internal case volume. My assumption is that if the external dimensions from one piece of brass to the next are the same, then if one piece weighs more, it must have less internal case volume. If this is true, then I should be able to expect the lightweight brass having more internal case volume to have a different point of impact on target than the heavyweight brass. I proceeded to experiment to determine the answer.

I built .308 Winchester cartridges using all the same specs except for brass weight. I built cartridges using lighter weight 152.1-grain brass,

Figure 7-34. Unfired medium-weight 152.5-grain brass.

Figure 7-35. Unfired heavyweight 153.2-grain brass.

medium cartridges using 152.5-grain brass, and heavy cartridges using 153.2-grain brass. I fired five-shot groups at 100 yards, 300 yards, and 600 yards to compare the difference in trajectory. As a benchmark, I used once-fired 153.0-grain brass, for which I already have established effective elevation data. A rough outline of my ballistic card for fired brass ranging from 152.5 grains to 153.0 grains is shown here:

Yards	MOA
100	1.75 down
200	0.0
300	2.5
600	13.75

With an adjustment of 1.75 MOA down at 103 yards, the point of impact was exactly the same between all brass weights, fired and unfired alike. As you'll see in Figures 7-32 through 7-36, things got interesting at the 300- and 600-yard lines.

The targets shown in Figures 7-32 through 7-35 were placed 304 yards from the firing line. The elevation adjustment for all shooting was 2.5 MOA up and there was no visible wind. You can see that *all* brand-new unfired brass hit .5 MOA too low. You may expect the unfired 153.2-grain brass to have the same point of impact as the once-fired 153.0-grain brass, but it's just not the case. Even the unfired brass of almost exactly the same weight hit lower than the once-fired brass. This tells me that

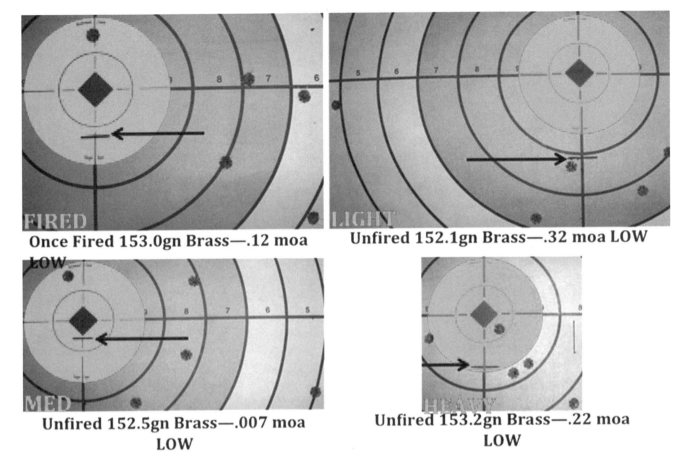

Once Fired 153.0gn Brass—.12 moa LOW

Unfired 152.1gn Brass—.32 moa LOW

Unfired 152.5gn Brass—.007 moa LOW

Unfired 153.2gn Brass—.22 moa LOW

Figure 7-36.

my idea that lighter-weight brass should have a lower point of impact due to more internal case volume was false. However, fired brass seems to hit higher than unfired brass. I believe this is a function of the carbon remaining on the inside of fired brass reducing the internal case volume, thus producing more muzzle velocity than unfired brass. As a result of this shooting event, I began keeping a completely separate ballistic card for unfired brass.

My assumption going into the 600-yard shoot was that the result would be similar to the 300-yard result: the unfired brass would hit lower than the fired brass, given the same elevation correction. This assumption proved partially true.

In Figure 7-36, the once-fired brass is on the top left. As stated previously, I already have good data for fired casings of this approximate weight. The day of this shoot was 04 August, 2012, and the temperature at the range—at Memphis Sportsman Shooting Association—was 98 degrees Fahrenheit.

Therefore, I didn't use my 13.75 MOA up adjustment for 600 yards, as my atmospheric benchmark for temperature is 50 degrees. After applying a .5 MOA down adjustment for temperature, my total elevation for all targets above sat at 13.25 MOA up.

The arrows in Figure 7-36 point to a line I drew on the targets after shooting them. The line is simply the vertical centerpoint of the shot group. You can see that with my once-fired brass, I hit .12 MOA low; the high or low impact indicators for the other three targets follow. As expected, the unfired light-weight and heavyweight brass hit lower than the fired brass did. Surprisingly, the unfired medium-weight brass hit 1/8-MOA higher than the fired brass . . . maybe a fluke, maybe not. Still, of six targets shot using unfired brass, five out of six targets yielded results indicating that unfired brass hits lower than fired brass at medium and long range.

You may have noted that I had a nasty "flyer" in the top right picture, sitting 6 inches left of the point of aim. Instead of reshooting, I chose to include the picture here in the spirit of remaining completely objective. The sun wasn't in my eyes, and I won't say the wind was kicking harder than I'm used to shooting in that day. I suppose that one was just my bad.

Knowing the above information, where does one go from there? You can either say, "Who cares? I'm not worried about .5 minutes of angle." And that attitude may be perfectly fine for a coyote hunter or the guy who spends most of his shooting time making metal targets sing. A hit is a hit, right? For those of you who want to be as perfect as possible, however, I would recommend one of two courses of action. Have two ballistic cards—one for fired brass, a second for unfired. Or simply make a note of the trajectory difference next to the adjustment on your existing ballistic card. All environmental corrections can remain the same as per wind, altitude, temperature, and air pressure change. Whether using the first or second course of action, you're taking steps to be more center-center on target than the guy next to you, and getting more enjoyment out of your shooting trips.

DETERMINING YOUR MOST ACCURATE CARTRIDGE OVERALL LENGTH

As a hand loader dedicated to achieving maximum accuracy, you're probably willing to take every step that has any chance of yielding more accuracy for you. After finding the most accurate bullet length for your rifle—based on your rate of twist, caliber, and muzzle velocity—you find the most accurate powder. Next, you determine the most accurate powder charge down to the nearest tenth of a grain. Hopefully you also lot your brass by weight and trim to the same length to the nearest thousandth of an inch every time. To get even more accuracy, you lot your bullets by length, and sub-lot them by weight, as I suggested earlier. After all that, there's yet another thing you can do—determine your most accurate cartridge overall length, or COAL.

A common discussion is whether it's most accurate to seat your bullets deep enough so that, upon chambering a cartridge, the bullet doesn't touch the lands; or whether it's most accurate to seat the bullets long enough so that they *do* touch the lands. If not touching the lands, how far off should the bullet be

from touching them? If engaging the lands, how far should the bullet engage them? It depends on the bullet and *your* rifle as usual. I put my rifle to the test.

When I started hand loading for precision rifles, I simply seated my bullets .002-inch shorter than magazine length so that all my cartridges would fit in the magazine. I didn't care if they were on or off the lands, so long as they fit in the mag. I measured from the bottom of the casing to the tip of the bullet. I was happy if I could get all of my .308 Winchester loads 2.828-inches long exactly. Years later, I started measuring from the bottom of the casing to the ogive of the bullet—that part of the bullet closest to the tip that measures .308 inches. By doing this, I ensured that each load had the same relationship into the lands or from the lands. I didn't care if my bullets were in or out of the lands as long as the relationship was the same each time I chambered a round. To determine that ogive cartridge overall length, I took a loaded cartridge with a 2.828-inch COAL and attached a .308 caliber bullet comparator to my calipers and observed the ogive COAL. The reading on the caliper was 3.258 inches. The comparator itself is 1.003 inches long (see Figure 7-38), so the actual ogive COAL for my loads was 2.255-inches long.

I finally got around to comparing different overall lengths for my cartridges, in the hope that I could squeeze a little more accuracy out of my rifle. My starting point was to determine where my current loads were seated in relation to the lands of the bore. A rifled bore has lands and grooves. The *lands* are that part of the rifling that touches the bullet as the bullet travels down the barrel.

I seated one of my 180-grain Sierra MatchKing

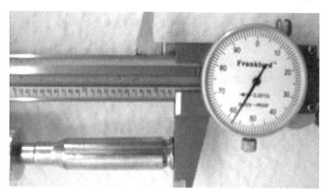

Figure 7-37. An ogive length of 3.258 inches with comparator.

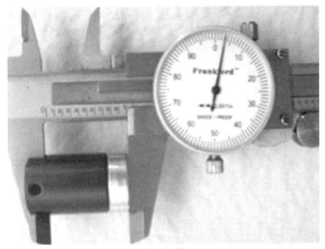

Figure 7-38. The bullet comparator measures 1.003-inches long.

Figure 7-39. Bullet seated to an ogive COAL of 3.331-inches long.

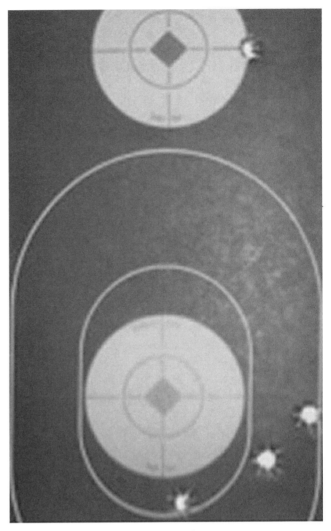

Figure 7-40.

bullets into a piece of unprimed brass. I kept the overall length way longer than I would ever intend to shoot so that when I chambered the round, I could then extract the round and observe the markings on the bullet produced by the lands.

As long as you seat the bullet long enough to engage the lands, you've done your part. You can see in Figure 7-39 that I marked the bullet with a permanent marker in order to see the smudge produced by the lands more clearly. I chambered this round, then extracted it. I measured the length of the smudge—yes, this is very technical, but it works. The smudge measured .082-inch long. The ogive cartridge length is 3.331 inches and the bullet is going .082 inch into the lands: therefore, if we subtract .082 inch from 3.331 inches, we get 3.249 inches. Using my bullet comparator, if I load rounds with a 3.249-inch COAL, each round that I chamber should just barely engage the lands. To compare the performance of cartridges with different lengths, I'll build five loads .002 inch off the lands, five loads .005 inch into the lands, five

loads (with my current recipe) .009 inch into the lands, and five loads .015 inch into the lands. The specifications for these loads are here:

Comparator COAL	Actual COAL	Reference to lands
3.247 inches	2.244 inches	.002 inch off
3.254 inches	2.251 inches	.005 inch into
3.258 inches	2.255 inches	.009 inch into
3.264 inches	2.261 inches	.015 inch into

I didn't think I'd notice much of a difference by shooting this comparison at 100 yards, so I took it out to 300 yards. In addition to the loads I brought for the COAL comparison, I brought four cartridges

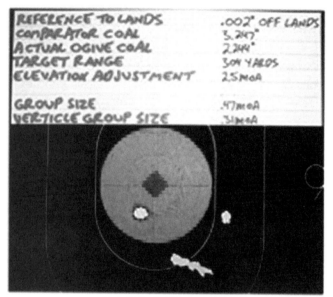

REFERENCE TO LANDS	.002" OFF LANDS
COMPARATOR COAL	3.247"
ACTUAL OGIVE COAL	2.244"
TARGET RANGE	304 YARDS
ELEVATION ADJUSTMENT	2.5 MOA
GROUP SIZE	.47 MOA
VERTICLE GROUP SIZE	.31 MOA

.002" Off Lands

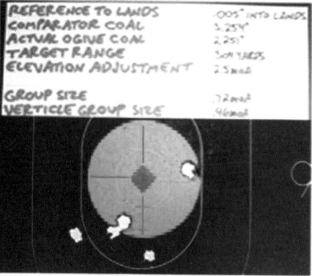

REFERENCE TO LANDS	.005" INTO LANDS
COMPARATOR COAL	3.254"
ACTUAL OGIVE COAL	2.251"
TARGET RANGE	304 YARDS
ELEVATION ADJUSTMENT	2.5 MOA
GROUP SIZE	.72 MOA
VERTICLE GROUP SIZE	.46 MOA

.005" Into Lands

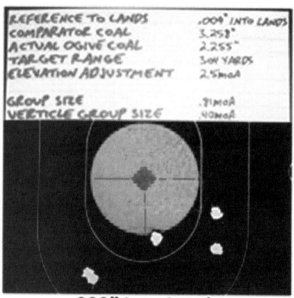

REFERENCE TO LANDS	.009" INTO LANDS
COMPARATOR COAL	3.258"
ACTUAL OGIVE COAL	2.255"
TARGET RANGE	304 YARDS
ELEVATION ADJUSTMENT	2.5 MOA
GROUP SIZE	.71 MOA
VERTICLE GROUP SIZE	.40 MOA

.009" Into Lands

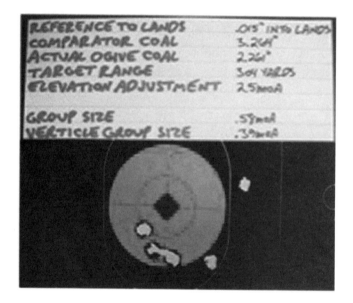

REFERENCE TO LANDS	.015" INTO LANDS
COMPARATOR COAL	3.264"
ACTUAL OGIVE COAL	2.261"
TARGET RANGE	304 YARDS
ELEVATION ADJUSTMENT	2.5 MOA
GROUP SIZE	.55 MOA
VERTICLE GROUP SIZE	.39 MOA

.015" Into lands

Figure 7-41.

that I had remaining from a previous shoot in order to gather some cold-bore data at 300 yards. Figure 7-40 shows the 300-yard cold-bore target.

As always for my clean-/cold-bore shot, I adjusted .5 MOA left for the first shot and set aside a completely separate point of aim for it. After the cold-bore shot, I fired three more rounds at a different bull's-eye. As a size reference, each target sticker in Figure 7-40 measured 2 inches across. Half of a minute of angle (.5 MOA) at 300 yards is 1.5 inches.

That's how much farther to the right the clean-/cold-bore shot would have been had I not made the necessary cold-bore adjustment. The shot wouldn't even be in view in Figure 7-40. In relation to the shot group shown in Figure 7-40, that .5 MOA left adjustment put the cold-bore shot right where the rest of the group ended up. After completing the cold-bore shoot, I proceeded with the overall cartridge length mission.

Figure 7-41 shows the four sets of five-shot groups fired at 304 yards. On the data cards on top of each 2-inch bull's-eye, I've added the ogive COAL and the group size in minutes of angle, among other data. I also measured the vertical group size in order to make the shift due to the presence of wind moot, in the event that it became necessary for the final comparison to pick the best load of the day. You can see that the group with the tightest group size also had the tightest vertical measurement. The target shot with bullets seated .002 inch off the lands had the tightest group size, of .47 MOA, and also had the tightest vertical group size—.31 MOA. Surprisingly, the COAL of 3.258 inches (.009 inch into the lands) that I had been using for so long yielded the worst shot group of .81 MOA. Even the vertical measurement of that group still put it in third place compared to the other groups.

As you can see, despite having been hand loading for many years, I can admit that I'm always learning and trying out new things. Some procedures prove to be a waste of time, and others don't. How detailed you get into hand loading is up to you. The question is, "How tight does that shot group need to be?" For me, the tighter the better.

More Cartridge Overall Length Testing

From the previous shoot, I was able to determine that seating my 180-grain Sierra MatchKings .002 inch off the lands yielded the best five-shot group at 300 yards, when compared to the other COALs in the previous section. Knowing that my rifle and ammunition prefers these bullets to be seated off the lands, I was curious to see whether or not there was another COAL that could yield even more accuracy for me, also seated off the lands—just a different amount.

I loaded up 10 cartridges with bullets seated .002 inch off the lands, and five cartridges seated .005 inch off the lands. I proceeded with the course of fire shown in Figures 7-42A through 7-42C.

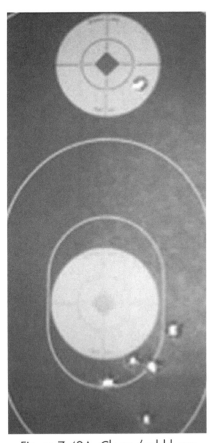

Figure 7-42A. Clean-/cold-bore (top target) .002 inch off lands (lower target).

All of the target stickers in Figures 7-42A through 7-42C measure 2.0 inches in diameter. The target distance was 304 yards. As usual, I dedicated a separate cold-bore target for my first shot of the day. I came .5 MOA left for the cold-bore shot, then zeroed the windage out for all shots following.

Number of inches off lands	Group size MOA / inches
Target 1: .002	.52 MOA / 1.658
Target 2: .002	.53 MOA / 1.697
Target 3: .005	.36 MOA / 1.172

You can see that the group size for the cartridges measuring .002 inch off the lands is consistent with the last shooting event at 304 yards. Last time, the .002-inch-off-lands cartridges yielded a .47-MOA group size. Today, the same cartridges measured a .525-MOA group size on average. Both days, I noticed the five-shot group accuracy hovering around .5 MOA. Today, the cartridges measuring .005 inch off the lands shot tighter than both shot groups fired using the .002-inch-off-land recipe; the .005-inch-off-land recipe measuring a .36-MOA shot group. Interestingly, that shot group impacted .285 MOA lower than the other two shot groups.

I couldn't give a scientific reason why seating my cartridges .005 inch off the lands yields more accuracy than seating my cartridges .002 inch off the lands. The important concept to grasp is that, for whatever reason, one is more accurate than the other.

As of this writing, my most accurate cartridge overall

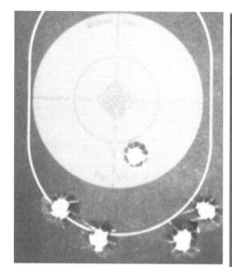

Figure 7-42B. Bullets seated .002 inches off lands.

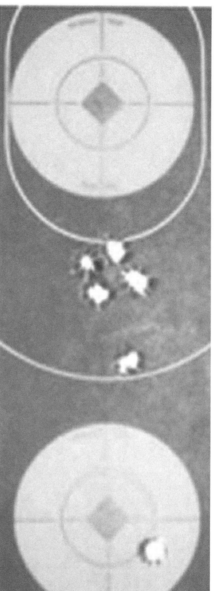

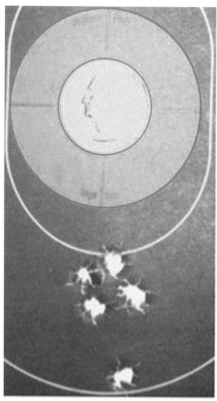

Figure 7-43. Inches off the lands: .005 inch; comparator COAL: 3.242 inches; actual COAL. 2.239 inches.

Figure 7-42C. The top target shows results using bullets .005 inch off the lands. The lower target shows the cold-bore shot before today's testing.

length yields a bullet that upon chambering sits .005 inch away from engaging my lands.

After firing another 200 or 300 rounds, I've learned that, as the lands nearest the chamber grow forward, the overall length test must be redone. This will allow me to return to this the same high level of accuracy. A 3.240" ogive overall length was great for me when I conducted the OAL test shown here. When the accuracy opened back up to .6 MOA, I redid the OAL test with the following loads:

Ogive OAL (inches)	Number of shots
3.238	5
3.240	6
	(one extra for the cold-bore shot)
3.242	5
3.244	5
3.246	5

The 3.244-inch ogive OAL tightened my loads back up to .3 to .4 MOA at 304 yards.

131

CHAPTER EIGHT

BARREL CARE: EXTENDING BARREL LIFE, ACCURACY, AND UNDERSTANDING COLD-BORE SHIFT

Some aspects of barrel care are somewhat consistent, given you're asking a trustworthy source. One aspect of barrel care that is generally agreed upon is that a high-grade rifle barrel should be "broken in."

Other aspects of barrel care seem to be a huge mystery for many people. There is a lot of debate over how to take care of a precision rifle barrel throughout its lifetime. In this section you will not find the end-all answer, but I *will* give you information that I've personally verified for myself in regard to yielding a consistent cold-bore shift, maintaining sub-MOA accuracy thousands of rounds beyond reported barrel life, and making your barrel last longer than any barrel company would ever want you to discover. Not only that, but you'll be able to take the information from this section and test it to see for yourself.

Many shooters are put off from buying magnum calibers, such as .300 Winchester Magnum and .338 Lapua Magnum, due to the fact that they *reportedly* only have around a 1,500-shot barrel life. If the barrel is never cared for the right way, I believe that report. However, how can so many shooters exceed 2,000 and even 3,000 rounds with these magnum calibers and still consistently print sub .5-MOA groups? These shooters didn't just get lucky or have magic barrels that defy physics. Rather, they likely understand the two factors that reduce barrel life: pits in the bore and throat erosion. Let's cover pitting the bore first.

AVOIDING PITTING THE BORE

A shooter goes to the range, has a successful shoot, comes home, and puts his rifle in the safe without cleaning the barrel. Next weekend he shoots again, sending bullets through the debris left in the bore from last time. He returns home and again doesn't clean the bore. He continues with this process for weeks. The risk is this—the only way to pit your barrel is to fire through the carbon that has been left behind. If you start each shoot with a clean bore, pitting your barrel—which in turn would reduce your accuracy—would not happen for a *very* long time. By simply cleaning your barrel in a proper manner, you can take a non-magnum caliber barrel from 2,500 rounds of barrel life to 7,000 plus, and can take magnum calibers at least two times beyond the standard reported 1,500 rounds. I'll share my method of barrel care, along with why I choose my specific method.

There is a critical concept to understand before getting into methods of barrel care. When shooting copper-jacketed bullets, two components are deposited into your barrel: copper from the bullets and carbon from the burnt powder. If a shooter removes the carbon and leaves the copper, he will experience a consistent, predictable cold-bore shift on his first shot during the next shooting event. If a shooter removes the carbon *and* all of the copper, he will experience a huge shot group during his next shooting event. Depending on the barrel, his crappy shot groups may remain for three rounds, six rounds, or more—and the placement from shot to shot will be unpredictable, until enough copper residue is laid back into his lands and grooves to tighten the accuracy back up. So knowing that, why would someone ever remove the copper? The answer is this: leaving copper in your bore will not result in barrel pitting, but over time a shooter will experience a partial loss in accuracy.

The original high level of accuracy can be regained if the copper is removed, followed by enough shooting to lay enough copper back into the bore to achieve tight shot groups once again. There are different cleaning compounds out there, and Hoppe's 9, for example, removes carbon primarily, and only a small amount of copper residue. Sweet's 7.62 Bore Cleaning Solvent, however, is specifically made to remove all copper residue from the bore of your rifle. My approach is to remove the copper from my bore when I've had 500 shots since my last copper-removing treatment, or when my accuracy degrades worse than .5 MOA consistently. No matter what performance my rifle is yielding, every time I come home from a shoot, I clean my bore with Hoppe's 9 to remove the carbon. The Hoppe's 9 will remove a small amount of copper residue, which is OK. More importantly it removes the carbon. Removing the carbon keeps your bore from getting pitted, which translates to extended barrel life. In addition, using a carbon remover such as Hoppe's 9 without a copper remover will also yield a consistent/predictable cold-bore shift.

CLEAN-/COLD-BORE ADJUSTMENTS

Track your cold-bore shots. Have a separate bull's-eye *just for that first shot of the day*. After cleaning with Hoppe's 9, I always have to adjust .5 MOA left for my first shot—my cold-bore shot or, more specifically, my clean-bore shot. In all shots following, I simply have to adjust .5 MOA back to the right. Each barrel is different and, therefore, the clean-/cold-bore shot for your rifle should require a

different adjustment than my rifle. It's too easy to determine your cold-bore shift after using a carbon removing solvent.

Figure 8-1 shows targets from two different shooting events. Note that there is a completely separate bull's-eye set aside to track the cold-bore shot, followed by a five-shot group to confirm zero. In both examples in Figure 8-1, I applied the .5 MOA left adjustment to the cold-bore shot. My gun requires this adjustment when I've cleaned the bore with Hoppe's 9 the day prior. You may think that it's a non-issue to have the first shot be half an inch off at 100 yards, but that deviation from my point of aim adds up over distance. For example, if my cold-bore correction isn't applied at 400 yards, I'm off to the right by 2 inches. If the cold-bore shot consistently hits in the same spot away from the main group, why not compensate for it?

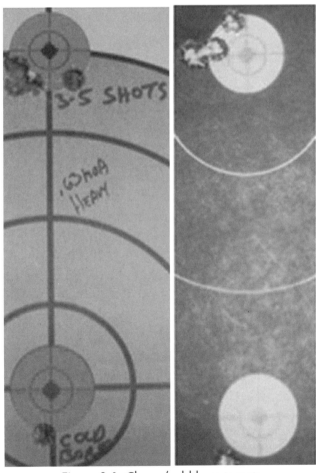

Figure 8-1. Clean-/cold-bore targets shot at 103 yards on different days.

Cold-bore shift is easy to track when carbon-removing solvent is used to clean the bore. When the time comes to clean the copper out, don't bother trying to track the cold-bore shift. You'll just have to shoot rounds through the bore until the copper gets laid back into the lands and grooves, and you get your accuracy back.

Figure 8-2 shows each three-round shot group at 103 yards after using Sweet's 7.62 Bore Cleaning Solvent (remember that this is a copper-removing solvent).

Both targets in Figure 8-2 are the same. The purpose of the image on the left is simply to identify that there are no more holes hiding under the information cards or the dime we used for scale. You can see that the first group was .80 MOA, the second group .55 MOA, the third group .43 MOA, the fourth group .46 MOA, and the fifth group .53 MOA. As ex-

pected, the first group was pretty bad. The first four shots of the day were unpredictable, but shots five through 18 were good as per size (hovering around .5 MOA) and consistent placement (.125 MOA right of the point of aim). After shooting the third and fourth group, I chose to adjust .25 MOA left before shooting the fifth shot group at the bottom in an attempt to get more center-center on the target.

Figure 8-3 shows my sixth shot group: shots 16, 17, and 18. The sticker is 2 inches across, like the one in the center of the first target in Figure 8-2. The sixth shot group measures .282 inches, which at 103 yards translates to .26 MOA. Therefore, after cleaning with Sweet's 7.62 Bore Cleaning Solvent, I can expect that my bore needs to be fouled with four shots before getting .5 MOA accuracy back, but after 15 foulers, .25 MOA accuracy is obtainable—not too shabby for a factory rifle. Prior to the treat-

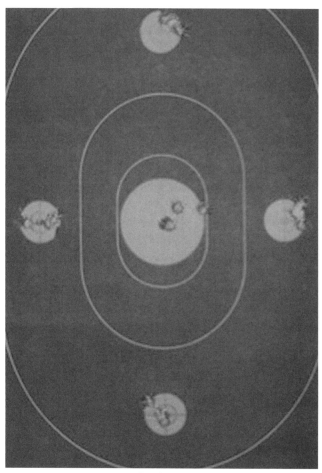

Figure 8-2. The first 15 shots after using Sweet's 7.62 Bore Cleaning Solvent.

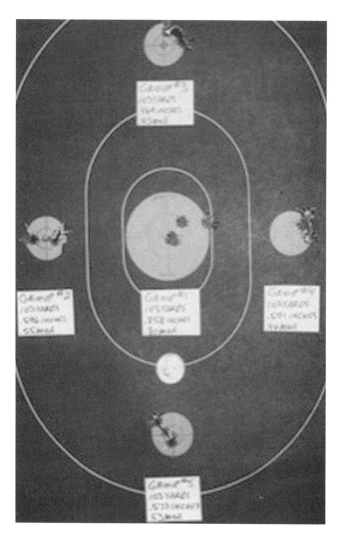

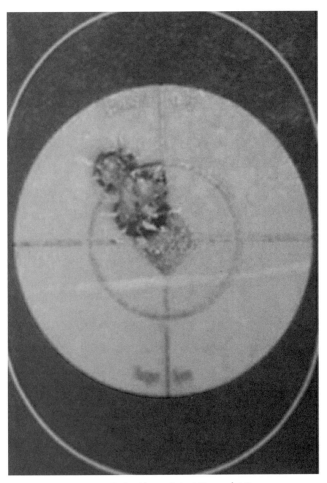

Figure 8-3. Shots 16, 17, and 18,
taken after using Sweet's 7.62 solvent.

ment with Sweet's 7.62 solvent, I was getting .6- to .7-MOA shot groups. It appears that it was, in fact, time to use the Sweet's after all.

BORE-CLEANING PROCESS

I never send any kind of brush through my bore. At the U.S. Army Sniper School, we were instructed not to, so I never even tried it out. I can imagine it would remove more copper than I wanted it to, though.

I remove my bolt and replace it with a bore guide. Then I use a Montana X-Treme cleaning rod, but any rod that has a rotating handle will be fine for you. This kind of handle allows the rod to twist with the lands of the bore during travel. Some folks use an eyelet with a patch. I use a jag with a cotton patch, as

this method allows for more surface-area contact between the patch and the inside of the bore.

After soaking the cotton patch with Hoppe's 9 and sending it through the bore, I discard the patch at the muzzle, unscrew the jag, and then remove the rod from the barrel. After removing the rod, I screw the jag back onto the cleaning rod. I do this because I don't want any metal-to-metal contact between the jag and the inside of the bore while pulling the rod out of the rifle bore. I let the bore soak no longer than three minutes and then attach a dry cotton patch to the jag and run it through the bore—again discarding the patch at the muzzle and unscrewing the jag before removing the cleaning rod. I repeat this process until the carbon has been removed from the barrel (no more black on the patches). Note that the longer the cleaning solvent sits in the bore, the more copper will be removed. Copper appears bluish-green on a used patch. After I'm getting no more black on the patches and I've run my final dry patch through the rifle, I send three to five more dry patches through the bore to ensure there is no solvent remaining. I let the rifle sit at least eight hours with the bolt open after cleaning before its next firing.

Using Hoppe's 9 only and cotton cleaning patches, I know that my clean and cold bore will require me to adjust .5 minutes of angle to the left for the first clean-/cold-bore rifle shot. I tracked the cold-bore performance for eight separate shootings in a row. The consistency was perfect, so I stopped tracking the cold-bore shift. I simply come .5 MOA left every clean-/cold-bore shot, and that adjustment sits the placement of my first shot with all shots following.

When it comes time to use the copper remover, I've already mentioned that I use Sweet's 7.62 Bore Cleaning Solvent. The directions on the bottle dictate to scrub the bore forward and back for one minute. Again, I don't pull anything backward through my bore. I use exactly the same method for Sweet's as I do for Hoppe's 9—discarding the patch at the muzzle, but I let the solvent soak in the barrel. To ensure understanding, Figures 8-4 through 8-11 illustrate the cleaning process.

In Figure 8-11 you can see the residue I was referring to. The entire cleaning process was done with Hoppe's 9. A healthy amount of copper remains in my lands and grooves, which will keep my

Figure 8-4. Elevate the rear of the rifle so that the barrel has a slight downward path.

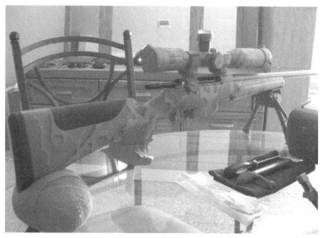

Figure 8-5. Remove the bolt and insert bore guide.

Figure 8-6. Rig a jag onto the cleaning rod, fix a patch, and add Hoppe's 9 to the patch.

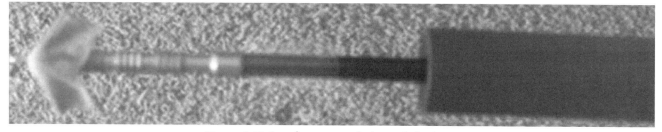

Figure 8-7. Run the wet patch through the bore.

Figure 8-8. Discard the patch at the muzzle.

Figure 8-9. Remove the jag.

Figure 8-10. Remove the cleaning rod.

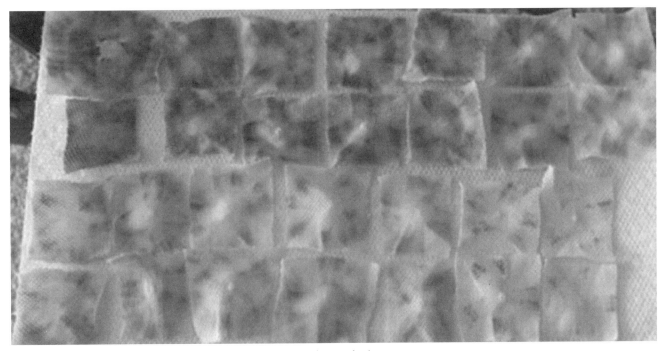

Figure 8-11. The bottom right patch shows my stopping point.

Figure 8-12. Clean-/cold-bore adjustment for first shot.

Figure 8-13. Adjustment for following shots (if no wind).

accuracy tight, starting with the very first shot during my next trip to the range. More than 95 percent of the carbon was removed, which will keep my barrel from getting pitted. Because my bore is now clean, I need to remember to make my clean-/cold-bore adjustment during my first shot next weekend.

AVOIDING THROAT EROSION

We've covered barrel pitting, how it reduces accuracy and barrel life, and how to mitigate it. The next factor that threatens barrel life is throat erosion. There are two primary contributing factors to accelerated throat erosion: trimming your brass too short and shooting loads too hot for your rifle.

Figure 8-14 shows the inside of a rifle chamber with a cartridge inserted. You can see that the case neck isn't jammed up against the bore. The case trim is as long as it can be without being jammed against where the chamber meets the bore. This type of "close but not touching" case trim will reduce throat erosion. When the case trim is too short, the hot gas produced by the burning powder has a greater heating effect on the throat—the first part of the bore that the bullet comes into contact with.

Figure 8-15 shows a case trim that is much too short. This will accelerate throat erosion and, thus, accuracy and barrel life. The trick here is to just stay within spec of your case length or trim the brass .001 inch to .002 inch shorter than the point at which the brass would impact the bore.

Figure 8-14. The inside of a rifle chamber.

Figure 8-15. This case trim is too short.

Figure 8-16. This case trim is too long.

In Figure 8-16, the case trim is too long. The brass is jammed up against the bore, bending the case mouth into the bullet. This puts pressure on the bullet, degrading accuracy.

Aside from a short case trim, we addressed how loads that are too hot cause accelerated throat erosion. If you are using a recommended powder for your caliber and bullet weight, you will never blow up your action with a hot load. The worst you could do is damage your brass and have to throw it away and/or quicken the throat-erosion process. There are a handful of identifiers for loads that are too hot, such as spent brass with bulging primers; a bulge at the base of the case; or case head separation warning rings on brass that should have many more firings left in its life.

When creating a safe hot load to give a mean edge in windy conditions during matches, I subtract 1.0 grain of powder from the first load that exhibits pressure signs. The best indicators of pressure signs I've seen are ejector marks on the case head of the brass coupled with a stiff bolt lift on a bolt-action rifle. If you determine your accuracy load at or under the maximum safe reported powder charge for your bullet weight and caliber, you'll be good in the department of avoiding throat erosion. Even if you exceed the maximum reported safe load by that bullet manufacturer or rifle powder company, mind the signs of overpressure, and you'll be fine as well.

The only instance that I'll shoot through cold carbon is during a hunting trip. At every target distance, my cold-bore shift for my primary bolt-action rifle is .5 MOA left. For cold-bore shots where I've cleaned with Hoppe's 9, my bore shift is still .5 MOA left—but only up to 250 yards. At 300-plus yards, I begin having elevation changes during the clean/cold-bore shot in addition to the .5 MOA horizontal movement. For example, at 600 yards my clean/cold-bore shot hits .5 MOA right and 1.25 MOA below the main group if uncompensated for. Because my dirty cold-bore shot is consistent at all distances, I'm willing to shoot through cold carbon for one or two important shots per year on game.

CHAPTER NINE

THE FUNDAMENTALS OF MARKSMANSHIP AND THE IMPORTANCE OF A STEADY FIRING POSITION

Up to this point, we've discussed gear selection and riflescope mechanics. We've covered the importance of gathering data and using that data correctly to maximize the precision of your future shots. You are now familiar with what is required of you in order to take a precision shot at high angle and how to adjust for environmental changes from those of your baseline weather conditions. All of that knowledge is critical for success in long-range marksmanship. Despite how vital the information prior to this chapter is, knowing and applying that information matters very little—if not at all—if you fail to achieve a steady firing position. Once you've achieved that all-important steady firing position, you then have to correctly execute the other fundamentals of marksmanship to maximize the accuracy and consistency of each shot. In this chapter, I will go into great detail about each fundamental of marksmanship to include the most important: steady position.

Learning to take a perfect precision rifle shot is like learning to execute a perfect golf swing. There are multiple things your body has to do at once but, like most people, you can only concentrate on two or three of those things at a time. In this chapter, I'll share what my opinion of "perfect" is for each fundamental of marksmanship. Do not be discouraged at the range if you cannot immediately execute each of them correctly all at the same time. You'll have to concentrate on two or three things at once until your muscle memory takes over the performance of those tasks. Then you can move on to concentrating on two or three new things, and so on. After you become proficient at doing all the little things you need to do to have a great shot, you'll find that there will always be one or two things you'll have to concentrate on no matter how much you shoot or how much success you have. Let's get started.

THE FUNDAMENTALS OF MARKSMANSHIP

The fundamentals of marksmanship are: trigger squeeze, breathing, sight picture, and steady position.

Trigger Squeeze

The goal here is to squeeze the trigger in such a way that your finger and firing hand do not move the rifle to the left or right in the least bit before, during, or after the shot rings out. Whether you're shooting a rifle with a traditional rifle stock or a vertical rear grip, you'll want to lightly pull the grip rearward with the middle finger and ring finger of your firing hand. Your pinky and thumb do almost nothing.

The trigger should be placed on the meaty portion of the tip of your trigger finger; not on the end of your fingertip and not on the joint of your finger. This, of course, is dependent upon the shooter's hand size and the width of the grip. A shooter with large hands and long fingers might have difficulty achieving that position, so he should simply place his finger on the trigger where comfortable (as long as squeezing the trigger does not cause the rifle to cant or sway left or right).

The trigger squeeze should be a slow, steady squeeze—not a quick pull, not a slap. The only time someone

Slight rearward pressure with middle finger and ring finger

Figure 9-1. This shooter's hand is in the ideal position.

would want to slap or pull the trigger quickly is if they were waiting for the reticle of their riflescope to go over the point of aim on the target. My argument for that is that if there is *any* movement in your reticle prior to taking the shot, you need to readdress your steady position before attempting to fire.

The process of squeezing the trigger should take no longer than two or three seconds. Any longer and you may begin to experience an undesirable slight shaking in your hand or body as a result of holding your breath for too long. Any movement in the rifle can translate to your shot placement. If the rifle is new to you, or you haven't shot it in a long time (shooting is a diminishing skill), executing a slow squeeze like this should yield a surprise to you when the rifle goes off. If you shoot your rifle often, it should absolutely *not* be a surprise when the rifle goes off. With practice and experience, you should know the exact point that your trigger breaks the shot. This is especially important for tactical shooters and hunters whose targets may move a bit. For stationary target shooters, it is also important not to be surprised with each shot. The more you experience surprise, the less relaxed you generally become.

Continue to squeeze the trigger rearward for one to two seconds after the shot rings out. This is follow-through—the act of performing all of the fundamentals of marksmanship for one to two sec-

onds after the shot has been fired. To practice, prepare a firing position and place your reticle on a target. With *no ammunition loaded*, dry fire the rifle. If the reticle doesn't move before, during, or after the "click," you've done your part.

For those of you AR-10 lovers who enjoy 1.5- to 3.0-pound triggers, be sure to increase the speed of your trigger squeeze faster than the extremely soft touch that you use on your bolt-action rifle trigger. Hold the trigger hard to the rear upon breaking the shot. By being soft and easy on an AR-10 trigger, you can easily bump-fire two shots in a row accidentally instead of just the intended single shot. Your sear is not faulty. Your trigger squeeze is.

Breathing

If you've achieved a perfect steady position for your rifle, the effect of your slow, relaxed breathing should yield little to no movement in the sight picture. You may notice, upon breathing in, that your sight picture moves slightly under your intended point of aim. Upon breathing out you may notice the reticle drifting a bit above your intended point of aim. Even if your eye detects no movement in the sight picture, you'll still want to pause your breath during your trigger squeeze, while the shot rings, and one to two seconds after the shot rings. This will ensure that the movement of your body is producing as little movement on the rifle as possible.

When there is no hurry and you're shooting for maximum accuracy and consistency, you'll want to pause your breath at the same point each time. If you take a handful of very good shooters, they may very well each tell you that they pause their breath at a different point. Army Sniper School instructors teach you to pause your breath after a full exhale, so that the amount of air in your lungs is the same every time you take a shot—this speaks to consistency, which translates to accuracy. Another excellent shooter may tell you that he pauses his breath with a full chest of air—that having more air in your lungs gives your body more time to squeeze the trigger before your body begins to shake slightly from oxygen deprivation. And yet another person may tell you he has great success by pausing his breath in the middle. His lungs aren't full, they aren't empty, but there is a comfortable amount of air in them, and that this relaxes him the most and has no negative affect on his consistency.

Having tried each method, I believe the most important thing is that "you"—the shooter—remain consistent with whatever you do. If you take a breath and hold before you shoot, do that each time. If you breathe out all your air before the shot, do that each time. Again, consistency translates to accuracy. I've found neither method to be superior to the other one. As long as you pause your breath before starting your trigger squeeze and you always have the same amount of air in your lungs during each shot, you've done well in the breathing department. Experiment with whether you prefer a full chest of air, an empty chest of air, or a partial chest of air. But decide on one and stick with it. To execute a good follow-through on the fundamentals of breathing, do not continue to breathe until one to two seconds has expired after you've sent your bullet.

Sight Picture

When shooting with a riflescope, you'll want to make sure that the ocular lens (the lens closest to your eye) is 3 inches from your eye. This is the most common eye relief, although some riflescopes vary.

Get down behind your rifle and achieve a sight picture. You should see the reticle clearly; if not, adjust the parallax. You should see your target clearly; if not, adjust the focus. After focusing on the target, bring the focus about 5 meters closer to you, so that the target is slightly blurred and the mirage just in front of the target is clear. This will be your most useful tool for adjusting for the presence of wind. A 14x or more magnification riflescope with quality glass is ideal for identifying mirage.

Acquire a full field of view, i.e., there should be no black ring around your field of view. At this time, slowly move your head backward away from the riflescope until you see that thin black ring around your sight picture. This is the perfect distance for your eye to be from the ocular lens. If the thin black ring around your field of view is of equal thickness the whole way around your sight picture, your eye is directly behind the riflescope and there is no parallax. If the thin black ring is thicker on one side than the other, you must readjust your head up, down, left, or right prior to taking the shot.

While actually taking the shot, you'll want to make sure that the thin black ring is visible and of equal thickness around the sight picture during your entire act of firing. This will help you ensure that your head is in the same place on the cheek rest every time. If you change the placement of your head, your zero will change. If you are using any muscles to hold your head far enough back to see the black ring or you are uncomfortable, you need to readjust the placement of your riflescope. You should be completely relaxed behind your rifle. So if you have to move the scope forward, move the scope forward. To prevent having to remount your optic, just do it right the first time.

One method is to attach your scope mount to your rifle and attach your lower ring halves to your scope mount. Get down into the prone supported firing position without the riflescope on the rifle. Achieve a steady firing position. Place your head on the cheek rest where most comfortable and natural with your eyes closed. Have a friend place your riflescope on the lower ring halves. Open your eyes—don't move your head at all. If you have no sight picture at all, adjust your cheek height by either building or purchasing a cheek rest. After achieving a sight picture whereby your body is comfortably positioned behind the rifle, tell your friend to move the scope forward or back until you achieve a perfect eye relief from the ocular lens—this is achieved if you see that thin black line around the outside of your sight picture. Tell your buddy to stop moving the optic when you have a thin black ring around the sight picture in your scope. At that point get off the rifle without moving the riflescope as it sits on top of the lower ring halves. Place a level on top of a flat portion of the receiver. Take note of what the level reads. Without moving the rifle, place the same level on top of the elevation knob of your riflescope. Turn the riflescope to the left or right to make the level read exactly the same as when you had the level on the flat portion of the receiver. After your riflescope is leveled, attach and torque down the upper ring halves to 15, 20, or 25 inch-pounds.

Note: Do not level your riflescope with the ground! Level the riflescope to the flat part of the receiver. As your rifle is resting on the ground or a table on its bipod, with a "sand sock" or bag under the buttstock, the gun itself may not be perfectly level with the ground. You'll likely try to get it perfect, but very close is as good as you'll probably get. As soon as you mount your optic, get behind the rifle, and prepare to shoot, the optic will be level with both the ground and the receiver if you follow the above instruction.

Steady Position

We've discussed in prior chapters the importance of keeping your shot groups as tight as possible at short- and medium-target ranges—the point being that the size of that 1/2-inch or 1-inch group at 100 yards multiplies in size over distance. For example, if you can achieve a 1-inch group at 100 yards, you can expect that the best you'll do at 400 yards with that same rifle is 4 inches, and at 600 yards is 6 inches. But if you can consistently print 1/2-inch groups at 100 yards, you can expect 2-inch groups at 400 yards, and 3-inch groups at 600 yards. The accuracy and consistency of your shooting should be dependent upon your rifle, ammunition, optics, and mounts . . . there should be no human error to reduce accuracy.

The most critical fundamental of precision rifle marksmanship to execute correctly prior to, during, and after shooting is steady position. If your reticle is moving *at all* while you're in the processes of breaking a rifle shot, that human error will be evident on your target by a poor shot group.

Moldable rifle rests are best for achieving a rock-solid steady position. Such rifle rests are very easy to make. I personally fill an unused, green GI sock with 6mm Airsoft pellets, then tie a knot in the sock to prevent any pellets from coming out. Any palpable material will work. I use plastic pellets because they are naturally waterproof and won't turn to mush in the rain or on wet ground, as popcorn kernels or rice would.

The best stable position is achieved by using sand socks in the front of the rifle, under the end of the stock, and under the buttstock of the rifle. The more distance you can put between the shooting rests, the more stable the shooting position will be. From the ground to the rifle, rests should go hard, soft, hard. The ground is hard and the rifle stock is hard. Therefore, resting the rifle stock on a raised piece of ground would yield a poor shooting position. There is not much reduction in accuracy by replacing your moldable shooting rest under the end of your stock with a bipod, but there *is* a slightly noticeable amount of movement yielded by using a bipod instead of a moldable rest such as sand socks.

Whether using sand socks under the stock and buttstock, or a bipod under the stock and a sand sock under the buttstock, the next step is to get the rifle as close to the shooting platform as possible. If you're in the prone firing position, this means compressing the sand sock/s—or lowering the bipod if using instead of sand socks—as much as possible without letting any part of the rifle touch the ground. If shooting from a bench, do the same thing. Get the lowest part of the rifle as close to the bench as possible without actually letting any part of the rifle touch the bench before, during, or after the shot. This is generally best achieved with a bolt-action rifle featuring a traditional comb. If using any rifle with a vertical rear grip or extended magazine, the rifle will have to be higher from the shooting surface. Therefore, more movement will be noticed in the reticle prior to shooting a high-center-of-gravity rifle. You should see zero reticle movement if you achieve a steady firing position with a low-center-of-gravity rifle. It is natural to see 1/8-minute of angle movement in your reticle after having achieved the best possible steady position with a high-center-of-gravity rifle.

As you can see in Figure 9-2, high-center-of-gravity rifles are the result of a vertical rear grip. Low-center-of-gravity rifles, such as the one shown in Figure 9-3, feature a more traditional comb. The gain from having a vertical rear grip is more ergonomics. A vertical rear grip makes for a more controllable trigger squeeze. It is up to you as the shooter to determine the costs and benefits of each.

Whether shooting from a bench or prone on the ground, orient your reticle on target. Wrap your nonfiring hand around the sand sock, which is under the buttstock. Squeeze the sand sock up as high as you can. Place the *entire* weight of your head

Figure 9-2. High-center-of-gravity rifle.

Figure 9-3. Low-center-of-gravity rifle.

on the cheek rest without letting the sand sock compress itself. The reticle of your riflescope at this point should be located below the bull's-eye of the target. Slowly release pressure on the sand sock until the reticle comes up to the bull's-eye of the target. As soon as your reticle is on target, only make the smallest of adjustments in elevation as required, using the sand sock in your nonfiring hand. If your rifle weighs 14 pounds or more, there should be zero movement in your reticle. You are now free to execute the rest of the fundamentals of marksmanship and send your bullet downrange. If your rifle is of lighter weight, the only movement you should notice in the reticle is from your heartbeat if you're wearing a thin shirt. By learning at what point your trigger breaks the shot, you can learn to fire between heartbeats—when your reticle is perfectly center-center on the bull's-eye.

When I achieve my steady position and pause my breathing, my reticle twitches from the center of the bull's-eye to the left edge of the bull's-eye in cadence with my heartbeat. I imagine my trigger finger is the second hand of an analog clock. Every time the crosshair is in the center of the bull's-eye, the second hand "ticks." So the only time my trigger receives rearward movement is when the crosshair is center-center on target. It takes practice to do this smoothly without jerking the gun during the shot, but it is a great tool for shooters firing high-center-of-gravity rifles.

When your perfect steady position is achieved, you'll notice that breathing in lowers your reticle on the target and breathing out raises your reticle on the target.

In Figure 9-4, the entire weight of the shooter's head is translated to the sand sock held in the nonfiring hand. Elevation of the rifle is controlled by squeezing and releasing the sand sock.

APPLYING THE FUNDAMENTALS

1) Get the rifle as low to the shooting platform as possible, using a moldable shooting rest.
2) Position the end of the buttstock in the pocket of your shoulder as inside on your chest as comfortable and with the least amount of bone contact. This is more easily achieved in the prone supported firing position as compared to shooting while seated from a bench.
3) Squeeze up the sand sock, which is under the buttstock, place the full weight of your head on

Figure 9-4.

145

the cheek rest, and bring the reticle of your riflescope on target by gently and slowly releasing tension on the sand sock. The reticle should arrive to the target from the bottom. Freeze when the reticle is at the desired elevation.

4) Exhale all of the air in your lungs and bring the reticle perfectly centered on the bull's-eye. Keep that same tension on the sand sock until one to two seconds after firing the shot.

   Note: As you breathe in, you should notice the reticle drift slightly below the bull's-eye. Upon exhaling, the reticle should drift back onto the bull's-eye.

5) You should be pulling the gun into your shoulder with medium pressure, using the middle and ring fingers of your firing hand.

6) You should have a thin black ring around your sight picture of equal thickness all the way around to ensure a parallax-free sight picture and confirm that your head is in the same place on the rifle stock every time.

7) When the reticle is perfectly centered on the bull's-eye, pause your breathing and squeeze the trigger softly, making the smallest of corrections necessary to keep the reticle center-center on the bull's-eye during the trigger squeeze. These subtle corrections should only be made using the tiniest of muscle movements. The tension of your hand around the sand sock should not change during the trigger squeeze. Freeze your trigger squeeze if your reticle drifts away from your ideal point of aim by the smallest bit. Resume when you bring the crosshair back to the target.

8) After the shot breaks, continue to keep the trigger in the rear position, let the reticle land where it lands naturally after the rifle comes down out of its recoil, keep your breath paused for one to two seconds after the shot breaks, and keep your cheek laid heavy on the cheek rest. This is follow-through.

9) If you were firing from the prone and the reticle jumped off target after the shot, you either did not have a perfect "natural position," or you were not directly behind the rifle. If you fired from a bench, it is normal for the target no longer to be in your field of view, as the majority of your body weight is not behind the rifle when shooting from this position.

NATURAL FIRING POSITION

A natural firing position is most easily achieved in the prone position, as the full weight of your body should be behind the gun. In the seated position, while firing from a bench, the recoil of the rifle will have greater effect on the movement of your body during and after the shot is fired.

To achieve a natural firing position while in the prone, achieve a steady firing position as if you were about to take a shot, to include getting the reticle on target and on the bull's-eye. Pause your breath as if about to fire. Close your eyes for 10 seconds and relax your body. Your muscles should be doing absolutely zero work to hold yourself up—the only exception being your nonfiring hand squeezing the proper amount of pressure on the sand sock under your buttstock. The highest portion of your chest should be in contact with the ground. You should be able to fall asleep on your rifle in this position. After 10 seconds have expired, open your eyes. With your body completely relaxed behind the gun, your reticle should still be on target. If off target, move your "belt buckle" left or right to adjust and start over.

♦

A FINAL WORD
TO THE READER

Herein, we've covered all concepts I feel you need to understand in order to achieve a high level of long-range precision rifle success. I hope that you have a solid understanding of all material covered, and that I've left you with few or no questions despite the immense amount of subject matter we've gone over.

As I said in the mission statement on the dedication page, this is the book I wish I'd had when I started this journey and had no one to ask questions of or to guide me. With any luck, your personal growth will be more quickly facilitated by having read this book than if you had attempted to tackle this great sport without it.

You know what to look for in a long-range rifle and the type of glass and rings to achieve your personal measure of success. You know how to gather data, build ballistic cards in increments of 10 meters out to your maximum effective range, and compensate for environmental conditions. You have an understanding of riflescope manipulation—using minutes of angle and mils to compensate for different rifle-shot scenarios. I've introduced you to manipulating ballistic software and the gains to be had by its proper application.

Hopefully, you'll log all of your shooting events in a data book, especially so you can refine that all-important known data page as you shoot more and more. We even discussed some more advanced firing techniques, such as high-angle shooting and shooting over and under obstructions. You have more than a basic knowledge of how to hand load precision rifle cartridges to yield the maximum level of accuracy for your rifle and ammunition combination. I've even given you some pointers on the fundamentals of marksmanship. But it's one thing to feel comfortable with all this knowledge; it's a whole other thing to be able to do it, and do it consistently well.

There is a wealth of knowledge out there in written form, on the Internet, and just by talking to those who have been shooting in this manner for a long time. As you grow, I'm sure you will figure out things on your own through trial and error, as we all do. Please don't stop your personal growth with the information you received here in this text. Shoot safely, keep pushing yourself, never stop learning, and I wish you best of luck!

✦
ABOUT THE AUTHOR

Anthony J. Cirincione II is a U.S. Army sniper and avid precision rifle and long-range rifle shooter, competitor, and enthusiast. He has 26 months' worth of combat deployments between Iraq and the highly kinetic Pech River Valley of northeastern Afghanistan.

Cirincione has trained multiple groups of squad-designated marksmen for his battalion in order to provide ground tactical commanders with just one more useful tool to achieve success on the battlefield. Many of his students had the privilege to exact their lethal toll on the enemies of our country, pushing their weapon systems up to and beyond their defined maximum effective ranges. He has provided his sniper section with basic sniper training to prepare selectees for school. He has forged an advanced sniper training program for his unit so that, in his absence, his section can continue to train new members of the team without them having to relearn lost information as its senior members depart and new faces gain the honor of entering the compound.

This book was written to provide U.S. military, U.S. coalition forces, and local law-enforcement personnel with a tool that they can use to properly set up their rifles and optics, and effectively employ them out to their maximum effective target engagement ranges. Having omitted certain tactical techniques and procedures that can potentially pose a threat to the operational security of our professionals, we're glad to say that this book is UNCLASSIFIED and is available to the law-abiding U.S. citizen. Cirincione says he wrote this book because he wants to take the mystery out of the trade. "I love it, and others want to enjoy it too. It's a little bit of art, mostly science, and is certainly a worthwhile craft. This stuff isn't witchcraft!"

Cirincione is a member of the National Rifle Association and the American Sniper Association. Recreationally, he takes on students from his local area in west Tennessee. He squares away their equipment, teaches them the ins and outs of riflescope mechanics, and improves their performance by pointing them in the right direction in their hand-loading practices and establishment of rock-solid shooting platforms. He welcomes any precision rifle or shooting questions at longrangeprecision@outlook.com.

If this book facilitates a successful shooting event or hunt, or adds effectiveness to your unit, please contact the author.